T0068280

An Effort of Inquiry

Larry Munger

August 11, 2013

authorHOUSE®

AuthorHouse™
1663 Liberty Drive
Bloomington, IN 47403
www.authorhouse.com
Phone: 1 (800) 839-8640

Published by AuthorHouse 01/05/2016

ISBN: 978-1-5049-7162-1 (sc)
ISBN: 978-1-5049-7161-4 (e)

Print information available on the last page.

KJV
Scripture quotations marked KJV are from the Holy Bible, King James Version (Authorized Version). First published in 1611. Quoted from the KJV Classic Reference Bible, Copyright © 1983 by The Zondervan Corporation.

NKJV
Scripture quotations marked NKJV are taken from the New King James Version. Copyright © 1982 by Thomas Nelson, Inc. Used by permission. All rights reserved.

NIV
Scripture quotations marked NIV are taken from the Holy Bible, New International Version®. NIV®. Copyright © 1973, 1978, 1984 by International Bible Society. Used by permission of Zondervan. All rights reserved. [Biblica

Any people depicted in stock imagery provided by Thinkstock are models, and such images are being used for illustrative purposes only. Certain stock imagery © Thinkstock.

This book is printed on acid-free paper.

TABLE OF CONTENTS

APPENDIX:

INTRODUCTION

As the mist rolls in from the sea, questions bring forth more questions and thus causes us a mental mist or fog in our minds. Analyzing questions often helps clear up the fog and mist surrounding them and helps get our minds clearer and more focused. I believeone should have a degree of curiosity about certain things in this life. To make an effort to satisfy this curiosity it would seem logical that one would be interested in putting forth some sort of inquiry into whatever it is that a person is curious about. The Church of Jesus Christ of Latter-day Saints has published works entitled "Joseph Smith Papers" which they make available for a price at their fully owned Deseret Book Store chain. It purports to be a study of various papers written by and about Joseph Smith.

This "Effort of Inquiry" is a study made to investigate these "papers" or writings and also to investigate circumstances surrounding them as there are many questions arising in the reading of these volumes published by the Church. What some of these questions are and possible answers to questions arising from the investigation of the publishing of these papers are herein contained.

The "effort" referred to herein is indeed just that - an effort. There are many questions that arise in this study and very few answers which in their own turn cause us to make further questions about this study.

Why are there so few answers? Why is there such uncertainty in the Church historians comments and their publishing? Why are there such inconsistencies in the historical records? Why do the historians seemingly evade certain questions concerning the very papers they are writing about?

Not only is this a study about the effort of inquiry into these and many other questions, but it is also a study of other records in an effort to show an accurate picture of what took place in the early days of the founding of the Mormon Church.

Was Joseph Smith told by God not to join any of the existing churches of his time? Why then did he join the Baptist and Methodist church? Did he really see God the Father and Jesus Christ? Or did he only see Jesus Christ. Why didn't he make others aware of his vision of the Lord appearing to him until twelve years later, after many other men of his time claimed to have similar revelations and indeed had published them in the area he lived? Who was Moroni? Who was Nephi? How did Joseph Smith see God the Father and live while the Bible repeatedly says this is not possible?

Great efforts have been made by many people to endeavor to convince people that Joseph Smith was a prophet of God and in fact spoke to God the Father face to face at least one time.

This is the beginning of much scriptural[1] contradictions and religious disputations between Joseph Smith's followers and many outside of

---

[1] *Joseph Smith told Nancy Rigdon "That which is wrong under one circumstance, may be, and often is, right under another. ... Whatever God requires is right, no matter what it is, although we may not see the reason thereof till long after the events transpire. ... even things which might be considered abominable to all who understand the order of heaven only in part, but which in reality were right because God gave and sanctioned by special revelation." Official History of the Church, Vol. 5, p.134-136, See also "The Letter of the Prophet, Joseph Smith to Miss Nancy Rigdon," Joseph Smith Collection, LDS archives. Why is 'whatever*

the church he founded. Also this has caused millions of people to believe in Joseph Smith as a prophet divinely called of God to restore His "only true church" upon the earth, if indeed there is such an organization anywhere.

The question seems to be why does God need a church of any kind on the earth? What is the purpose of having a church for God anyway? Does God want us to worship Him? Is this why he created us, so we can worship him and praise him forever? Wouldn't it seem easier for Him to simply create androids that would accomplish the same purpose without ever committing any sins or transgressions against God? There is a teaching in the Mormon Church that Lucifer met with God in a great council prior to the creation of this earth and offered to God a plan that would guarantee the salvation of all of his children however Lucifer asked that the glory for this salvation be his, not God's. We do not appear to have enough information about this

---

God requires' right? Doesn't God have to follow His own laws and rules? Would they really be rules and laws if they could be broken whenever God wants to? When God proclaims He is the same yesterday, today and forever is he telling us the truth? If He is really the same yesterday, today and forever wouldn't it be necessary for His rules and laws to also be the same yesterday, today and forever? Where does Joseph Smith get the idea that 'that which is wrong under one circumstance, may be, and often is, right under another'? Don't we need some examples of what he is trying to communicate to us here? When Jesus Christ said "...except a man be born of water and of the Spirit, he cannot enter into the kingdom of God" do you think Joseph Smith believes that may not be true under certain circumstances? And what about all the other teachings of Jesus Christ? Are they not always true under every circumstance? What about the ten commandments? What about the Articles of Faith of the Mormon church?

Is it possible Joseph Smith meant that while these commandments "may be right under one circumstance they may be (and often are) wrong under another circumstance"? Is this perhaps why he had his character Nephi in his Book of Mormon kill Laban? Was there no way God could have given the plates of Laban to Nephi other than to have Nephi kill Laban? This despite the commandment "Thou shalt not kill?" Is there a circumstance wherein we should not do justly or love mercy or walk humbly with God?

council and Lucifer's plan to adequately understand why God elected to deny Lucifer's plan in favor of another plan that would apparently give all the glory to God.

Many people have given their lives to further the growth of the Church throughout the world and indeed many have admitted that even if God Himself were to visit them and suggest Joseph Smith was not really His messenger, they would not believe him, but would rather believe in Joseph Smith. This type of belief is indicative of how this belief has grown and perhaps that it may well be considered in the realm of "cultism" as well as simple religion?

This type of belief is not limited to the Mormon Church. Indeed you find it in the Catholic Church and many of the southern Baptist churches and other protestant faiths throughout the world and certainly in the Moslem religion. It would seem it is indicative of the human race.

Some people have tried to convince us that a cult is an evil organization while in reality it simply is an organization that has certain rules and regulations pertaining to its continued existence. It may or may not be evil or good, depending on what the particular cult's aims or goals are. Since the time of the founding of the Church of Jesus Christ of Latter-day Saints (first called the Church of Christ) by Joseph Smith on April 6, 1830 the Church has sent missionaries throughout the world proclaiming that God has established His church through Joseph Smith.

For whatever reason, it appears that Jesus Christ may have had a church that he established when he lived on earth but there are many questions about this. The Apostle Paul wrote epistles or letters to many churches and to the people in Corinth he clearly stated "Now God hath set some in the church…" (1 Cor 12:28-31) Was this God's church or Jesus Christ's church? There is no mention that these churches had the same name and certainly no reference that any of them carried the name "The church of Christ".

Throughout the scriptures 'church' and congregation refer to people, never to a building. The Church, the body of Christ, is a congregation of members of the church, and is made up of people who feel they are called to follow Jesus Christ.

Everything God requires of His people and every tenet of right living in the Bible is founded on two basic principles – loving God and loving our fellow man. These, according to Jesus, are the two great commandments given for us to follow.

God has given us directives to live by that have nothing to do with a church. Ecclesiastes 12:13 tells us "Let us hear the conclusion of the whole matter: Fear God, and keep his commandments, for this is the whole duty of man". Do you see any mention here about any church in the "conclusion of the whole matter"? What do you think the "whole matter" is?

Micah 6:6-9 "Wherewith shall I come before the Lord, and bow myself before the high God? Shall I come before him with burnt offerings, with calves of a year old? Will the Lord be pleased with thousands of rams, or with ten thousands of rivers of oil? Shall I give my firstborn for my transgression, the fruit of my body for the sin of my soul? He hath shewed thee, O man, what is good; and what doth the Lord require of thee, but to do justly, and to love mercy, and to walk humbly with thy god?" Again, do you find any mention of any church in what the Lord requires of us?

Christ told Peter that he would build his church upon "this rock" Matt. 16:18 What rock is he talking about? Some feel he meant Peter was the rock. Others feel Christ was referring to Peter's revelation being the rock from God that Christ is the Son of the Living God. In either event it is clear that Christ intended to set up a church. This would mean the "rock" Christ was referring to is perhaps the rock of revelation, not a particular individual. Is revelation a "rock" then?

Acts 1:21-22 "Wherefore of these men which have companied with us all the time that the Lord Jesus went in and out among us. Beginning from the baptism of John, unto that same day that he was taken up from us, must one be ordained to be a witness with us of his resurrection." From this reference we may infer that others had been "ordained" to be a witness of his resurrection and now one more must be "ordained" for such a purpose as Judas had removed himself from their group by committing suicide.

We have already been told the "conclusion of the whole matter" and been given the two great commandments in the law and been told just what the Lord requires of us. Is it necessary to have a church also? Was Jesus Baptized into a church? While some had been ordained, does that mean they had to belong to a church? Paul said that God had set "some in the church, first apostles, secondarily prophets, thirdly teachers, after that miracles, then gifts of healings, helps, governments, diversities of tongues: (1 Cor 12:28-31) His church was to have apostles first and then prophets second.

When Paul said God had set some in the 'church' he also said not all were apostles, prophets, etc. but encouraged the people to covet "earnestly the best gifts, and yet shew I unto you a more excellent way". Then he proceeds to tell us "and now abideth faith, hope, charity, these three: but the greatest of these is charity". (1 Cor; 13:13) which apparently is the "more excellent way" than the apostles, prophets, etc. that he had just told us about God setting up these people in the church.

It appears the human race has always endeavored to set up a God for them to believe in, whether it was a belief or a super race of God's chosen people. We are taught the Bible is the Word of God from the time we are small children and many of us feel we need to have an organization to follow God's instructions. Actually God has already given us the directions we need for our time in mortality as outlined above. It is not the purpose of this study to condemn anyone for establishing various organizations or churches to satisfy their needs for such organizations to let them worship God. It is instructional however to make an attempt to keep open our minds and hearts to what God has said to us in the Bible.

Hundreds of thousands of people have contributed their time and their finances to serve missions as the Mormon Church has never seen fit to finance them even though they labored for the Church's benefit. Is it not difficult to imagine any business with such a powerful work force at its disposal for free not becoming extremely prosperous?

Thus the Church has now published Volume 1 of the Joseph Smith Histories 1832-1844. In this effort much study has been done by many different people to develop this historical record and it is forcefully presented as an official work of the Church of Jesus Christ of Latter-day Saints, copyright 2012 by Intellectual Reserve, inc. which from the copyright page indicates it is fully an outgrowth of the Church Historian's Press, a fully accepted subsidiary of the Church of Jesus Christ of Latter-day Saints.

Thus it appears to be a logical and meaningful effort to study this latest official presentation of the Church of Jesus Christ of Latter-day Saints to ascertain the validity of the Church's claims and what actually happened to bring this great Church into being. Certainly the Church has no opposition to this type of activity or would it ever have published such a work as this?

The fact of it appearing in the Church's official bookstore would be a positive indication that the Church would indeed like as many as possible to purchase this book and thoroughly study it. From the price they charge for these volumes it is also obvious the church is publishing these volumes for a profit and not as an effort to freely tell everybody about its history. This study includes a fairly extensive introduction as well as 686 additional pages of historical information for us to study.

This research is being done in an effort to thoroughly review what has been written and compare it to other statements that have also been written which may conflict with each other from time to time. Indeed there are even some areas where a belief is indicated where there is no written documentation as to where this belief comes from, i.e. temple garments, temple ceremonies, temples themselves, Danites, Council of Fifty, etc. and in these cases it is most interesting to note none of these things are mentioned anywhere in the Book of Mormon. Yet the Book of Mormon is claimed by Joseph Smith to contain the fullness of the Gospel. In point of fact, many of these items just mentioned are given little or no consideration in the book "Histories" either.

The study of Joseph Smith's experience with polygamy is an interesting dichotomy of alleged facts. One set of facts historically portrays Joseph Smith's activities in this area through writings of what are truthful statements of other early church leaders who remained faithful to the Mormon Church for their entire lives, some of them even becoming the President of the Church in their lifetimes. A second set of statements, not the least of which is made by Joseph Smith himself (alleged by him from what seem to be reliable sources) deny the same ideas put forth in the first set of statements.

It becomes confusing in these instances to understand why the historians chose to ignore these additional statements of Joseph Smith so we must ask, aren't these Joseph Smith's papers also? When differences like this occur it is difficult to know what to believe.

In the book under review many significant historical sources have been ignored which is unfortunate. Indeed one of the very reasons

Oliver Cowdery left the church[2] was due to his utter disgust at Joseph Smith's sexual involvement with a 16 year old girl named Fanny Alger which Oliver described as "a nasty, filthy dirty" situation which he didn't approve of and this became a stumbling block to his remaining with the Mormon Church in 1838 when he separated himself from the church.

This will be examined in more detail throughout this study. Oliver Cowdery had great respect and admiration for Joseph Smith and refused to openly accuse Joseph Smith of being involved in such a relationship by accusing him of adultery.

The authors of this history book try to bring together many of the histories written about Joseph Smith and in so doing present many differences in this history. You will see these different histories and how they differ from each other as you read through this study. There will be at least ten different histories presented herein.

The inconsistencies in the ten different histories are seemingly ignored by the very historians presenting them to us. They seem to gloss over them by simply saying Joseph Smith gave additional information, or made a 'redaction', regarding his revelations as time went by.

The reader will be able to read each of these ten "versions" of the histories and judge for themselves regarding the obvious differences in each version.

Source: The Joseph Smith Papers "Histories" Volume 1 Joseph Smith Histories 1832-1844 On page 4 the historians state a tear was mended by cellophane tape which was not invented until 1930. In reality, cellophane tape was invented in 1908 and made available to the

---

[2] *See appendix Account of Oliver Cowdery's excommunication. The second charge against him by the Church was that he was seeking to destroy the character of President Joseph Smith, Jr., by falsely insinuating that he was guilty of adultery. In Oliver Cowdery's answer to the charges he didn't respond to this particular one*

public by 1919. This minor point simply shows the historians were not entirely accurate in details, which may lead one to question their accuracy throughout.

There are at least two sides to every situation of course. What are the "fruits" of Mormonism? Do its followers truly show forth an increase of love to those who have been excommunicated from their faith? Do they show forth any love to others that they do not see at their church meeting? There seems little doubt they feed the hungry and help the poor and we should not belittle these efforts even a little. Do not other churches do the same?

We have very bad men like Warren Jeffs, the leader of the Fundamentalist Church*[3], who makes life a terrible experience for many people and yet his beliefs spring from Joseph Smith. He has denied he is a prophet at one time, and then reclaimed this title and makes his followers do absolutely unbelievable things. Lately he has predicted the end of the world by the end of the year 2012 which cannot we all say was a completely false prophecy? He used young boys and girls for his sexual gratification and yet his followers continue to support and sustain him in his apparent wickedness. He has instructed his followers to only allow 15 picked men to sexually impregnate the women in his group, even if they are married to other men, in order to continue to propagate his followers in the manner he wishes. Are there any instances whatever in the scriptures that permit, much less encourage, men to break their marriage vows? In the temple he built in Texas, the upper room was especially designed for his sexual fantasies.

Ervil LeBaron was another one who left the main stream of Mormonism for the Apostilic United Brethren Church, also a splinter

---

[3] *The Apostilic United Brethren Church was a splinter group off of the main Church of Jesus Christ of Latter-day Saints, and the Fundamentalist Church of Jesus Christ of Latter-day Saints was a splinter off from the Apostilic United Brethren Church.*

group off of the Mormon Church*, and then left it also and then masterminded the plot to kill Rulon C. Allred, their leader. LeBaron was eventually convicted of the crime and sentenced to life in prison at the Point of the Mountain State Prison in Draper, Utah. He died in prison on August 16, 1981 of an apparent heart attack and interestingly enough his brother died in Mexico in a car crash a few hours after Ervil died in Utah.

It might seem incredible that people actually believe in such ridiculous and outrageous men but there are many who do and there are many more splinter groups off of the Mormon Church which either still exist or did exist at one time or another (See Splinter Groups in the appendix).

There are other splinter groups from the Mormon Church who do very questionable things but the main stream that exists from Joseph Smith until today is the Church of Jesus Christ of Latter-day Saints, the Mormons, headquartered in Salt Lake City, Utah.

Joseph Smith was a human being and subject to the temptations of the flesh as we shall see. He stated "a prophet is a prophet only when he is acting as such". Teachings of the Prophet Joseph Smith, Section Five 1842-1843. P 278 What does he mean "when he says only when he is acting as such"? Is there ever a time when a prophet would not act like he was a prophet? Did he say this to excuse his somewhat excessive sexual activities with many different women? How about instead saying, "Once a prophet, always a prophet"? Weren't the prophets of the Bible always prophets?

Today the Mormon church does many good things that are beneficial to mankind. They feed the hungry and needy and provide financial aid to some and medical assistance to others and give clothing to the needy. They provide a great society of fellowship for millions of people that allow great fellowship and friendships between many people. They furnish interesting and meaningful activities for their members to participate in such as social gatherings, dinners, meetings, temple activities and genealogy studies. Their teachings seem to provide comfort to many and answer many of life's questions regarding the purpose of existence. The church has its problems and certainly teaches what may appear to be false and deceiving doctrines but they also teach many uplifting doctrines and teach many true and uplifting ideals.

The Church assists nations and peoples who suffer from natural disasters and provide jobs for many people thus allowing them to provide for their families through their own efforts. They certainly give people direction and guidance to live good and meaningful lives. Despite Joseph Smith's many apparent sins and transgressions, the outcome of his activity in starting the Mormon church is resulting in many good and helpful benefits to many people. So the statement of Christ, "By their fruits ye shall know them" is not totally accurate in Joseph Smith's case. While he may have broke some of the ten commandments[4] and disobeyed many of his own revelations, there are many people who are very happy and content in their belief that Joseph Smith was truly a prophet of God.

Sam Walter Foss wrote the following poem which seems to express how people behave in their lives, unable to perceive reality but instead content to follow what others have told them is the truth. However conclusive the evidences that are shown herein, yet few if any will accept them and will continue to believe what they already believe to be truth.

---

[4]   See Appendix *"Did Joseph Smith break any of the Ten Commandments?"*

By **Sam Walter Foss** (1858-1911)

One day, through the primeval wood a calf walked home, as good calves should;
But made a trail all bent askew a crooked trail, as all calves do.
Since then three hundred years have fled and, I infer, that calf is dead.
But still he left behind his trail and thereby hangs a moral tale.
The trail was taken up next day by a lone dog that passed that way;
And then the wise bellwether sheep pursued the trail o'er vale and steep,
And drew the flock behind him, too as good bellwethers always do.
And from that day, o'er hill and glade through these old woods a path was made,.

And many men wound in and out and dodged and turned and bent about,
And uttered words of righteous wrath because 'twas such a crooked path;
But still they followed — do not laugh —the first migrations of that calf,
And through this winding wood-way stalked because he wobbled when he walked.

This forest path became a lane that bent, and turned, and turned again.
This crooked lane became a road where many a poor horse with its load
Toiled on beneath the burning sun and traveled some three miles in one.
And thus a century and a half men trod the footsteps of that calf.

The years passed on in swiftness fleet. The road became a village street,
And soon, before men were aware, A city's crowded thoroughfare,
And soon the central street was this of a renowned metropolis;
And men two centuries and a half trod in the footsteps of that calf.

Each day a hundred thousand rout followed the zigzag calf about,
And o'er his crooked journey went the traffic of a continent.
A hundred thousand men were led by a calf near three centuries dead.
They follow still his crooked way and lose one hundred years a day,
For thus such reverence is lent to well-established precedent.

A moral lesson this might teach were I ordained and called to preach;
For men are prone to go it blind along the calf-paths of the mind,
They work away from sun to sun to do what other men have done.
They follow in the beaten track and out and in, and forth and back,
And still their devious course pursue to keep the path that others do.
They keep the path a sacred groove along which all their lives they move;
But how the wise wood-gods must laugh who saw that first primeval calf!
Ah, many things this tale might teach —but I am not ordained to preach.

CHAPTER 1

JOSEPH SMITH'S FIRST VERSION OF HIS FIRST VISION

We began our study with this statement: "Joseph Smith circa Summer 1832 is the <u>only</u> narrative of the foundational spiritual events of Joseph Smith's early life that includes his own handwriting". (Page 4 Histories). If this is the only narrative of the foundational spiritual events of Joesph Smith's early life, why do we have nine different versions of him claiming Christ or God and Christ appeared to him under different conditions? With this initial statement being made by the historians in the book Histories it becomes imperative that we continue to return to this history that has been written in Joseph Smith's own handwriting. Shouldn't any conflict between his own handwritten documents and other histories be considered highly suspicious? If different, should any other accounts be considered false? Why do all of the other nine versions claim to be Joseph Smith writing them himself? Who actually wrote the other nine versions? We shall look into this further in this study.

On page 6 of Histories the historians write that in the early 1830's, when this history was written, it appears that Joseph Smith had not broadcast the details of his first vision of Deity. They go on to say

1

his history began to be written November 27, 1832. However the term circa gives us a broad area to become aware of him writing his own personal history. Prior to his writing his own personal history he wrote down many revelations he claimed to have received from God about various subjects but these had nothing to do with his own personal history. Even the entire Book of Mormon was written down prior to his recording his own personal claim of God visiting him. In reality he wrote very little himself but appointed scribes and historians to write what he told them to write.

The church was established in 1830 and Joseph Smith claimed John the Baptist,[5] and Peter, James and John had all appeared to him and restored the Aaronic Priesthood and Melchizedek Priesthood[6] before he ever got around to writing about his first vision.

There is reference to the office of Priest, but none claiming High Priest. Joseph Smith makes only a passing reference to Peter, James and John appearing to him on the banks of the Susquehanna River and telling Joseph Smith that they (Peter, James and John) had the Keys of the Kingdom and of the dispensation of the fullness of times![7] Nowhere else do we find any revelation or story about this event actually happening.

---

[5] *Doctrine and Covenants Section 13 May 15, 1829*

[6] *There is no mention of a Melchizedek Priesthood with the office of Elder or Seventy that is passed on to anyone recorded anywhere in the Bible. We have no record that Jesus Christ ever ordained any individual to be a priest in the order of Melchizedek. There is no evidence Peter, James and John ordained a leader into the order of Melchizedek. There is no evidence John the Baptist ordained any leaders for Aaronic Priesthood offices anywhere in the Bible. Hebrews 7:1-28 See Report at end of this study entitled "Priesthood". Nowhere in the Book of Mormon which Smith states contains the fullness of the Gospel) does it talk about the Melchizedek and Aaronic Priesthood.*

[7] *Doctrine and Covenants, Section 128:20*

It is interesting to note that Joseph Smith claimed to have many revelations and heavenly messengers visiting him prior to his writing about his first vision in 1820 (or 1823 depending on whose account you wish to believe). Yet the historians clearly state that the circa Summer 1832 version was Joseph Smith's first narrative that was in his own handwriting.

All of the revelations and appearances of heavenly messengers referred to above seem to be his words, accounting for what happened to him, yet the historians maintain his circa Summer 1832 history was his first handwritten statement and this was not published until March 1, 1842 (page 565 Histories), over 12 years after the establishment of his church and the appearance of angels and heavenly messengers and over 20 years after it allegedly happened. Why do you think Joseph Smith published this personally handwritten account of his first vision in 1842 long after eight other accounts had already been published and released and all of them are different than his own handwritten account? Was this the actual handwritten version Joseph Smith wrote down that was published in 1842 or the revised version written at a later date?

Why did Joseph Smith write this in 1832 and not publish it for ten more years? Why did Joseph Smith allow other versions of his first vision to be published prior to 1842 that show obvious disagreement with his own hand written version claimed to be written in 1832?

The historians writing the Joseph Smith Papers actually speculate that John Whitmer, one of the first church historians, was not even aware of Joseph Smith's claims of having been visited by God the Father and Jesus Christ and John Whitmer left the church in 1838 which was 8 years after the church was founded and 18 years after Joseph Smith claimed he experienced talking face to face with God the Father and Jesus Christ.

Should we believe what the historians have written or should we believe all of these other revelations and accounts of heavenly messengers appearing to Joseph Smith were actually true accounts written by Joseph Smith? Was he dictating to a scribe who wrote them down? Why did he wait until 1842 to publish his first personal story of what happened to him in 1820, 22 years later?

It is interesting to note that at one point Joseph Smith attempts to write his history himself, and yet later claims he has dictated it to certain scribes he appoints to be church historian.

He claimed to have 19 revelations from God prior to his starting his church which he caused to be written down and eventually published in the Book of Commandments which later turned into the Doctrine and Covenants. In none of these 19 revelations does he claim that God appeared to him.

Now the historians make an interesting statement on page 6 of the book that in the early 1830s, when this history was written, it appears that Joseph Smith had not broadcast the details of his first vision of Deity. The history of the church, as it was then generally understood, began with the gold plates. John Whitmer mentions in his history[8] (What history? The historians said Whitmer refused to deliver his history up to anybody)* the commencement of the church history commencing at the time of the finding of the plates suggesting that Whitmer was either unaware of Joseph Smith's earlier vision or did not conceive of it as *foundational*'. Records predating 1832 only hint at Joseph Smith's earliest manifestation.

---

[8] *There is a history kept by John Whitmer entitled "The Book of John Whitmer Kept by Commandment" typescript by Pauline Hancock, BYU-A Holograph is located in RLDS Archives. He states he began this history June 12, 1831. This is when Joseph Smith had him appointed Church historian and scribe. Vol 2 of Histories says he was appointed April 9, 1831 Page 5*
*Could this be the history John Whitmer refused to deliver up to the Church of Jesus Christ of Latter-day Saints? See "Book of John Whitmer" appendix at the end of this report. *In volume 2 of the Joseph Smith Papers the historians now come up with a detailed history of John Whitmer's historical writing*

CHAPTER 2

IMPORTANCE OF JOSEPH SMITH'S FIRST VISION

D oes it appear that the historians are clearly stating that Joseph Smith's first vision of the Lord appearing to him was not considered foundational to the organizing and building of the Church? Does it appear Whitmer was unaware of any revelation given to Joseph Smith regarding the appearance of either God the Father or Jesus Christ personally appearing to Joseph Smith at any time? What records predating 1832 hint at Joseph Smith earliest manifestation? And why do they only hint at this?

They even suggest that John Whitmer perhaps was not even aware of Joseph Smith's first vision. If this is true, how important can this first vision of Joseph Smith really be? Has it not been suggested by others that the main doctrine of the church became the Book of Mormon and later polygamy? and when polygamy was discontinued in 1890 the church began to replace this major doctrine (polygamy) with the story of the first vision of Joseph Smith as the most important story of the Mormon Church?

Confirming this idea, the very first lesson taught by missionaries in proselytizing their faith to others is the story of Joseph Smith's first vision. This is taught before any other church doctrines and indeed you will now read of several presidents of the Mormon church stating the importance of the first vision.

In 1998 Gordon B. Hinckley, then Church President and Prophet, declared that the Mormon church's entire case as members of the church of Jesus Christ of Latter-day Saints rests on the validity of the glorious First Vision. It was the parting of the curtain to open this, the dispensation of the fullness of times. ***Nothing is more important than this***. He says that he submits that if Joseph Smith talked with God the Father and His Beloved Son, then all else of which he spoke is true. This is the hinge on which turns the gate that leads to the path of salvation and eternal life.

   November 1998 Ensign

Hinckley earlier stated that either Joseph Smith talked with the Father and the Son or he did not. If he did not, the Mormon church leader says the church is engaged in a blasphemy. Likewise in a January 2007 interview conducted for the PBS documentary, The Mormons, Hinckley said of the First Vision that it is either true or false. "If it's false, we're engaged in a great fraud. If it's true, it is the most important thing in the world… That's our claim. That's where we stand, that's where we fall. But we don't. We just stand secure in that faith."

   Improvement Era December 1961

David O. McKay, the ninth president of the LDS Church, also declared the First Vision to be the foundation of the faith.

   Gospel Ideals, 1951

Hugh B. Brown, an apostle of the Mormon Church, said "The first vision of the prophet Joseph Smith constitutes the groundwork of the church which was later organized. If this first vision was but a figment of Joseph Smith's imagination then the Mormon Church is what its detractors declare it to be – a wicked and deliberate impostor". The Abundant Life P. 310-311 Aug 15, 1999.

We seem to have arrived at a major disagreement between Gordon B. Hinckley, David O. McKay, Hugh B. Brown and the historians who wrote the Joseph Smith Papers Histories book.

The historians suggest John Whitmer, one of the early leaders of the church, indeed the church historian in charge of keeping church records, may not have even been aware of the story of the first vision. Yet Hinckley, McKay and Brown say exactly the opposite about the importance of the first vision.

Which line of belief are we to follow? Was the first vision foundational or not? Why would John Whitmer, the official church historian, not be aware of this claim of Joseph Smith's first vision?

Gordon B. Hinckley places the importance of the first vision above anything else the church teaches. Wouldn't this include the teaching of the Book of Mormon? Wouldn't this include temple work and the wearing of special undergarments? Yet would the historians have us believe the story of the first vision was perhaps not well known and the Book of Mormon was perhaps the most important belief of the Church when it was founded?

Does it not appear that we need some very substantial clarification on this disagreement between Prophets of the Church and the Historians accurate confirmation of the ignorance of the first vision? As already pointed out, the Joseph Smith Papers certainly appears to be an official publication of the current Mormon Church and would therefore be their official position on everything published therein.

CHAPTER 3

JOSEPH SMITH DID NOT COMPLETE SEVERAL JOURNALS AND DOCUMENTARY ENDEAVORS

The historians tell us that with the assistance of Frederick G. Williams, Joseph Smith first set about recording his own history in the summer of 1832 (Page 7 Histories). In it he recorded for the first time in writing his first vision of Deity and the discovery of the gold plates. This was not published until 1842. Two years later another project, the 1834-1836 history, was started. This history grew largely on existing records, including Oliver Cowdery's account of the translation of the Book of Mormon and the conferral of priesthood authority. Like the 1832 history mentioned earlier, this manuscript also remained unfinished.

A partial reason that his manuscript remained unfinished might be found in the many lawsuits placed against Joseph Smith which took a great deal of his time as well as establishing newspapers and a bank in Kirtland, Ohio and finally fleeing from the law in New York, Ohio, Missouri, and Illinois.

The historians fail to point out that Joseph Smith Jr.s work initially involved treasure seeking in the ground. He hired out to different people promising to find gold or buried treasure and when he failed to do some of these activities, people took him to court for what they felt was fraudulent actions. Indeed, when Joseph Smith was refused membership in the Methodist Church in 1828, he was accused of necromancy.[9] and was asked to leave the Methodist Church if he refused to admit necromancy was not a true doctrine and should not be followed which he refused to do.

John Whitmer was appointed historian of the church on June 12, 1831 and was excommunicated March 10, 1838. He was part of the mass exodus of apostles and members of the church who were excommunicated[10] upon losing a lot of money in the Kirtland Safety Society Anti-bank scheme that you will read of later. Then John Corrill and Elias Higbee were both appointed as church historians. Heber C. Kimball said of this anti-bank scheme failing that he believed there could not be found twenty people who still believed Joseph Smith was a prophet of God at that time.

We may admit the historians have left us confused by their apparent indications that we had no way to read John Whitmer's history as we later find out his history was turned over to the Reorganized Church of Jesus Christ of Latter-day Saints and has been published in that organization.

---

[9] *Necromancy is a claimed form of magic involving communication with the decesased – either by summoning their spirit as an apparition or raising them bodily – for the purpose of divination, imparting the means to foretell future events or discover hidden knowledge. The term may sometimes be used in a more general sense to refer to black magic or witchcraft*

[10] *Joseph Smith excommunicated many of his closest friends and associates over a period of time. He stated clearly that the Book of Mormon contained the fullness of the Gospel yet there is no mention of temple ceremonies or temple garments anywhere in the Book of Mormon, nor polygamy, nor excommunciations.*

John Whitmer continued to add to his history until after Joseph Smith's death in 1844 but Whitmer refused to give up his record. (Page xvii) Corrill was excommunicated in 1839 – a year after his appointment. So now we realize John Whitmer did indeed keep his records and made them available but not to the Mormon Church. However they are available for us to study now.

CHAPTER 4

INTERESTING ITEMS REGARDING JOSEPH SMITH RELATIVES

Joseph Smith Sr., Joseph Smith Jr's., father, had at least seven revelations or visions or dreams, which took place prior to Joseph Smith's first stated vision and some occurring after his vision. The second vision of Joseph Smith Sr. reported by Lucy Mack Smith (Joseph Smith Jr's., mother) "exhibits many similarities to the Tree of Life vision which Joseph Smith, Jr. would later dictate as part of the Book of Mormon (Bushman 2005 p. 36). Bushman tells us also (Page 54 Rough Stone Rolling) "Joseph Sr. was not fully adequate in his responsibility for family leadership. …He was a gentle, disappointed man with an inclination to compensate for his failures with magic and drink". Continuing he tells us, that Joseph Jr. eventually restored his father's dignity by giving him an honored place in the church. If there was any childhood fantasy at work in Joseph Jr.'s life, it was the desire to redeem what he felt was his flawed, loving father, but was this enough to make him a prophet?

Like many other Americans living on the frontier at the beginning of the 19th century, Joseph Smith, Jr. and his family believed in visions, dreams, and others claimed to have mystical communications with

God. For example, in 1811, Joseph Smith, Jr.'s maternal grandfather, Solomon Mack, described a series of visions and voices from God that resulted in his conversion to Christianity at the age of seventy-six.

Before Joseph Smith, Jr. was born, his mother Lucy Mack Smith went to a grove near her home in Vermont and prayed about her husband Joseph Smith Sr.s rejection of religion. That night she said she had a dream which she interpreted as a prophecy that Joseph, Sr., would later accept the "pure and undefiled Gospel of the Son of God." She also said that Smith, Sr. had a number of dreams or visions between 1811 and 1819, the first vision occurring when his mind was "much excited upon the subject of religion." Joseph Sr.'s first vision confirmed to him the correctness of his refusal to join any organized religious group.[11]

This shows that Joseph Smith, Jr.s family had a history of visionary experiences claimed both by his father and his grandfather and his mother. It might appear that these types of reported visions give a person leave to "borrow" some events as they wish to rather than tell what actually happened which, as we shall see, was exactly the liberties Oliver Cowdery felt he could take whenever he wished. In any event we see that there was acceptance by Joseph Smith Jr.s family of his claimed visions and we can see why they were not surprised by them since they had such a history of these types of claims in their own family history.

---

[11] *See Joseph Smith Sr. Visions – Appendix end of this report*

CHAPTER 5

MORE UNCERTAINTIES

On page xiv we read that even before the April 1830 injunction to keep a church record, Joseph Smith began recording sacred texts, including the extensive Book of Mormon translation. So he recorded sacred texts before he broadcast the details of his first vision of Deity?

Footnote 4 page xiv Histories we find that William W. Phelps[12] reported hearing Joseph Smith speak on the subject "This is my beloved son' hear ye him", which likely included an account of his first visionary experience. Phelps reported: "He preached one of the greatest sermons I ever heard-it was about 3 ½ hours long-and unfolded more mysteries than I can write at this time." June 2, 1835 is when Phelps wrote this and it is therefore unclear what date he is

---

[12] *William Wines Phelps (February 17, 1792 – March 7, 1872) was an early leader of the Latter-day Saint movement. He was an assistant president of the church in Missouri and scribe to Joseph Smith, Jr. and a church printer, editor and song writer. Don't you think with these credentials he could have made at least a few notes about this sermon he claimed as "one of the greatest sermons I ever heard"? After all, wasn't he a reporter for the newspaper also? He was excommunicated March 17, 1838 and rebaptized in 1840, then excommunicated again Dec. 9, 1847 and rebaptized 2 days later.*

speaking of when he heard Joseph Smith deliver this sermon. Was he not an editor, printer and song writer? Was he not trained to write things down which he both heard and saw? Yet he says Joseph Smith unfolded more mysteries than I can write"? Maybe just even a little writing brother Phelps?

Note above it states "which <u>likely</u> included…" An uncertainty. Maybe it did **not** include an account of his first visionary experience as the authors merely say "which likely included"? Why didn't Phelps write down what Joseph Smith claimed in his first vision? If Joseph Smith preached for 3 ½ hours, does it not seem possible Phelps could have written down at least a great deal of what he heard? Why didn't he at least try to mention a few of the things Joseph Smith preached about, especially his first vision?

On page 5 of Histories, footnote 10 we read about the John Whitmer, History, 25, in JSP, H2:36; see also Historical Introduction to Whitmer, History in JSP, H2:8. Again we must ask, what history of Whitmer? If he refused to give up his history where does this Whitmer History come from? Is the Book of Whitmer referred to earlier the actual history, then, that John Whitmer recorded and refused to surrender to the Church when he was excommunicated in 1838? Why do not the Historians offer this as a possibility in this study? Further, on page 6 the historians again quote from Whitmer's history and we continue to ask where this historical information came from as the authors have already told us that Whitmer refused to give up his records. Are we safe in accepting the Book of Whitmer as actual historical accuracies of Joseph Smith's history? [13]It would seem so.

---

[13] *and footnote #5 (Page 2 abaove) The authors of the "Histories" book make it clear that John Whitmer refused to deliver up his history papers when he was excommunicated in 1838 and we are led to ask why they bring this up and then quote from his book later?*

Further the historian says there is a suggestion that Whitmer was either unaware of Joseph Smith's earlier vision or did not conceive of it as fundamental. Page 6 (Histories) "Record predating 1832 only <u>hint</u> at Joseph Smith's earlier manifestation". Help! How could Whitmer have possibly not conceived Joseph Smith Jun. personal handwritten story of his first vision, fundamental? What could be more fundamental? Haven't we already read from other Prophets about how fundamental the story of the first vision is? Is there any mention of Joseph Smith's first initial vision in the Book of Whitmer?

Why not?

Didn't Gordon B. Hinckley say of the First Vision "It is either true or false. If it's false, we're engaged in a great fraud?"

The historians state on page 6 that records predating 1832 *only hint* at Joseph Smith's earliest manifestation. Really? Section 1 verse 17 of the Doctrine and Covenants written November 1, 1831 says "Wherefore, I the Lord, knowing the calamity which should come upon the inhabitants of the earth, *called upon my servant Joseph Smith*, Jun., and spake unto him from heaven, and gave him commandments."[14]

Is this only a '*hint*' that the Lord spoke to Joseph Smith Jun. from heaven prior to 1832? Isn't this a direct call from God to Joseph Smith?

Interesting to note the Lord says that he "called upon my servant Joseph Smith, Jun.", not the other way around although Joseph Smith, Jun. says it was him (Joseph Smith Jun.) that called upon the

---

[14] *Wherefore, I the Lord, knowing the calamity which should come upon the inhabitants of the earth". The Lord knew of a calamity that "should come upon the inhabitants of the earth"? There was no great calamity that has ever come upon the inhabitants of the earth. Even the World Wars that occurred almost a century to a century and a half later did not destroy as many people as did the black plague of 1348 to 1350 See prophecies of Joseph Smith appendix*

Lord. Which was it? If the Lord spoke to you from heaven and gave you commandments, do you suppose you would consider this just a hint? Maybe the historians are trying to be humorous and I just missed their point?

Understanding the production of the circa 1832 history is further complicated by the possibility that it was copied from an earlier manuscript, a possibility suggested by the record-keeping practices of Joseph Smith and Frederick G. Williams, in whose alternating handwriting the history is inscribed. In the same time period they jointly copied six revelations from 1831 and 1832, some of which Joseph Smith originally dictated to Williams, into the beginning of a compilation of revelations.

The historians speculate on page 6 that initially, Joseph Smith may have considered this vision to be a personal experience tied to his own religious explorations. So Joseph Smith **may have** considered this vision to be a personal experience? What *else* could he have considered this to be? Why do they say that he "may have considered this"?

What do the historians mean here? Joseph Smith "may have considered this vision to be a personal experience? Are they really suggesting Joseph Smith might possibly have also considered this to be an **impersonal** experience? How could this be?

He was not accustomed to recording personal events and he did not record at first the vision. Only when Joseph Smith developed his thoughts to include historical records did he write down a detailed account of the vision he experienced as a youth. The result was a simple unpolished account of his first marvelous experience, written largely in his own hand.

The account was not published or widely circulated at the time, though in later years he told the story more frequently.

The historians do not declare their beliefs about whether Frederick G. Williams wrote part of Joseph Smith's first vision which they have stated is "written largely in his own hand," so we are led to believe the circa Summer 1832 version is Joseph Smith's own personal account of what he claimed happened to him.

He didn't record the vision as he later did the sacred texts at the center of his attention? He said (nine years later) he told his father[15] about it the next day. There is no definite record of the date Joseph Smith Jun. first wrote down his version of what transpired during his first vision. The historians speculate that they believe it was written sometime during 1832 with the assistance of Frederick G. Williams but this is merely guesswork. The only thing definite that can be said of this hand written version by Joseph Smith, Jun is that it was written in his own personal handwriting or largely in his own hand.

The authors do state on page 7, "Other textual evidence, however, indicates that the circa Summer 1832 history may be the original inscription." Unfortunately for us the authors do not reveal what this other textual evidence may be.

Then later they write "The history also contains several significant contemporaneous revisions in Joseph Smith's handwriting, which <u>may</u> indicate that Joseph Smith was composing original narrative. …Joseph Smith and Williams may have been modifying the circa summer 1832 history as they copied it from an earlier text"

---

15 *He claimed he told his father of the vision of the angel that appeared to him by night. The historians state on page 6":In the early 1830's, when this history was written, it appears that JS had not broadcast the details of his first vision of Diety." Hadn't he <u>broadcast</u> this event to his father the morning after it happened? Remember, he didn't tell us this until 9 years later. He ordained Oliver Cowdery to be church historian and two months later he appointed John Whitmer as historian. Yet the historians tell us he was not accustomed to recording personal events. Wasn't the translation of the Book of Mormon a personal event?*

CHAPTER 6

COMPARISONS IN JOSEPH SMITH'S LIFE

Consider some comparisons between events in Joseph Smith's life and events in the Book of Mormon. Wasn't the translation of the Book of Mormon a personal event from what we can see below? Are we to believe the occurrence of God the Father personally appearing to Joseph Smith was not worthy of his reporting such an event? The Book of Mormon was more important than God appearing to him?

Joseph born fourth living child

Nephi born fourth living child

Joseph has brother named Samuel

Nephi has a brother named Sam

One of the Smith children named Joseph

One of Lehi's children named Joseph

Joseph taken south to Palmyra By his father at about age 11

Mormon carried south to Zarahemla by his father at age 11

Joseph claims he is visited of the Lord in his 15th year

Mormon claims he is visted of the Lord at age 15

Joseph searches for hidden Treasures in the earth

Inhabitants begin hiding treasures in the earth

Doesn't it seem that if they were copying from an earlier text it would have had to be a text written by Joseph Smith prior to Joseph Smith and Frederick G. Williams writing this circa summer 1832 history or at least someone who had written down Joseph Smith's first vision and who could that have been? Where are these "significant contemporaneous revisions"? There are few records of Joseph Smith writing down revelations until after he met Oliver Cowdery so it is possible Oliver Cowdery wrote something down that Joseph Smith could have later copied from, but if he did we are left to wonder why his hand written account is so different from that written by Oliver Cowdery? Could this explain the Historians comments about whether his circa Summer 1832 history may have been copied instead of being completely original?

We have the authors statements of "other textual evidence" indicating the circa Summer 1832 history may be the original inscription. Then the authors tell us that Joseph Smith and Frederick G. Williams may have copied it from an earlier text.

Joseph Smith and Frederick G. Williams "divided inscription work when they copied JS's 27 November 1832 letter to William W. Phelps, which JS originally dictated" Page 6 Histories.

Oliver Cowdery, Warren Cowdrey, Warren Parish and Frederick G. Williams kept a history of the church which may have included a version of Joseph Smith's first vision but we have no written record of this. We refer to this as the 1834 to 1836 history. Oliver Cowdery makes definite reference to Joseph Smith's first vision but does not give us a detailed account such as Joseph Smith himself has done in his circa Summer 1832 account or as Oliver Cowdery did in reporting Joseph Smith's meeting with Joshua, the Jewish Minister.

In the front of the Book of Mormon we find several statements of interest that are herewith written for the readers additional information:

Joseph Smith states, "I returned to my father in the field, and rehearsed the whole matter to him. He replied to me that it was of God, and told me to go and do as commanded by the messenger (no mention of the name of the messenger)."

Earlier on the same page the messenger "added a caution to me, telling me that Satan would try to tempt me (in consequence of the indigent circumstances of my father's family), to get the plates for the purpose of getting rich. This he forbade me, saying that I must have no other object in view in getting the plates but to glorify God, and must not be influenced by any other motive than that of building His kingdom; otherwise I could not get them."

Was Joseph Smith interested in the plates because they were gold and he could sell them for a great amount of money? Did he forget God was using him to reveal things to mankind and that everything he was directed to do was from the Lord? Was he interested in them for selling them to someone who could interpret them and tell the history of the people of the land he was in? Remember, his job at the time was digging for money and precious metals. This is one reason Emma Hale's (JS wife) father (Isaac) didn't like him. He had paid him money to find treasure on his land and Joseph Smith had failed.

He was certainly interested in money because when it turned out he couldn't sell the gold plates he then planned to sell his translation of the plates and sent representatives up into Canada to sell the copyright to the Book of Mormon. Hiram Page and Oliver Cowdery went to Toronto for this purpose, but they failed entirely to sell the copyright, returning without any money.[16]

So according to Oliver Cowdery are we led to believe Joseph Smith was very avaricious and selfish in his desire to find these gold plates so he could accumulate great wealth, not to follow Gods directions?

---

[16] (*Comprehensive History of the Church* Vol. 1 pp. 162-66).

Oliver Cowdery said that any young man in this situation would want to sell the gold plates to get rich and it was just normal for Joseph Smith to have these types of thoughts. Isn't it interesting to note that when Joseph Smith tried to sell the Book of Mormon he showed himself as the author of the book, and when he failed to sell it he had it changed to show he was the translator instead of the author?

CHAPTER 7

THE FIRST VISION OF JOSEPH SMITH

The first vision and forgiveness of his (Joseph Smith's) sins came when he was 14 (or 15? Or 16?), in the early spring of 1820 (or 1821) when at a later date he remembers this heavenly vision (12 years later?).

The reason these different ages and dates are shown here are due to the many versions Joseph Smith and Oliver Cowdery gave regarding the occurrence of his first vision.

Let us record for this study Joseph Smith's handwritten version of his first vision as found in the book Histories, pages 11-14. (Note: I have copied it as exactly as I could, complete with the misspellings and lack of punctuation)

Version number one as written "largely in his own hand".
I was born in the town of Charon (Sharon) in the (State) of Vermont North America on the twenty third day of December AD 1805 of goodly parents who spared no pains to instruct(ing) me in (the) Christian religion(.) at the age of about ten years my Father Joseph Smithy Seignior moved to Palmyra Ontario County in the state of New York and being in indigent circumstances were obliged to

labour hard for the support of a large Family having nine children and as it required their exertions of all that were able to render any assistance for the support of the Family therefore we were deprived of the bennifit of an education suffice it to say I was mearly instructed in reading and writing and the ground (rules) of Arithmatic which const(it)uted my whole literary acquirements.

At about the age of twelve years my mind became seriously imprest with regard to the all important concerns for the welfare of my immortal soul which led me to searching the scriptures believeing as I was taught, that they contained the word of God thus applying myself to them and my intimate acquaintance with those of different denominations led me to marvel exceedingly for I discovered that (they did not) adorning their profession by a holy walk and Godly conversation agreeable to what I found contained in that sacred depository this was a grief to my Soul thus from the age of ***twelve years to fifteen*** I pondered many things in my heart concerning the situation of the world of mankind the contentions and divi(si)ons the wicke(d)ness and abominations and the darkness which pervaded the minds of mankind my mind become exceedingly distressed for I become convicted of my sins and my searching the scriptures I found that (mankind) did not come unto the Lord but that they had apostatized from the true and living faith and there was no society or denomination that built upon the gospel of Jesus Christ as recorded in the new testament and I felt to mourn for my own sins and for the sins of the world for I learned in the scriptures that God was the same yesterday to day and forever that he was no respecter of persons for he was God for I looked upon the sun the glorious luminary of the earth and also the moon rolling in their magesty through the heavens and also the stars shining in their courses and the earth also upon which I stood and the beast of the field and the fowls of heaven and the fish of the waters and also man walking forth upon the face of the earth in magesty and in the strength of beauty whose power and intelligence in governing the things which are so exceeding great and marvelous even in the likeness of him who created (them) and when I considered upon these things my heart exclaimed well hath the wise man said (it is a) fool (that) saith in his heart there is no God my heart exclaimed all these bear testimony and bespeak an omnipotent and omnipresent power a being who makith Laws and decreeth and bindeth all things in their bounds who fileth Eternity who was and is and will be from all Eternity to Eternity and when (I) considered all these things and that (that) being seeketh such to worship him and worship him in spirit and in truth therefore I cried unto the Lord for mercy for there was none else to whom I could go and to obtain mercy and the Lord heard my cry in the wilderness✱ and while in (the) attitude of calling upon the Lord (in the 16ᵗʰ year of my age) a piller of light above the brightness of the sun at noon day come down from above and rested upon me and I was filled with the spirit of god and the (Lord) opened the heavens upon me and I saw the Lord and he spake unto me saying Joseph (my son) thy sins are forgiven thee, Go thy (way) walk in my statutes and keep my commandment, behold I am the Lord of glory I was crucified for the world that all those who believe on my name may have Eternal life (behold) the world lieth in sin and at this time and none doeth good no not one they have turned aside from the gospel and keep not (my) commandments they draw near to me with their lips while their hearts are far from me and mine anger is kindling against the inhabitants of the earth to visit them according to their ungodliness and to bring to pass that which (hath) been spoken by the mouth of the prophets and Ap(o)stles behold and lo I come quickly as it (is) written of me in the cloud (clothed) in the glory of my Father and my soul was filled with love and for many days I could rejoice with great Joy and the Lord was with me but could find none that would believe the heavenly visions nevertheless I pondered these things in my heart but after many days I fell into transgressions and sinned in many things which brought a wound upon my soul and there were many things which transpired that cannot be written and my Fathers family have suffered many persecutions and afflictions and it came to pass when I was seventeen years of age I call again upon the Lord and he shewed unto me a heavenly vision for behold an angel of the Lord came and stood before me and it was by night…..

Now we have it recorded in this report let us examine it a little. Then we will also record the official version of this same vision as recorded in the Pearl of Great Price under "Joseph Smith – History" plus perhaps a few others.

He states "…I cried unto the Lord for mercy…and the Lord heard my cry in the wilderness* and while in the attitude of calling upon the Lord (in the 16th year of my age), a pillar of light above the brightness of the sun at noon day come down from above and rested upon me and I was filled with the spirit of God and the (Lord) opened the heavens upon me…and I saw the Lord and he spake unto me saying Joseph (my son) thy sins are forgiven thee, go thy (way) walk in my statutes and keep my commandments" Nothing said here about some power of darkness that was trying to overcome Joseph Smith while he prayed and received this vision. In fact from his telling this, isn't it clear there was **not** something like that (power of darkness etc.) happening to him?

He "cried" to the Lord? When you pray to God do you feel you are really "crying" instead of praying? Or both? Is it possible he was trying to make himself appear to be tearfully pleading with God? He was trying to find mercy from God? Mercy from what? He simply says "and I saw the Lord and he spake unto me saying Joseph (my son) thy sins are forgiven thee, go thy (way) walk in my statutes and keep my commandments"

Let us make a few significant observations here:

From when he was ten years old to when he was fifteen "he pondered many things in my (his) heart concerning the situation of the world of mankind the contentions and divi(si)ons the wicke(d)ness and abominations and the darkness which pervaded the minds of mankind my mind become exceedingly distressed for I become convicted of my sins and my searching the scriptures I found that (mankind) did not come unto the Lord but that they had apostatized from the true and living faith and there was no society or denomination that built upon the gospel of Jesus Christ as recorded in the new testament and I felt to mourn for my own sins and for the sins of the world for I learned in the scriptures that God was the same yesterday today and forever." It appears he is fifteen years old when he experiences his first vision, from what he states in largely his own hand.

He further confirms his age to be 15 as he states in this same version: "and while in (the) attitude of calling upon the Lord (in the 16th year of my age) a pillar of light above the brightness of the sun at noon day come down from above and rested upon me and I was filled with the spirit of god and the (Lord) opened the heavens upon me and I saw the Lord".

There was no mention or any indication that any power of darkness was present during this event or had any part of his first vision. The idea of being bound by some mysterious dark power binding his tongue didn't become part of the first vision account until some time after Charles G. Finney came out with his account of a vision he had of the Lord in 1821 wherein he tells about a dark power binding his tongue and a rustling in the leaves behind him, etc. which now becomes part of Joseph Smith's first vision according to Oliver Cowdery. It is confusing to read it, as it reads as if Joseph Smith himself is telling this yet in reality it is Oliver Cowdery composing and publishing this particular account.

There is no mention made of any angels present during his vision.

There is no mention made of any other personage, such as God the Father, appearing at this time and telling him to listen to his son. The idea of seeing both God the Father and Jesus Christ was related by a Norris Stearns in 1815 in a vision he claimed he had. Neither Norris

Stearns nor Joseph Smith could account for the many scriptures saying nobody could see the face of God and live. They didn't seem to feel it was necessary to explain this predicament at all, not at all. Nowhere does the Lord tell him not to join any of the churches around there.

Joseph Smith says nothing about reading from the 5th Chapter of James in the New Testament about anybody lacking wisdom should ask God. He is very precise in stating his concerns about what other churches were teaching and gives these concerns as the reason he went and prayed to the Lord, not because he had read the 5th chapter of James in the Bible.

Richard Bushman, one of the editors and historians writing this Histories, dismisses all of these later additions to Joseph Smith's visitation by stating "When he described the First Vision he abbreviated the experience" (Bushman, Rough Stone Rolling page 40) Bushman gives no reason for this statement. Why does he say it was abbreviated?

Wasn't this first recorded vision of Joseph Smith given in the actual handwriting of Joseph Smith? Where does Bushman come up with the idea that Joseph Smith could later change his original story and add other parts to his vision? Isn't it obvious to Bushman, a historian, that all of these alleged additions and changes Joseph Smith later makes to his original story, are all recorded in alleged revelations given to Norris Stearns, Alexander Campbell, Asa Wilde, Charles G. Finney, Solomon Chamberlain and Elias Smith? These men all wrote down their accounts which were all available to Joseph Smith many years prior to his claiming the same things happened to him.

CHAPTER 8

OTHER REVELATIONS CLAIMED BY MEN IN HIS VICINITY

Now it might be interesting to the reader to be made aware of the following revelations given to certain individuals in the area where Joseph Smith lived and grew up.

Note: All of these accounts appeared in print before Joseph's first vision was published.

An account of Norris Stearns published in 1815 in Greenfield, Massachusetts, not far from where the Joseph Smith Senior family lived in Vermont

"I saw two spirits, which I knew at the first sight. But if I had the tongue of an Angel I could not describe their glory, for they brought the joys of heaven with them. One was God, my Maker, almost in bodily shape like a man. His face was, as it were a flame of fire, and his body, as it had been a pillar and a cloud. In looking steadfastly to discern features, I could see none, but a small glimpse would appear in some other place. Below him stood Jesus Christ my Redeemer, in perfect shape like a man---his face by a vision of the night. That man heard a voice in the woods, saying 'Thy sins be forgiven thee'. A third saw his Savior descending to the tops of the trees at noon day" (The Christian Baptist. Vol 1. pp 148-49)

Norris Stearns herein claims to have seen God the Father and his Son Jesus Christ in his vision.

Now we have Alexander Campbell claiming he experienced a vision "of the night" and "heard a voice in the woods saying, 'Thy sins be forgiven thee'. In Joseph Smith's first version in his own handwriting he claimed the Lord appeared to him and told him his sins were forgiven.

Asa Wild on October 22, 1823 had a similar story published in the Wayne Sentinel (the paper to which the family of Joseph Smith subscribed).

"It seemed as if my mind, though active in its very nature, had lost all its activity, and was struck motionless, as well as into nothing, before the awful and glorious majesty of the Great Jehovah. He then spake to the following ourport; and in such a manner as I could not describe if I should attempt. -- He told me that the Millennium state of the world is about to take place; that in seven years literally, there would scarce a sinner be found on earth; that the earth itself, as well as the souls and bodies of its inhabitants, should be redeemed, as before the fall, and become as the garden of Eden. He told me that all of the most dreadful and terrible judgments spoken in the blessed scriptures were to be executed within that time, that more than two thirds of the inhabitants of the world would be destroyed by these judgments; some of which are the following -- wars, massacres, famine, pestilence, earthquakes, civil, political and ecclesiastical commotions; and above all, various and dreadful judgments executed immediately by God, through the instrumentality of the Ministers of the Millennial dispensation which is to exceed in glory every other dispensation; a short description of which may be seen in the last chapter of Isaiah, and in other places. He also told me, that every denomination of professing Christians had become extremely corrupt:"

We can readily see his claimed revelation has serious errors contained in it. The "Great Jehovah" allegedly told him that the "Millennium state of the word is about to take place; that in seven years literally, there would scarce a sinner be found on earth" etc. which obviously never happened, however his statements sound familiar to what Joseph Smith claimed in his first vision, after being altered by Oliver Cowdery etc.

In 1816 Solomon Chamberlin "As all others had failed I thought I would go to God and plead for mercy, and if I went to hell, I would go praying, and I cried unto the Lord night and day, for the forgiveness of my sins. Like Enos of old, till at length the Lord said, "Solomon, thy sins are forgiven thee. Go in peace and sin no more." My heart then leaped for joy unspeakable, I now joined the Methodist Order, and thought they were the rightest of any on the earth."

In 1816 a minister by the name of Elias Smith published a book in which he told of his conversion. Notice how similar it is to Joseph Smith's first account:

"…I went into the woods…a light appeared from heaven…My mind seemed to rise in that light to the throne of God and the Lamb… The Lamb once slain appeared to my understanding and while viewing him, I felt such love to him as I never felt to any thing earthly… It is not possible for me to tell how long I remained in that situation…" (The Life, Conversion, Preaching, Travels, and Sufferings of Elias Smith, Portsmouth N.H. 1816 pp 58-59)

Here Elias Smith claims he saw Jesus Christ and makes no mention of any other personage evident in his vision.

Alexander Campbell wrote the following on March 1, 1824, concerning a "revival in the state of New York". Enthusiasm flourishes… This man was regenerated when asleep, vision an angel, who told him that all the existing churches were corrupt and that God would soon raise up an apostolic church. This comes from Richard Bushman one of the authors of the Joseph Smith papers.

The account of Charles G. Finney can also be examined and found to be very similar to Joseph Smith's first vision account. This vision occurred to Finney in 1821.

"North of the village, and over a hill, lay a piece of woods, in which I was in the almost daily habit of walking, more or less, when it was pleasant weather…instead of going to the office, I turned and bent my course towards the woods, feeling that I must be alone, and away from all human eyes and ears, so that I could pour out my prayer to God. …I then penetrated into the woods, I should think, a quarter of a mile…and found a place where some large trees had fallen across each other, leaving an open place between. There I saw I could make a kind of closet. I crept into this place and knelt down for prayer. As I turned to go up into the woods, I recollect to have said, 'I will give my heart to God, or I never will come down from there'…

But when I attempted to pray I found that my heart would not pray… when I came to try, I was dumb; that is, I had nothing to say to God' or at least I could say but a few words and those without heart. In attempting to pray I would hear a rustling in the leaves, as I thought and would stop and look up to see if somebody were not coming. This I did several times…"

Compare this with what Joseph Smith claimed happened to him: " One account said he heard a noise behind him like someone walking towards him and then, when he tried to pray again, the noise grew louder, causing him to spring to his feet and look around, but he saw no one."

We continue, "The question of when, that is of the present time, seemed to fall heavily into my heart. I told the Lord that I should take him at his word; that he could not lie; and that therefore I was sure that he heard my prayer and that he would be found of me. Next morning, on the way to the office, he had as clear a view of the atonement of Christ as he ever had afterwards. The Holy Spirit seemed to present Christ: hanging on the cross for him. The vision was so clear that almost unconsciously he stopped in the middle of the street for several minutes when it came to him. North of the village and over a hill lay a piece of woods, or forest, and he decided to go there and pour out his heart in prayer. So great was his pride, he kept out of sight so far as possible for fear that some one should see him on the way to the woods and should think that he was going there to pray. He penetrated far into the woods where some large trees had fallen across each other leaving an open space between. Into this space he crept to pray. "But when I attempted to pray," says he, "I found that my heart would not pray." He was in great fear lest someone should come and find him praying. He was on the verge of despair, having promised God not to leave the spot until he settled the question of his soul's salvation, and yet it seemed impossible to him to settle the question. "Just at this moment," says he, "I again thought I heard some one approach me, and I opened my eyes to see whether it were so. But right there the revelation of my pride of heart, as the great difficulty that stood in the way, was distinctly shown me. An overwhelming sense of my wickedness in being ashamed to have a human being see me on my knees before God, took such powerful possession of me, that I cried at the top of my voice, and exclaimed that I would not leave that place if all the men on earth and all the devils in hell surrounded me." He was completely humbled in soul by the thought of his pride. Then the most comforting verses of Scripture seemed to pour into his soul. He saw clearly that faith was not an intellectual state but a voluntary act, and he accepted the promise of God. He than gave me many other promises, both from the Old and the New Testament, especially some most precious promises respecting our Lord Jesus Christ...

I continued thus to pray, and to receive and appropriate promises for a long time, I know not how long. I prayed till my mind became so full that, before I was aware of it I was on my feet and tripping up the ascent toward the road."

"After dinner we (Squire Wright and himself) were engaged in removing the books and furniture to another office. We were very busy in this, and had but little conversation all the afternoon. My mind, however, remained in that profoundly tranquil state. There was a great sweetness and tenderness if my thoughts and feelings. Everything appeared to be going right, and nothing seemed to disturb me or ruffle me in the least."

"Just before evening the thought took possession of my mind, that as soon as I was left alone in the new office, I would try to pray again - that I was not going to abandon the subject of religion and give it up, at any rate; and therefore although I no longer had any concern about my soul, still I would continue to pray."

"By evening we got the books and furniture adjusted; and I made up, in an open fire-place, a good fire, hoping to spend the evening alone. Just at dark Squire Wright, seeing that everything was adjusted, bade me goodnight and went to his home. I had accompanied him to the door and as I closed the door and turned around, my heart seemed to be liquid within me. All my feelings seemed to rise and flow out; and the utterance of my heart was, 'I want to pour my whole soul out to God'. The rising of my soul was so great that I rushed into the room back of the front office to pray."

"There was no fire, and no light, in the room, nevertheless it appeared to me as if it were perfectly light. As I went in and shut the door after me, it seemed as if I met the Lord Jesus Christ face to face. It did not occur to me then, nor did it for some time afterward that I was wholly a mental state. On the contrary it seemed to be that I saw Him as I would see any other man. He said nothing, but looked at me in such a manner as to break me right down at His feet. I have always since regarded this is as a most remarkable state of mind; for it seemed to me a reality, that he stood before me, and I fell down at His feet and poured out my soul to Him."

As stated above, all of these accounts were in print and available to Joseph Smith prior to his announcement of his first vision, several prior to Joseph Smith's 1820 claim for his first vision and several after, but all were in print before Joseph Smith "broadcast" his first vision and put it in writing.

It is interesting to note that most of the alleged visions these men had were at night. It is also interesting to note that most of these visionaries are men, not women although there are a few sprinklings of a few women claiming to have experienced visions also.

CHAPTER 9

OTHER VERSIONS OF JOSEPH SMITH'S FIRST VISION

Now we continue on with the Histories. From page 25 we read that the 1834 – 1836 is a composite historical record consisting of genealogical tables, journal - like entries, and transcripts of newspaper articles. .

In this 1834 – 1836 version of the history of the church Oliver Cowdery wrote a series of letters to William W. Phelps who published them in the Messenger and Advocate of which he was in charge of at that time. He makes vague and passing comments about Joseph Smith's first vision but does not attempt to write it down in this version of the history of the church. However, he does go into significant detail about Joseph Smith's second vision of the angel Nephi or Moroni, relative to the gold plates. We shall consider that later.

The Book of John Whitmer says nothing about Joseph Smith's first vision. Indeed this shows why the authors of the History Papers question whether Whitmer was even aware of any visions Joseph Smith had. Now we have Joseph Smith's version of his first vision written "largely in his own hand", we have John Whitmer's history which doesn't mention Joseph Smith's first vision, and Oliver Cowdery, Warren Parrish, Warren Cowdrey and Frederick G. Williams history which only lightly touches on Joseph Smith's first vision.

It is interesting to note what the historians say about Oliver Cowdery's style of writing. Page 38 "Employing florid romantic language, frequent scriptural allusions, and much dramatic detail", etc. This is pointed out to show that not only could I easily tell this about Oliver Cowdery, but also the entire staff of history writers that were involved in the publication of Histories The Joseph Smith Papers. Now we are going to explore another version of what Joseph Smith said he experienced.

On Page 13 (Histories) footnote 45 "Joseph Smith later recounted that he saw two personages, that one appeared after the other, and that 'they did in reality speak unto me, or one of them did'. What does he mean "*or* one of them did"? In later accounts he claimed God the Father said "This is my beloved Son, hear him". Then Christ also reportedly talked to him. Why is it so difficult for Joseph Smith to remember God talking to him?

Other accounts identify the two personages as the Father and the Son. (JS History, vol. A-1 p.214 of Histories under Draft 2) JS Journal, 9-11 Nov. 1835, in JSP Jr. 1:87-88. These are yet other versions of his first vision, which we will consider later in this report being called the 1838 – 1839 Histories.

On Nov. 9, 1835 he met with Joshua, the Jewish Minister and gave an account of his first vision. This was 15 years after his first vision actually happened. Joshua's real name was Robert Matthews (1788-ca. 1841) From Page 608 Histories we read "carpenter, joiner, merchant, minister, Born at Cambridge, Washington Co., New York,

Raised in Anti Burgher Secession Church. Married Margaret Wright, 1813, at New York City. Adopted beliefs of Methodism and then Judaism. Moved to Albany, ca 1825. Claimed to be God the Father reincarnated in body of Matthias, the ancient apostle. Prophesied destruction of Albany, 1830. Left Albany and his family to embark on apostolic preaching tour through eastern and southern U.S. Upon returning to New York, recruited local religious figures Elijah Pierson and Benjamin Folger. Committed to hospital for the insane at Bellevue, New York City, for a time. Little is known of Matthews after his 1835 visit with JS at Kirtland, Geauga Co., Ohio. Reported to have died in Iowa Territory."

Page 115 Nov. 9, 1835 "While sitting in his (JS) house this morning between the hours of ten an(d) eleven, a man came in and introduced himself to him calling himself Joshua, the Jewish Minister. His appearance was something singular, having a beard about three inches in length which is quite gray. His hair was also long and considerably silvered with age. He had the appearance of a man about 50 or 55 years old. He was tall and straight, slender frame, blue eyes, thin visage, and fair complexion. He wore a green frock coat and pantaloons of the same color. He had on a black fur hat with a narrow brim. When speaking he frequently shut his eyes and exhibits a kind of scowl upon his countenance.

Joseph Smith gave him a relation of the circumstances, connected with the coming forth of the Book of Mormon. This is the second account of his first vision and it is recorded on page 115 of the Histories book as follows:

"Being wrought up in my mind respecting the subject of Religion, and looking at the different systems taught the children of men, I knew not who was right or who was wrong, but considered it of the first importance to me that I should be right, in matters of such moment, matter involving eternal consequences. Being thus perplexed in mind I retired to the silent grove, and there bowed down before the Lord, under a realizing sense, (if the bible be true) ask and you shall receive, knock and it shall be opened, seek and you shall find, and again, if any man lack wisdom, let (him ask) of God who giveth to all men liberally & upbraideth not. Information was what I most desired at this time, and with a fixed determination to obtain it, I called on the Lord for the first time in the place above stated, or in other words, I made a fruitless attempt to pray. My tongue seemed to be swollen in my mouth, so that I could not utter. I heard a noise behind me like some one walking towards me. I strove again to pray, but could not; the noise of walking seemed to draw nearer; I sprang upon my feet and looked round, but saw no person, or thing that was calculated to produce the noise of walking. I kneeled again, my mouth was opened and my tongue loosed. I called on the Lord in mighty prayer. A pillar of fire appeared above my head, which presently rested down upon me, and filled me with unspeakable joy. A personage appeared in the midst of this pillar of flame, which was spread all around and yet nothing consumed. Another personage soon appeared like unto the first; he said unto me thy sins are forgiven thee. He testified also unto me that Jesus Christ is the son of God. I saw many angels in this vision. I was about 14 years old when I received this first communication."

Hopefully, dear reader, you can see the similarities of the above account to that of Charles G. Finney's revelation in 1821 to Joseph Smith Jr.s recounting his second version of his first vision in 1835, fourteen years later. Significantly Charles Finney's account was printed in 1821 and Joseph Smith had ample opportunity to read it and incorporate it into his own life should he have desired to do so.

When he later recounted about seeing two personages he still did not identify them as one of them being God the Father. So we have his first account where the Lord appears to him, and then in his recounting his story (and this 'recounting' occurred after Oliver Cowdery came on the scene and began writing as if he was Joseph Smith), a second being appears after the first and identifies the first being as Jesus Christ.

So now we have two very different versions of his first vision. Even the historians cannot be certain whether in the circa Summer 1832 version Joseph Smith was introducing this for the first time or was copying from some earlier writings. They give no evidence about any such writings so we are left in the dark as to where Joseph Smith would have obtained earlier writings of his first vision. Isn't it very clear that these first two versions, Joseph Smith's and Oliver Cowdery's, were very different from each other?

Oliver Cowdery wrote his version as if he were Joseph Smith speaking himself, so does it not appear very confusing to read two very different accounts of what Joseph Smith said happened to him? Especially when we are asked to believe they are both Joseph Smith talking in each version?

The version printed in the Documentary History of the Church Vol 1, pp 5-6 is very different than the version Joseph Smith wrote in his own handwriting. In the Documentary History of the Church version it says nothing about Joseph Smith's sins being forgiven and claims two personages appeared to him at the same time, not one after the other. It would appear from the official version of the Mormon Church that one personage was God the Father as it is recorded "One of them spake unto me, calling me by name, and said-pointing to the other-This is my beloved Son, Hear him".

Although this appears to be Joseph Smith's own words, it is actually written by Warren Cowdery and Warren Parrish in 1835. Oliver Cowdery has confused the issue by stating in his letter to Wm. W. Phelps that Joseph Smith was 17 years old when he first had a vision from God, not 14 years old as Warren Cowdery and Warren Parrish now state and what Joseph Smith himself wrote in the circa summer 1832 account. We now have Joseph Smith's circa summer 1832 account, Oliver Cowdery's account, and Warren Cowdery and Warren Parrish's account, none of which agree with each other plus Joshua the Jewish Minister's account which also does not agree with any of the others. It is not clear however that possibly the account of Joshua the Jewish Minister was written by Warren Cowdery and Warren Parish also. It is clearly someone relating an occurrence and not Joseph Smith either writing or dictating what happened. (Page 115 Histories). From the Historians stating that the circaSummer1832 account was the only one written in Joseph Smith's own hand can we now assume none of these other accounts were actually written by Joseph Smith himself?

Joseph Smith in his presentation to Joshua the Jewish Minister, said the Lord appeared to him and said there were many angels present. Oliver Cowdery writing as if it was Joseph Smith talking said God and Christ appeared and there was no mention made of angels. Warren Parrish and Warren Cowdery, also writing as if they were Joseph Smith himself state that a personage appeared to him followed by another personage, neither of which is identified, yet the first version said it was the Lord and the second version said it was two personages. Now in Joshua the Jewish Minister version one personage appears and another one appears later. One allegedly said that "Jesus Christ is the Son of God" but in this version neither personage is identified. He said that he called on the Lord in "mighty" prayer. Nowhere do we find a definition of "mighty" prayer compared to other types of prayer so we are left to wonder what "mighty" prayer means. Does it sound like he is trying to use unnecessary adjectives in an effort to be more impressive?

On page 124 of "Histories" footnote 279 we see his recounting of the first vision of angels corresponds with the vision he described earlier in the week to Robert Mathews (the Jewish Minister, also called Robert Mattias, wherein he saw two "personages" and "many angels" when he "was about 14. We are left to wonder whether to believe Joseph Smith stating his age "about 14" or Oliver Cowdery stating Joseph Smith was about 16? Or Joseph Smith stating he was in his 16th year making him 15? Refer to Histories Page 56 where Oliver Cowdery in a letter to William W. Phelps said it was in the 17th year of Joseph Smith's life that the great religious controversies took place and therefore it was in his 17th year that he would have had his first vision experience.

Was Joseph Smith 14, 15, 16 or 17 years of age when he claimed to have his first vision? Where is the detail needed in these related stories?

In the circa summer 1832 version, of which we are not sure if he was copying from an earlier written statement or was composing at this time, he stated that "…and I saw the Lord" etc. Warren Cowdery adds to this account after he received the journal from Warren Parrish in early April 1836. It was during this writing that the addition of the powers of darkness trying to hamper Joseph Smith in his first vision comes about.

Alexander Campbell's account of his vision had been in publication about ten years by this time wherein he detailed the powers of darkness apparently hindering him in his attempt to pray. In Joseph Smith's first writing of this it was Jesus Christ (the Lord) who appeared to him, not two personages, one after the other. From page 116 of Histories Warren Cowdery's gives his version of what happened to Joseph Smith.

Again he writes as if he is Joseph Smith himself talking to Robert Mathews, the Jewish Minister.

"I made a fruitless attempt to pray. My tongue seemed to be swollen in my mouth, so that I could not utter. I heard a noise behind me like some one walking toward me. I strove again to pray, but could not; the noise of walking seemed to draw nearer. I sprang upon my feet and looked round, but saw no person, or thing that was calculated to produce the noise of walking. I kneeled again, my mouth was opened and my tongue loosed; I called on the Lord in mighty prayer. A pillar of fire appeared above my head; which presently rested down upon me, and filled me with unspeakable joy. A personage appeared in the midst of this pillar of flame, which was spread all around and yet nothing consumed. Another personage soon appeared like unto the first: he said unto me thy sins are forgiven thee. He testified also unto me that Jesus Christ is the son of God. I saw many angels in this vision."

We have already compared Charles Finney's account of his vision with this one by Warren Parish aka Joseph Smith with regard to the noise of one walking behind him, etc.

Isn't this very different than Joseph Smith's own handwritten account of what transpired? Nowhere does he mention angels appearing to him in his first account. While he doesn't specifically say he is Jesus Christ, he does say "I am the Lord of glory I was crucified for the world that all those who believe on my name may have Eternal life", so it would appear we can safely conclude this is Jesus Christ. Nowhere does he mention his tongue being swollen and that he couldn't utter. Nor does he mention hearing any noise behind him like someone walking.

The second forgiveness of his sins came Sept 21, 1823 by an angel appearing to him. There is serious confusion about the name of this angel as we shall see later on in this study. Is it possible for an angel to forgive sins?

The third forgiveness of his sins came April 10, 1830 or perhaps four days earlier when he reported receiving a revelation regarding the starting of a church. Joseph Smith says he had received a "remission of his sins" but is not clear who gave him this remission. Could it have been Jesus Christ? Or the angel? Or God the Father?

In this study, it becomes necessary for me to insert additional information that I believe is necessary for the reader to be able to better understand this effort. It may be helpful to the reader to know some additional information about some of the individuals involved in this study of Joseph Smith Papers.

First let us investigate Joseph Smith from the standpoint of the historian Whitney R. Cross in his book "The Burned-Over District". Page 142 "The entire family (Smith's) was at least barely literate. Hyrum had attended a Vermont seminary, and Joseph had some part of a few years' schooling in Palmyra, possibly increased by brief attendance at Bainbridge in 1826. He had belonged to the young men's debating society in Palmyra. Though he read easily, his writing was at best halting and he attained only the rudiments of arithmetic.

Probably the family budget had required his labor a good deal of the time when he might have been in school. Despite testimonials to the contrary, it must be concluded that neither Joseph nor any of his family was especially ignorant according to the standards of the place and time. Interest in things marvelous and supernatural they certainly had abundantly, but even this made them differ only in degree from their neighbors. After all, Joseph's peeping stone attracted loyal followers. The rest of the family, though perhaps not the prophet himself, behaved like others in attending services in revival seasons."

"It seems entirely plausible, as his most recent biographer claims, that Joseph became a prophet in quite accidental fashion. Having risen above his own early experiments in necromancy his imagination wandered into new realms. "When he found others taking his new hobby seriously, he had to live up to expectations and spend the remainder of his short life learning to assume the consequent responsibilities. In so doing he improved and demonstrated his naturally dynamic character.[17] "This was no more than happens to any man who enjoys the great responsibilities which fate thrusts upon

[17] *O. Turner, History of the Pioneer Settlement of Phelps and Gorham/s Purchase etc. (Rochester, 1852) cited in Evans, Smith, 38; Orson Pratt, Remarkable Vision quoted by Henry Mayhew, History of the Mromons, etc. (Augusrn 1853, 19 ff Palyra Herald, Oct. 8 1822 and Western Farmer, July 11, 18, 25,, 1821.*

him, though religious leadership demands somewhat rare personal qualities. It might have happened to almost anyone of Joseph's fellow Yankee migrants. The fundamental condition leading to the new faith was the credulity and spiritual yearning which made people anxious to follow a prophet, whoever he might be."[18]

"It should be added, however, that interest in Mormonism was no necessary indication either of extraordinary ignorance or of unusually febrile imaginings. Converts like Brigham Young, Heber Kimball, J. J. Strang, William Phelps, Sidney Rigdon, Orson Pratt and Lorenzo Snow to name only a few, had on the whole superior education for their times, and most of them proved to be as vigorously realistic pillars of the church as anyone might desire. The man who exercised primacy over these individuals approached some kind of genius, however it may have been inspired."[19]

For additional insight into Joseph Smith and the Mormon Church, see the appendix at the end of this study titled **"Joseph Smith"**

Isaac Hale, the father of Emma Hale – Joseph Smith, Jr's wife – gave his opinion of Joseph Smith and this is found in the appendix of this report under **Isaac Hale's affidavit.**

A statement by Peter Ingersoll, a friend of Joseph Smith at this same time is found at the end of this report under the appendix **"Peter Ingersoll".**

Certainly it seems critical to this study to know something about Oliver Cowdery also in order to better understand how he fits into the Joseph Smith history.

---

[18] *(Mayhew), Mormons. 36*

[19] *Brodie, No Man Knows, passin, Whitney R. Cross "Mormonism in the "Burned Over District", New York History XXV (July, 1944) 326-338*

* The Burned Over District page 143*Footnote17 The burned over District page 1143

Oliver Cowdery was a school teacher who moved from place to place and lived with different families as he taught school which was customary at that time. He was born Oct. 3, 1806, within about a year of Joseph Smith Jr.'s birth (Dec. 23, 1805)

The Cowdery family attended the Congregational Church of Poultney, VT, where Ethan Smith was pastor for several years. At that time, Ethan Smith was writing a book called View of the Hebrews (1823) one of many books written by him during the period speculating that Native Americans were of Hebrew origin. Interestingly enough 1823 was the year Joseph Smith claimed the angel Nephi appeared to him and told him about the gold plates. The name of this angel was Nephi but sometime after 1855 someone changed it to be Moroni but there is no record of who did this or why. More on this to follow.

In 1828 it is reported that Oliver Cowdery lived with the Joseph Smith Sr. family although he didn't meet Joseph Smith, Jr. until April 5, 1829. Joseph Smith apparently lived about 300 miles away from his father's house at this time. It appears Oliver was always of a frail nature and succumbed to many illnesses easily. Indeed, this may have been why he died March 3 1850 of complications from what may have been tuberculosis.

Although few Mormons are aware of it, Oliver Cowdery and the Mormon Prophet Joseph Smith, Jr. were second cousins, both via Smith's mother, Lucy Mack and through a second, even lesser known kinship. This same family connection also makes Warren Cowdrey a second cousin of Joseph Smith, Jr. Warren appears to have changed the spelling of the name Cowdery to Cowdrey.

Upon meeting Oliver Cowdery, Joseph Smith said he had been promised by the Lord that he would be given an assistant to help him in furthering the Lord's work upon the earth and upon meeting Oliver, Joseph said this was the man the Lord had sent to him. Nothing more is said about Oliver engaging in any school teaching activities from that time forth and when he eventually was separated[20] from the church he practiced law for seven years.

From 1838, the date of his excommunication from the Church, to 1848, Cowdery put the Latter Day Saints church behind him. He studied law and practiced at Tiffin, OH, where he became a civic and political leader.

Cowdery also joined the Methodist church there and served as secretary in 1844. He edited the local Democratic newspaper until it was learned that he was one of the Book of Mormon witnesses; then he was assigned as assistant editor. In 1846, Cowdery was nominated as his district's Democratic party candidate for the state senate, but when his Mormon background was discovered, he was defeated.

Oliver worked with Joseph on the writing of the Book of Mormon from April 1829 when he first met Joseph on June of 1829 when the work was completed. The Church was organized in April of 1830, almost a year later. For additional information on the Book of Mormon, see the appendix at the end of this report titled "Book of Mormon".

On June 9, 1830 Oliver Cowdery was appointed "the church record and conference minutes" (strange wording) yet in the Fall of 1830 he was sent on a "Proselytizing" mission to the west, effectively ending his early work to keep church records.

Oliver Cowdery was one of the six initial members of the Church of Christ when it was organized by Joseph Smith on April 6, 1830.

At a conference June 9, 1830 (the one appointing Cowdery church clerk) there is a record of ten ministerial licenses that were issued. It is unclear what these licenses were for but it seems they were priesthood licenses.

---

[20] *See the end of this report for list of charges brought against Oliver Cowdery in his excommunication hearing and his letter in response to the charges.*

It was incorporated April 6, 1830 so it would seem the church had the authority to issue whatever licenses it wished. It would seem this would give an individual authority for this church to act as a minister and perform those duties normally conducted by ministers of any registered or incorporated church of whatever denomination **except** marriages. To perform marriages a person had to be licensed by the state. There is no official title of "minister" in the Church of Jesus Christ of Latter Day Saints, so this may have been a license given certain individuals certifying them as priesthood holders of the Mormon church.

It is clear they did not have the authority to perform marriages as on October 25, 1835 (5 years later) it states on page 103 footnote 199 Brunson (Seymour) had obtained a license in Jackson County, Ohio to solemnize weddings, may have been the only Latter-day Saint with such a license at this time[21].

Let us return to the "Histories". On page 7 the historians speculate that the fact that the extant history exists in a record book and not as loose leaves suggest it is a copy. (Joseph Smith circa summer 1832) "It may not be…" "…suggesting he was copying rather than composing". What would he be copying from?

On page 6 it states the circa summer 1832 history possibly was copied from an earlier manuscript, then on page 7 it states "other textual evidence however indicates that the circa summer 1832 history may

---

[21] *Seymour Brunson obtained a position as Justice of the Peace and in this office was able to perform marriages and other legal duties that went with this position. Born Sept. 18, 1798 in Orwell, VT and served in the war of 1812. He joined the Mormon Church in early 1831. He served as a missionary for the church. Died August 10, 1840. Seymour brought charges against Oliver Cowdery and David Whitmer causing them to be excommunicated from the church.*
To have legally recognized clergy status in Ohio, one must have ordination papers from a church recognized in Ohio. In May 1830, the other Mormons from New York came to Kirtland. This small town near Cleveland became the headquarters of the Church from January 1831 to December 1837.

be the original inscription." Continuing, "The history also contains several significant contemporaneous revisions in Joseph Smith's handwriting which <u>may</u> indicate that Joseph Smith was composing original narrative".

What "contemporaneous revisions" and where can we find them? What "earlier manuscripts" were available to him at this time?

Back we go again, "likewise Joseph Smith and Williams <u>may</u> have been modifying the circa summer 1832 history as they copied it from an earlier version." So was it copied or was it composed? And how can we understand anything about "an earlier version"? The author of this history has already clearly stated Joseph Smith circa Summer 1832 is the only narrative of the foundational spiritual events of Joseph Smith early life that includes his own handwriting. We are still asking whether the circa Summer 1832 history was an original account of Joseph Smith's first vision or was it copied from some other writing? What other writing could it have come from?

So we have words like "suggest, …may,… possibly". So there are other alternatives available to us in this study. How can we be convinced of the validity of any of the items mentioned in this book when they are stated to be "possibly, may, suggest. Etc."? Is this book based merely on possibilities and speculations?

"Frederick G. Williams first met Joseph Smith in the summer of 1831 but there is no evidence he began work as a scribe before 16 February 1832." Page 7, 8

Page 8 ""…it is not <u>implausible</u>…" "Joseph Smith <u>probably</u> followed…" continued comments about this history being very uncertain and full of guess work.

July 8, 1832 Sidney Rigdon surrenders his Priesthood license. "At a Sunday morning meeting held in Kirtland on 8 July 1832, Joseph

Smith demanded that Rigdon surrender his priesthood license because Rigdon had declared three days earlier that the 'keys of the kingdom' had been taken from the church and that he alone retained them.'" Histories Page 9 Footnote 23. Then he got it back three weeks afterwards and Joseph Smith reinstated him in the church presidency.

For additional history about Sidney Rigdon I have added the following in an effort to better understand who he was and how he fits into this history study.

He was born in St. Clair Township, Allegheny Count, PA about 10 miles south of Pittsburgh. Sidney remained on his fathers farm until 1818 when he apprenticed himself to a Baptist minister named Andrew Clark. Rigdon received his license to preach for the Regular Baptists in March of 1819. He moved in May to Trumbull County, Ohio where he jointly preached with Adamson Bentley from July 1819. He married Bentley's sister Phoebe Brook in June 1820, and remained in Ohio until February 1822 when he returned to Pittsburgh to accept the pastorate of the First Baptist Church there under the recommendation of Alexander Campbell.

Sidney Rigdon and Adamson Bentley went to meet Alexander Campbell in 1821, for the purpose of learning more about the Baptist who preached his idea that the New Testament should hold priority over the Old Testament in the Christian Church. After engaging in many discussions, both men joinied the Disciples of Christ church that was associated with Alexander Campbell. Some disaffected members of this church forced his resignation in 1824. For the next two years Rigdon worked as a tanner to support his family, while preaching on Sundays in the Pittsburgh courthouse. In 1826 he was invited to become the pastor of the Baptist Church in Mentor, Ohio. Many of the prominent early Latter-day Saint leaders, including Parley P. Pratt, Isaac Morley and Edward Partridge, were members of Sidney Rigdon's congregations prior to their conversion to the Church of Christ, which became the Church of Jesus Christ of Latter-day Saints.

Parley P. Pratt stopped in Palmyra, where he first learned about the Book of Mormon. In early September 1830, Parley P. Pratt was baptized into Joseph Smith's Church of Christ. In October Pratt and Ziba Peterson were called on a mission to preach to the American Indians or "Lamanites". In December 1830, Sidney Rigdon traveled to New York where it is reported he met Joseph Smith. There is considerable disagreement as to when Sidney Rigdon really met Joseph Smith and there is some evidence they knew each other as early as 1828. Sidney Rigdon was a very good preacher and immediately called by Smith to be the spokesman for the church.

A December 1830 revelation to Joseph Smith counseled members of the church in New York to gather to Kirtland, Ohio and join with Sidney Rigdon's congregation there. Many of the teachings of Rigdon's group experimented with, including living with all things in common and later found expression in Joseph Smith's church. When returning to Ohio from New York in early February 1831, Joseph Smith convinced Sidney Rigdon's church to abandon the common-stock principle for the more perfect law of the Lord. On February 9, 1831, Joseph Smith announced God's revealed Law of Consecration about having all things commonly owned by eveeryone. Members were advised that "all things belong to the Lord" and were asked to deed all their personal property to the bishop of the Church.

When Joseph Smith organized the Church's First Presidency, he set apart Jesse Gause and Sidney Rigdon as his first two counselors. Joseph Smith and Sidney Rigdon became close partners, and Sidney Rigdon seemed to take over Oliver Cowdery's place as the original "Second Elder" of the Church. However, Oliver Cowdery was still called "Assistant President of the church".

Jesse Gause was a Quaker who moved to North Union, Ohio at the same time Latter-day Saints from New York were also emigrating to Ohio, settling in the area of Kirtland, Ohio, some fifteen miles east of North Union. It is unknown just when Jesse Gause came into contact with these Latter-day Saints, but some time after October 1831 he was baptized as a Latter-day Saint himself. Jesse Gause rose quickly to a position of prominence in this new faith; in an early record book it states that on March 8, 1832, Joseph Smith "chose this day and ordained brother Jesse Gause and brother Sidney Rigdon to be my counselors of the ministry of the presidency of the High Priesthood". (Kirtland Revelation Book, p. 10, LDS Church Archives, Salt Lake City, UT). A week later, Joseph Smith received a revelation concerning Gause's selection as a counselor in what later became known as the First Presidency, as well as giving him additional instructions concerning his new assignment. Both Jesse Gause and Joseph Smith's other counselor, Sidney Rigdon, had previous experience living in communal societies. Gause accompanied [22]Joseph Smith to Jackson County, Missouri, between April and June 1832, to set up the Law of Consecration. It is not known what happened to cause him to lose faith in Mormonism, but by the end of 1832 he had 'denied the faith' and was excommunicated from Joseph Smith's church on December 3, 1832.

Jesse Gause's role in Mormon history went unacknowledged for many years. The revelation given about him in 1832 was changed by replacing his name with his replacement in the First Presidency, Frederick G. Williams. His name was finally recognized in the 1980 edition of the Doctrine and Covenants, but then only in the historical introduction to the revelation; Frederick G. Williams name remained in the text itself. Only after historians demonstrated his role in the formation of Mormon hierarchy, beginning with Robert J. Woodford

---

[22] *Joseph Smith 'recounted' his first story? What does this mean? Is this just an attempt to admit his first story was not true? By using the word 'recounted' can he change his initial story to anything he wants to say at this point? He counted wrong the first time? He only counted one person so he needed to recount? By changing his first account he shows his memory is very poor or he couldn't really remember what happened when he first told us about it. Do you think if you saw and talked to God that you would have trouble remembeering how many beings were present at that time?*

in 1975 and D. Michael Quinn in 1983, was his name restored to the church's list of General Authorities.

Sidney Rigdon became a strong advocate of the construction of the Kirtland Temple. When the Church founded the Kirtland Safety Society[23], Sidney Rigdon became the bank's president and Joseph Smith served as its cashier. When the bank failed in 1837, Sidney Rigdon and Joseph Smith were both blamed by Mormon dissenters.

So continuing on, nobody seems to know where the circa summer 1832 history came from and in fact the authors state on page 10 "regardless of when it was created…" so after ten pages we still don't know where the circa summer 1832 history came from. Was it originally written by Joseph Smith and Fredrick G. Williams, or copied from an earlier record? "…but it does preserve details of those visions not recorded elsewhere".

Now dear reader, hold on here just a minute please. Details of visions not recorded elsewhere? What can this possibly mean? Are we to believe these "details of visions" in the circa summer 1832 history are accurate and should be believed? What? You say you are confused? Dear reader, the title of this historical document is "The Joseph Smith Papers". This is purported to be a historical record of Joseph Smith's papers. The historians writing or compiling this work have here added something about visions not recorded elsewhere. It would seem necessary after making such a statement to give us a little more enlightenment about these "other visions". Please note that these historians clearly state that this circa summer 1832 history "does preserve details of those visions not recorded elsewhere". Details? Oh really? You think you are confused now. Wait until you see the additional "details" added to Joseph Smith's "details" by Oliver Cowdery.

---

[23] *For more detailed information on the Kirtland Safety Society, or Joseph Smith's attempt at banking, see the appendix at the end of this report Kirtland Safety Society Anti-Bank*

CHAPTER 10

NO MAN HAS SEEN THE FATHER

When Joseph Smith was fourteen (or 15, or 16?) years old he says "…I saw the Lord and he spake unto me…" Earlier in our study we read "Joseph Smith later recounted[24] that he saw two 'personages'" Yet aren't we told nobody can see the face of God and live?

"And the LORD said, "I will cause all my goodness to pass in front of you, and I will proclaim my name, the LORD . . . But, "he said, "you cannot see my face, for no one may see me and live. " (Exodus 33:19-20, NIV)

It states clearly here "for no one may see me and live" (Ex ch 33) but back in chapter 6 God is reported to say "and I appeared unto Abraham unto Isaac, and unto Jacob". And Job says "but now my eyes see You". Could a possible explanation be that it is Jesus Christ speaking about appearing to these prophets, not God the Father? Doesn't he refers to Himself often as the one God relating to the prophets?

---

[24] *The historians say Joseph Smith 'recounted' that he saw two personages? If he indeed saw two personages from the start why didn't he say so in the first place?*

". . .He who is the blessed and only Potentate, the King of kings and Lord of lords . . . dwelling in unapproachable light (where the Father lives), whom NO MAN has seen or can see . . ." (1Timothy 6:15-16, NKJV)

"Then Job answered the Lord and said: "I know that You can do everything, and that no purpose of Yours can be withheld from You . . . I have heard of You by the hearing of the ear, but now my eye sees You." (Job 42:1,5, NKJV)

"No one has seen the Father except the one who is from God; only he has seen the Father." (John 6:46, NIV)

"For the law was given through Moses; grace and truth came through Jesus Christ. No one has ever seen God, [the Father] but God the One and Only, who is at the Father's side . . . " (John 1:17-18, NIV)

Exodus 33:20 "And he said, Thou canst not see my face; for there shall no man see me, and live." KJV

Exodus 6:2-3 And God spake unto Moses, and said unto him, I am the Lord: (3) And I appeared unto Abraham unto Isaac, and unto Jacob, by the name of God Almighty, but by my name JEHOVAH was I not know to them".

And without the ordinances thereof, and the authority of the priesthood, the power of godliness is not manifest unto men in the flesh, For without this no man can see the face of God, even the Father, and live. D&C 84"21-22

Joseph Smith taught in the Lectures on Faith Doctrine and Covenants 1835 Edition that "The Father being a personage of Spirit" and that Christ had a physical tabernacle. In other writings he claimed God had a body of flesh and bones.

Now remember Oliver Cowdery stated Joseph Smith was in his 17th year, not his 16th year as Joseph Smith said earlier. If Oliver Cowdery is correct, Joseph Smith would be 16 years old, not 15 as he says he was. It should be noted here that nowhere does Joseph Smith state that when he went to pray a terrible dark power tried to overcome him. Details? In fact, just the opposite is stated. Everything is glorious and light as soon as he enters a prayer to God. He continues "…many things which transpired that cannot be written…" Why not? Is there ever a time when God dangles information in front of people through his prophet and after going through many things that transpire between God and his prophet he tells his prophet "many things… that cannot be written?" One may be left to wonder what "details" are preserved in the circa summer 1832 history that are not already written down in the Joseph Smith Papers history?

CHAPTER 11

JOSEPH SMITH SINS AND TRANSGRESSIONS

From page 89 Oliver Cowdery informs us "I do not pretend that he (Joseph Smith) is not a man subject to passions like other men, beset with infirmities and encompassed with weaknesses". And as noted earlier in this account Joseph Smith himself continued to claim he committed many sins and transgressions. Oliver Cowdery attempts to excuse these sins and transgressions by saying "but if he is, all men were so before him". He shows a very ample case of ignorance concerning mans behavior as from all the court actions and prison inmates we see that all men are indeed very different from one another and cannot be excused from their sinful actions by simply saying "all men were so before him". Would this ever be accepted in a court of law anywhere in our land or any other land as a reason for sinful acts against society?

From Joseph Smith's own words, he claims he committed many sins and transgressions and continued to claim this until he was at least 35 to 36 years old. Perhaps dishonesty was one of his sins or transgressions as he reported how all the sects united to persecute him when he told about his vision? However it should be noted that this is all speculative as there is nowhere that Joseph Smith details the nature and disposition of his sins and transgressions.

If his report that "all the sects...united to persecute me" were accurate, one would expect to find some hint of this in the local newspapers, narratives by critics, and in the affidavits D. P. Hurlbut gathered in 1833. The record is nevertheless silent on this issue. No one, friend or foe, in New York or Pennsylvania remembers either that there was 'great persecution' or even that Joseph claimed to have had a vision. Not even his family remembers it.

This is not to say Joseph Smith did not have serious problems with society. He had to flee New York to Kirtland, Ohio to avoid prosecution of the law for his dishonesty. He was not persecuted by other religious sects but by the law itself for his violations against society.

Also his claim that all of the churches were crying "lo here" and "lo there" as to them being the only true church appears incorrect. The churches of his day were friendly with each other as has been clearly shown above and indeed none of them made any claim that they were "the only true church". Members of one church would visit another denomination freely and without any animosity and on any given Sunday a person could be found in a Baptist, Congregational or other denominational church. This is not to say the various churches were not trying to get new members to join them as they were trying to build their congregations as they are doing to this day. They all wanted their own building to worship in but there was no evidence of any of the churches claiming they were the only one and true church of God and everybody else was wrong. The only one actually claiming such a belief was Joseph Smith and his claim came after he had started his own church and was making such a recall of memory some twenty years after it had allegedly occurred.

After receiving a revelation wherein the Lord appeared to him now Joseph Smith apparently sees no reason to continue to try to communicate with God any longer, nor does God seem interested in revealing Himself to Joseph Smith again. After three long years go by, and he is now 18 years old (Oliver Cowdery claims these dates were misprinted and that would make Joseph Smith 19 by now or possibly 20?), he says "but after many days I fell into transgressions and sinned in many things which brought a wound upon my soul and there were many things which transpired that cannot be written". Since he continues by stating he is now seventeen years old (or 19 if we believe Oliver Cowdery), we may safely conclude his "many days" was a three year period. During this time he transgresses the law repeatedly and sins in many things.

We are not told what his transgressions were, nor what sins he committed [25] during this period of time but we must assume they were important or he would not have continued admitting to these activities. He says "there were many things which transpired that cannot be written". Why not? Was he too busy sinning and transgressing the law to write them all down? Does it not seem this would be the logical conclusion one would come to from what he has written?

In the Mormon publication, Messenger and Advocate (of which Joseph Smith was the editor) Vol. 1 November 6, 1834 p. 40 we read: Joseph Smith stating:

"At the age of ten my father's family removed to Palmyra, New York, where, and in the vicinity of which, I lived or, made it my place of residence, until I was twenty-one; the later part, in the town of Manchester. During this time, as is common to most of all youths, I fell into many vices and follies: but as my accusers are, and have been forward to accuse me of being guilty of gross and outrageous violations of the peace and good order of the community, I take the occasion to remark that, though as I have said above, 'as is common

---

[25] ***He said "sins and transgressions" earlier, not vices and follies***

to most, or all youths,' I fell into many vices and follies [26], I have not, neither can it be sustained in truth, been guilty of wronging or injuring any man or society of men, and those imperfections to which I allude, and for which I have often had occasion to lament, were a light, and too often, vain mind, exhibiting a foolish and trifling conversation".

We still don't know what his "sins and transgressions" were. Now he compounds his sins and transgressions with vices and follies and again will not tell us what they were. Why? What sins and transgressions or vices and follies are "common to most, or all youths? Why are we left to guess what he means? Did he break any or all of the ten commandments? Did he commit moral sins or transgressions? We know he was taken to court for dishonesty in obtaining money from people under false circumstances in his money digging operations… was this what he meant by sins and transgressions? He claims he was subject to "vices and follies" and "sins and transgressions" yet claims his sins were "not great or malignant".

Apparently he felt he had a list of vices and follies, sins and transgressions, etc. which he could define as really not great or malignant. Although since he does not mention such a list we are left to wonder how he could determine himself which sins were great or malignant and which sins were not. He later claimed that Jesus

---

[26] ***"His sins were not "great or malignant", he later said, but "I was guilty of levity and sometimes associated with Jovial company etc. not consistent with that character which ought to be maintained by one who was called of God as I had been." From time to time he drank too much. Joseph regretted his "gratifications of many appetites offensive in the sight of God," without specifying which ones. Bushman, Rough Stone Rolling Page 43 Remember earlier JS said a prophet was only a prophet when acting as one? Here he says something about that character which ought to be maintaned by one who was called of God…"***

Christ told him that He (God) could not look upon sin "with the least degree of allowance" so would it not seem to mean his sins and transgressions were indeed very serious?

A Rev. Wesley Walters discovered documents in the basement of the Chenango County, New York, jailhouse at Norwich, New York in 1971. The records, affidavits, and other data show that Joseph Smith was arrested, went to trial, and was found guilty as an imposter and disorderly person in the Stowell matter of 'glass-looking'.

Continuing from page 18 Joseph Smith says "…when I was seventeen years of age I called again upon the Lord and he shewed (sp) unto me a heavenly vision for behold an angel of the Lord came and stood before me and it was by night and he called me by name, and said the Lord had forgiven me my sins and he revealed unto me… there were plates of Gold upon which there was engravings which was engraven by Maroni (later changed the name to Moroni, Elders Journal July 1838, 42-44) & his father…in ancient days and deposited by the commandments of God…and thus he appeared to me three times in one night and one on the next day…"

CHAPTER 12

NAME OF ANGEL (MORONI, NEPHI, MARONI?)

Here let us take a break to learn more about the name of this individual, Maroni, Moroni or who? … Was this really Nephi, the prophet at the beginning of the Book of Mormon? Now, we have promised you we would address this concern so here we go.

The Times and Season Volume III pages 749, 753
"When I first looked upon him I was afraid, but the fear soon left me. He called me by name, and said unto me that he was a messenger sent from the presence of God to me, and that <u>his name was Nephi</u>. That God has a work for me to do. …He said there was a book deposited written upon gold plates, giving an account of the former inhabitants of this continent, and the source from whence they sprang."

Joseph Smith was the editor of the Times and Seasons. As editor he was responsible for the content of this publication. He allowed this statement to be printed with him being the editor of the publication. Doesn't this seem like he agreed to the content of the information in his own paper? Can't we rely on the historical documents from the Times and Seasons to reflect what was actually published back then in history? The study of the book "Joseph Smith Papers" investigates many different historical documents. Doesn't it appear we are expected to believe these historians and their statements throughout this book? Doesn't it appear the "Papers" book is a historical research project?

Millennial Star was the Church's newspaper printed in England, and published Joseph Smith's story stating that the angel's name was "Nephi". Millennial Star. Volume 3, page 53. On page 71 of the same volume we read that the "message of the angel Nephi…opened a new dispensation to men…". Again, Joseph Smith was in charge of this newspaper, even if it was printed in England. From the fact that this newspaper published the same story as that in the Times and Seasons, does it not seem that the information printed therein was what Joseph Smith wanted people to believe?

In 1853 Joseph Smith's mother, Lucy Mack Smith, also said the angel's name was Nephi.

The name Nephi was also published in the 1851 edition of the Pearl of Great Price. "He called me by name and said unto me, that he was a messenger sent from the presence of God to me, and that his name was Nephi." Pearl of Great Price, 1851 edition page 41. The Pearl of Great Price is considered one of the four major scriptures of the Church of Jesus Christ of Latter-day Saints. Had we been alive in 1851 or earlier, do you think you would have believed what was printed in this scripture of the Church?

We are left to wonder if this angel was named Nephi or Moroni and why there is such difficulty in Joseph Smith getting this name correct. In his own handwriting he says the plates were written on by Maroni but does not assign a name for the angel at this time. His own mother recalled him saying the angel's name was Nephi, the Pearl of Great Price – an official scripture of the Church – claims the angels name was Nephi and in the Times and Season and the Millennial

Star (both Church newspapers) all claim that he names this angel as Nephi, not Moroni. From a study of the Book of Mormon it is clear that Nephi and Moroni are two separate individuals, one appearing at the beginning of the book and the other being the last one to write on the plates.

Joseph Smith lived for two years after this 'mistake' but he never printed a retraction.

So we are left having to believe this angel was named Nephi, not Moroni however, the Mormon Church felt a need to change the angels name to Moroni for some reason. Why can't they tell us the reason for this? They actually changed what is recorded in Joseph Smith's second and subsequent historical accounts to make it read the angels name was Moroni, not Nephi. Why? The historians stated Joseph Smith 'recounted' his version of his first vision so why couldn't Joseph Smith also have changed the name of the angel from Nephi to Moroni? Joseph Smith seemed to tell a different story about his first vision. Isn't it obvious he told different stories at different times?

Isn't it clear he changed his version of his first vision many times? If he could change such an earth shaking account of what he claimed he experienced, how difficult do you think it would be to simply change the word Nephi to Moroni in his publications?

On page 223 of History footnote 56: "A later redaction[27] in an <u>unidentified</u> hand changed "Nephi" to "Moroni" and noted that the original attribution was a "clerical error". Clerical error? We have clearly shown Joseph Smith said the angel was "Nephi" and yet today all the records have been changed making it appear that Joseph Smith said the angel was "Moroni". This certainly sounds

---

[27] *What do the historians mean by the word "redaction"? The dictionary says the meaning of the word redaction is putting something in writing. Where is this 'redaction' coming from?*

like much more than a simple "clerical error". Who said this was a clerical error and why?

The Millennial Star, the Times and Seasons, Joseph Smith's mother and the 1851 edition of the Pearl of Great Price all clearly state the name of this angel was Nephi. Where is the 'clerical error' here? Doesn't this seem like a very significant "error" that deserves serious attention? And perhaps some corrections?

Early references often did not name the angelic vision, but those people naming Moroni include Oliver Cowdery's historical letter published in the April 1835 LDS Messenger and Advocate, an expanded version of an August 1830 revelation, as published in the 1835 edition of the Doctrine and Covenants and a Joseph Smith editorial published in the Elders Journal in July 1838. The present history is the earliest existing source to name Nephi as the messenger, and subsequent publications based on this history perpetuated the attribution during Joseph Smith's lifetime. So we see it is Oliver Cowdery claiming this angel was named Moroni although Joseph Smith maintained his name was Nephi all through Joseph Smith's life.

Notice in the circa summer 1832 history Joseph Smith said the writing was done by Maroni but did not identify the angel appearing to him by any name. Later versions alledgedly made by Joseph Smith claim Joseph Smith said the angel told him his name was Nephi, then later versions than these versions said the angel told Joseph Smith his name was Moroni.

There is a city named "Moroni" in the Comorros islands off Madagascar in southeast Africa. It was founded sometime in the 10th century. It is interesting the similarity of Comorro to Cummorah as well as the actual name Moroni. Is it possible perhaps this is where Joseph Smith came up with the Angel Moroni or the Hill Cummorah?

There is unfounded speculation that Blackbeard the Pirate buried some of his stolen treasures near Moroni [28] on the Comorro Islands. It is thought that possibly Joseph Smith made some purchases of various items from China that were stolen by Blackbeard the Pirate, which is where Joseph Smith learned the name Moroni and Comorro. There is some possible connection somewhere as Joseph smith was always looking for buried treasure and Blackbeard the Pirate was burying his treasures in different places also.

As will be seen later after Oliver Cowdery took over writing history, things seemed to change dramatically, even conflicting directly with Joseph Smith's own handwritten accounts of what happened to him. Oliver Cowdery however does not feel it a necessary stipulation to explain this difference in naming the angel and we are left to wonder why and who really changed the name from Nephi to Moroni? Before the Book of Mormon was written the angel was named Nephi and could it not be argued that Moroni would be better qualified to be the keeper of the plates than Nephi, as he was the last one to actually handle them? Since he was the one who buried the plates in the ground it would it not seem plausible he would be able to show the place to Joseph Smith better than Nephi? If the angel was sent by the Lord however, would he have any trouble locating where the plates were buried in any event?

Also, where does the Mormon Church come up with the idea Moroni played a musical instrument? On many of the temples there is a statue

---

[28] **With the golden statues of Moroni on so many LDS Temples doesn't it seem important to know who made this 'redaction' and what the circumstances surrounding it are? We may wonder why the statue is not of Elijah instead of Moroni? Elijah was the one concerned with temple work, not Moroni. More importantly, why any statue on a temple? God was angry with Israel and punished them for building a golden calf. Is it possible he is not so unhappy because the Mormon's place a golden man on top rather than a golden calf?**

believed to be a likeness of Moroni blowing on some type of horn. To my knowledge there is no recorded revelation to any of the Presidents of the Mormon church stating why Moroni is blowing on a horn and why his statue needs to be placed on the pinnacle of the temples of the Latter-day Saints. Why not have him playing a trombone? Or maybe a Bass Trombone? From what we have learned, perhaps should it at least be the angel Nephi, not Moroni? As long as we are wondering about this, why not Jesus Christ being the statue that should be placed on the Mormon temples? Or God the Father? And while we are wondering, why not explain why this individual is blowing on a horn? And why does there have to be a golden idol of any nature on top of the Mormon temples? Who decided what type of horn he was playing? Do other religions use statues or idols of Christ to help them identify with Christ? Perhaps placing them on dashboards of their cars? Or Buddah? If it is Christ's church wouldn't you think the statue on all of His temples would be Him, not one of his angels? And why is Moroni clean shaven while God the Father and Jesus Christ are portrayed with beards? It makes a person wonder why the Mormon's dislike the symbol of the cross so much when they have their own symbol of a person on their temples, much like churches have crosses on top of their church building. Don't most churches use crosses or statues of Christ on the cross?

CHAPTER 13

OBTAINING THE GOLD PLATES

L et us continue however, " and then I immediately went to the place and found where the plates was deposited. …and straightaway made three attempts to get them (the plates)." Now comes a little 'doublespeak' on his part as he says "…then being exceedingly frightened I supposed it had been a dreem (sp) or Vision but when I considered I knew that it was not…" What is this supposed to mean? He says he made three attempts to get them and becomes exceedingly frightened but does not say why he is so frightened. So in the same sentence he says "I knew that it was not (a dream) therefore I cried unto the Lord in the agony of my soul (agony of his soul? agony means wretchedness, bitterness, misery, anguish, desolation, heartache grief, despair – I question he was crying to God in agony-and what would agony of his soul mean anyway?) why can I not obtain them?" Now the angel appears to him again and perhaps this is the appearance of the "next day" he alluded to earlier.

Peter Ingersoll, a close personal friend of Joseph Smith relates this story: "As I was passing, yesterday, across the woods, after a heavy shower of rain, I found, in a hollow, some beautiful white sand, that had been washed up by the water. I took off my frock, and tied up several quarts of it, and then went home. On my entering the house, I found the family at the table eating dinner. They were all anxious to know the contents of my frock. At that moment, I happened to think of what I had heard about a history found in Canada, called the golden Bible; so I very gravely told them it was the golden Bible. To my surprise, they were credulous enough to believe what I said. Accordingly I told them that I had received a commandment to let no one see it, for, says I, no man can see it with the naked eye and live. [29] However, I offered to take out the book and show it to them, but they refused to see it, and left the room." Now, said Joe, "I have got the damned fools fixed, and will carry out the fun." Notwithstanding, he told me he had no such book, and believed there never was any such book, yet, he told me that he actually went to Willard Chase, to get him to make a chest, in which he might deposit his golden Bible. But, as Chase would not do it, he made a box himself, of clap-boards, and put it into a pillow case, and allowed people only to lift it, and feel of it through the case.

PETER INGERSOLL.

State of New York, Wayne County, ss:

I certify, that on this 9th day of December, 1833, personally appeared before me the above named Peter Ingersoll, to me known, and made oath, according to law, to the truth of the above statement.

TH. P. BALDWIN,
Judge of Wayne County Court.

The angel tells him "…you have not kept the commandments of the Lord which I gave unto you (what commandments?) therefore you cannot now obtain them for the time is not yet fulfilled therefore thou wast (sp) left unto temptation…" Oliver Cowdery in 1835 wrote

---

[29] ***How did Joseph Smith get to see these "plates" with the 'naked' eye then and not be killed by God? Didn't he say "No Man"…and wouldn't that include him?***

"that Joseph Smith was 'sensibly shocked' each time he attempted to remove the plates from their repository. (Olivery Cowdery, "Letter VIII", LDS Messenger and Advocate. Anybody want to try to explain what "sensibly shocked" means? Oliver Cowdery will try to explain that Joseph Smith received electrical shocks at this time.

Now Joseph Smith said the angel had appeared to him three times the night before and had told him his sins had been forgiven him. Immediately after the angel's three appearances he went to the place where the plates were. Now the angel again appears to him and tells him he has not kept the commandments of the Lord. What? In the space of time between the third visit of the angel and his immediately going to the place where the plates were he somehow did not keep the commandments of the Lord? This would have been about 20 to 30 minutes a distance or just under three miles. Joseph Smith does not say anything except he "immediately" went to the place. This would preclude him from stopping at a tavern, meeting another person to visit with, stopping for a bite to eat, etc. He "immediately" went to the place-no turning to the right or twisting to the left. Again we may wonder what commandments the angel gave him?

It was only two or three miles and could be traveled in less than half an hour so we are left to seriously wonder what commandments he did not keep from the time the angel said he was forgiven of his sins and his immediate journey to where the plates were. The angel said to him "…You have not kept the commandments of the Lord which I gave unto you…" Joseph Smith said nothing about this angel giving him any commandments during any of his three visits the night before. Even if the angel did give him "commandments of the Lord", when did he have time to break any of these commandments from the time he had his third visit of the angel and then his immediately going to the place the plates were? He hadn't even been given enough time to tell us what the purpose of the other two visits were for and what "commandments of the Lord" the angel had given him as his departure was so "immediate" when the angel left him.

Joseph Smith said on at least three occasions he was a transgressor of the law and a sinner. Is it possible even for him to have committed sins and transgression during a time of "immediately"? Remember, the angel had clearly stated that Joseph Smith had been forgiven for his sins when he first started talking to him. Oliver Cowdery, in his letter to Wm. W. Phelps, (Page 74) states clearly about this angel's words *"…by hearing that his own sins were forgiven and his former transgressions to be remembered against him no more"*. This is Oliver Cowdery writing of Joseph Smith's experience and he is stating the same thing Joseph Smith stated in his circa summer 1832 history. It is not clear how Joseph Smith could have committed any sin or transgression in the simple act of obedience to the angels instructions to go directly to where the plates were. Well, now, we first have the angel stating the Lord had forgiven Joseph Smith and his sins and his transgressions would "be remembered against him no more". Second, we have an angel of the Lord, Joseph Smith (and Oliver Cowdery) stating he (Joseph Smith) could not obtain the plates because **"you have not kept the commandments of the Lord which I gave unto you".** Doesn't it seem obvious that not keeping the commandments of the Lord are both a sin and a transgression? And isn't it clearly stated by Joseph Smith in his own handwriting, and also written down by Oliver Cowdery, that Joseph Smith had been told directly by the angel that he (Joseph Smith) could not obtain the plates since he had not kept the commandments of the Lord? *It is very plain that his sins and transgressions had indeed been remembered by the Lord* as this is the **single vital reason** the angel tells him he cannot obtain the plates, and this is the same angel that just a short time earlier had assured him his sins had been forgiven and his former transgressions would "be remembered against him no more". What is going on here?

I don't understand. Something is very definitely wrong here as we have two perfectly contradictory accounts regarding Joseph Smith's sins and transgressions. Let us not get further confused by someone trying to tell us we are trying to make a man an "offender for a word". If anything, we are making an angel, Joseph Smith, and Oliver

Cowdery an offender for quite a few words. Did not the apostle Paul admonish us to "prove all things and hold fast to that which is good (1 Thessalonians 5:21) "?

Joseph Smith included in the thirteenth Article of Faith that "indeed we may say that we follow the admonition of Paul." Is someone lying? It has to be either the angel or Joseph Smith doesn't it? Oliver Cowdery can be excused as he was merely relating what Joseph Smith told him to say, right? (or did he?).

First the angel said Joseph Smith's sins were forgiven him, then this same angel says he cannot obtain the plates because Joseph Smith had committed sin by not keeping the commandments of the Lord. Which one is correct?

Did Joseph Smith not go "immediately" from the angel to where the plates were, and instead stopped long enough to commit at least one sin or transgression against God?

Did the Angel forget he had just told Joseph Smith his sins had been forgiven him? Why are we left to speculate on this matter? Is Joseph Smith so confused about it all that he couldn't keep it clear in his own mind? Well, as earlier in the matter of the name of the angel who appeared to Joseph Smith, we are again left confused.

When he was twenty-two years of age, on January 18, 1827 he married Emma Hale, and on Sept 22, 1827 he obtains the plates. (Page 14, 15) Emma's father refused permission for him to marry Emma and so he talked Emma into eloping with him.

During the two years he worked in the area where Isaac Hale lived with his family, Joseph twice asked Isaac Hale for permission to marry Emma, but was refused both times because he was a stranger,[30]

---

[30] **See Isaac Hale's affidavit in the appendix section at the end of this report**

Emma was twenty two years old the previous July and Joseph was twenty two the previous December when they married on January 18, 1827. They moved to Manchester, New York to be near his parents. In the fall of 1827 Joseph finally obtained the plates he had been seeking. [31]

He then claimed he was always being sought after by other people seeking to steal his gold plates and he moved with Emma back to Harmony, Pennsylvania to seek privacy as he translated the plates. Despite his eloping with Emma, her parents still welcomed her to their home. Joseph bought a small farm from her father but only worked it sporadically as he wrote the Book of Mormon. Emma was his first scribe. She was never to see the plates but handled them in their protective cover. They moved back to Fayette, New York where in June 1829 the translation was completed.

In December of 1827 Joseph Smith moves to Susquehanna "by the assistance of a man by the name of Martin Harris…" who "because of his faith and this righteous deed (giving Joseph Smith $50.00) the Lord appeared unto him (Martin Harris) in a vision and shewed (sp) unto him his marvelous work which he was about to do". (Page 15)

Oliver Cowdery "was ordained an assistant president to Joseph Smith in the general church presidency and placed ahead of Joseph Smith's other assistants. He <u>may</u> have begun the 1834-1836 history in response to his new appointment". Page 25, 26

The 1834-1836 history "passed from Oliver Cowdery to Frederick G. Williams to Warren Parrish to Warren Cowdrey. Finally it returned to Parrish." (Page 25-Histories) Oliver Cowdery "began this new historical record in early December 1834".

---

[31] *Joseph Smith got the plates Sept. 22, 1827. He worked on translating them until he met Oliver Cowdery April 5, 1829 and within two more months the entire Book of Mormon was completed*

The revisions in Joseph Smith's history do not attempt any explanation as to why they are necessary, especially since they change significantly the original writing of Joseph Smith himself. We are left to decide if we wish to believe Joseph Smith's original version of his vision or believe those of his followers made some years later. We remember that it took Joseph Smith over twelve years to "broadcast" his first vision. Oliver Cowdery, Frederick G. Williams, Warren Parrish and Warren Cowdrey took four years to "broadcast" their different versions of what happened to Joseph Smith.

Oliver Cowdery first meets Joseph Smith Sunday April 5, 1829 (Page 41) in Harmony, Susquehanna County, PA. Two days later he began to write the Book of Mormon and it was finished in June of that same year. Oliver Cowdery has just come from Poultney, VT and was familiar with Ethan Smith and his ideas on where the American Indians originated, i.e. from the Jews.

Doesn't it seem probable that Oliver Cowdery told Joseph Smith about Ethan Smith's ideas and Joseph incorporated these ideas into his writing the Book of Mormon? He and Joseph Smith experienced a vision of John the Baptist appearing to them giving them the authority to baptize.

Although Cowdery had no firsthand knowledge of church history or Joseph Smith's history prior to April 1829, Cowdery assured his readers that "our brother J. Smith Jr. has offered to assist us…Some passages in the …narrative seem to have been related to Cowdery by Joseph Smith, since Cowdery recounted events in which only Joseph Smith participated."

Page 41 footnote 41 says that Oliver Cowdery boarded with Joseph Smith's family in Manchester, New York, beginning in fall 1828. This was after Joseph Smith had moved with Emma to Harmony, Pennsylvania, a distance of almost 300 miles.

Footnote 40 on Page 40 says "one of the 'authentic documents' Cowdery relied on may have been Joseph Smith's circa summer 1832 history." If so, why did Cowdery change it substantially in the 1834-1836 version of his history of the church? Is it possible Joseph Smith couldn't remember exactly what happened until fourteen years later? Or is it equally possible that Oliver Cowdery wrote what he himself wanted to make it appear?

Interesting sidelight here, from page 46 Oliver Cowdery is quoting: "The fact is as Terrullian said, no man ever looked carefully into its (religion) consistency and propriety without embracing it. It is impossible: That light which enlightens man, is at once enraptured: that intelligence which existed *before the world was, will unite, and that wisdom in the Divine economy will be so conspicuous, that it will be embraced, it will be observed, and it must be obeyed!*"

This is prima face totally incorrect as is testified to by the many different religions in the world and especially the many different churches all claiming to be Christ's churches as well as the many individuals and organizations which claim to be agnostic or atheistic in their beliefs. There is little, if any, consistency and propriety among the many different religions and Christian churches. In point of fact, this was one reason Joseph Smith gave for seeking out the Lord, to help him determine which church he should join."

Oliver Cowdery seems to be a very flowery type writer and I believe he added to Joseph Smith's narrative as he imagined it could have happened, rather than reporting how it actually happened. Given the choice of Cowdery's version of Joseph Smith's visions and Joseph Smith's own handwritten version, aren't Joseph Smith's own handwritten versions more believable than Cowdery's more flowery plus the many changes from Joseph Smith's versions? As the historians stated, Oliver Cowdery's writings were "Employing florid romantic language, frequent scriptural allusions, and much dramatic detail", etc.

Read this "flowery" (and incorrect) comment of Oliver Cowdery's (Page 46) "Religion has had its friends and its enemies; its advocates and its opponents. But the thousands of years which have come and gone, have <u>left it unaltered</u>; millions who have embraced it, and are now enjoying that bliss held forth in its promises, have left its principles unchanged, and its influence upon the honest heart, unweakened".… And he goes on and on. Religion has been altered significantly over the years, contrary to what he says above, and I question that millions who have embraced religion are now enjoying that bliss he mentions. Rather they are brainwashed in their beliefs making them feel complacent in their beliefs. But I digress…

Oliver Cowdery takes it upon himself to relate Joseph Smith's feelings and also speaks about conditions generally in the area Joseph Smith lived. P. 53 "It is necessary to premise this account by relating the situations of the public mind relative to religion, at this time:…Large additions were made to the Methodist, Presbyterian, and Baptist churches. …For a length of time the reformation seemed to move in a harmonious manner, but, as the excitement ceased, or those who had expressed anxieties, had professed a belief in the pardoning influence and condescension of the Savior a general struggle was made by the leading characters of the different sects, for proselytes. Then strife seemed to take the place of that apparent union and harmony which had previously characterized the moves and exhortations of the old professors, and a cry – I am right – you are wrong was introduced in their stead."

As this claim about various religions became such an important part of Joseph Smith's story about why he even went to God in prayer in the first place, it is necessary to introduce factual evidence about religion at or about the time of Joseph Smith's 15th year. For this purpose I refer the reader again to the book, "The Burned-Over District" by Whitney R. Cross 1950 published by Cornell University Press. In the preface, "Burned-over district was a name applied to a small region, during a limited period of history, to indicate a particular phase of development. …I have tried…to produce a reliable and broadly meaningful bit of general American history" says Cross.

Critics chiefly concerned with the habitual revivalism occurring in a much wider area came to call it (Western New York) the "burnt" or "Burned-over District," adopting the prevailing western analogy between the fires of the forest and those of the spirit. (Page 3) "… fervent revivalism concentrated in western New York as in no other portion of the country during its pioneering era. Emotional religion was thus a congenital characteristic, present at birth and developed through out the youth of the section." P. 4 Burned Over District

CHAPTER 14

BURNED OVER DISTRICT

The various denominations goal was to "reinforce that religious doctrine which would in practice stress emotionalism at the expense of reason. Edwards and the New Lights made conversion the exclusive test of church membership." Thus there was none of this "lo here-lo there" type of arguing among the churches as Oliver Cowdery and Joseph Smith seem to claim. "It mattered little whether he (anyone) was nominally Congregational, Baptist, or Methodist. He might in the young country change affiliations several times as one sect or another held services nearby, or seemed to enjoy particular manifestations of heaven-born agitation. [32]

"Evidence concerning the development of the burned-over District churches before 1825 is unreliable, but it suffices to indicate similar patterns of growth among the several denominations. ... the winter of 1799-1800 was in western New York long called the time of the Great Revival, just as it was in Kentucky."[33]

---

[32] **P. 8, 9 Burned Over District**
[33] **P. 9 Ibid**

"After 1800 excitement diminished, rose again to a lesser peak in 1807-1808, and slumped once more during the war years. But even the least promising seasons saw awakenings in a few localities. …The religious upheavals following the War of 1812 surpassed all previous experiences. …The Presbyterians of Utica made nearly as many converts in 1815 as in the Finnery revival a decade later, and added large numbers again in 1819 and 1821."[34]

"Since the first climax of 1800, distinct peaks of fervor had now occurred twice with intervals of quiet interspersed. Another low point in the cycle was destined to follow 1820". Yet it was during this "low point" in revivalism that Joseph Smith claims was the height of religious agitation among various churches. "Most Methodist circuits showed declining membership in two of these five years (following 1820) and only slight growth in a third. But substantial gains came in 1821, and in 1824 rapid development began once more, led by the district about Western, in Oneida County." …Since the peak of fervor reached in 1826 is often attributed to Charles Finney's single-handed influence, Presbyterian revivals in the immediately preceding years are particularly significant. …The series of crests in religious zeal begun by the Great Revival formed the crescendo phase of a greater cycle. Strenuous evangelism mounted irregularly from the 1790's to reach a grand climax between 1825 and 1837.,,,The Baptist General Tract Society, formed in 1824,…"[35]

"The Baptists and Methodists maintained forthright denominational connections, perhaps limiting their appeal by so doing. The Plan of Union groups, in part perhaps because of the non sectarian make up but probably more largely because of the wealth and prestige of their Congregational and Presbyterian members, had far greater influence in western New York."[36]

---

[34] **Footnote 7 P 11 Ibid**
[35] **Footnote 8 p 24-25 Ibid**
[36] **Footnote 9 p. 26 Ibid**

Man's ability to be saved was a matter of his own will, yet actual conversion was supposed to be exclusively the work of the Holy Spirit. Complete submission to the will of God would somehow put one in the way to be saved."

There was none of this "lo here-lo there" type of preaching claiming one particular church was right or another one was right as Joseph Smith claims and Oliver Cowdery also claims. There were differences of opinion on doctrinal matters as shown above and in matters of whether predestination or free will were the correct doctrines, having nothing to do with which church was right or wrong. Indeed "the Baptists generally in this Western Country…are of the opinion that ministers should take no thought how or what they should speak…for it is not they that speak, but the Spirit which speaketh in them. And one of the Ministers told me that I must let the Holy Ghost study my sermons for me. David Rathbone May 1812".

Let us pause briefly to read from the Doctrine and Covenants Section 20 verse 45 "The elders are to conduct the meetings as they are led by the Holy Ghost, according to the commandments and revelations of God". Yet Joseph Smith said the Lord told him all other churches were an "abomination" in His sight, but what is the difference between what they claimed that they should be led by the Holy Ghost, and Joseph Smith stating the Apostles in his church are to be "led by the Holy ghost" also? The ministers of that day claimed this in May 1812 and Joseph Smith claimed it for the Apostles of his Church in 1830, 18 years later. Yet Joseph Smith claims the Lord said these other people were an abomination in his eyes. For doing the very same thing? And why then did Joseph Smith join the Baptist (in 1824) and later the Methodist church (in 1828) after God told him to join none of them?

Fayette Lapham said that about 1830 Joseph Smith Sr. told him that Joseph had joined the Baptist Church in 1824 and was baptized into it. Historical Magazine, Vol 8, No. 5 May 1870.

CHAPTER 15

JOSEPH SMITH TRIES TO JOIN METHODIST CHURCH

Another report reads as follows: In 1822 Joseph Smith caught a spark of Methodism and became a very passable exhorter in the evening meetings". (History of the Pioneer Settlement of Phelps and Gorham's Purchase, 1851, p. 214)

Emma Smith's uncle, Nathaniel Lewis, preached and acted as a lay minister of the local Methodist Episcopal church. His congregation met in the homes of the members for Sunday services. On Wednesdays a regular circuit preacher visited Harmony. In the spring or summer of 1828 Joseph Smith asked the circuit rider if his name could be included on the class roll of the church. Joseph "presented himself in a very serious and humble manner" and the minister obliged him.

When Emma's cousin, Joseph Lewis, discovered Joseph's name on the roll, he "thought it was a disgrace to the church to have a practicing necromancer" as a member. He took the matter up with a friend, and the following Sunday, when Joseph and Emma arrived for church, the two men took Joseph aside. "They told him plainly that such character as he…could not be a member of the church unless he broke off his sins by repentance, made public confession, renounced his fraudulent and hypocritical practices, and gave some evidence that he intended to reform and conduct himself somewhat nearer like a Christian than he had done. They gave him his choice to go before the class, and publicly ask to have his name stricken from the class book, or stand a disciplinary investigation." Joseph refused to comply with the humiliating demands and withdrew from the class. His name, however stayed on the roll for about six months, either from oversight or because Emma's brother-in-law, Michael Morse, who taught the class, did not know of the confrontation."[37]

As stated above, "Complete submission to the will of God would somehow put one in the way to be saved. Righteous behavior was both a token of the persons correct state of mind and a symbol of Heavenly favor." Does this sound like these people were an "abomination" in God's sight? Do you think it is an "abomination" to submit to the will of God?

Nowhere in any of the religions of that day can we find any claims or statements indicating that any particular religion was right or wrong. Doesn't it seem the only one making such a claim was Joseph Smith? Haven't we learned that the "great revival" that he said was going on in 1823 did not exist until 1825? Doesn't his story about a great revival and competitions between churches claiming to be the only true church are made up of full cloth, completely fictitious and without foundation?

Richard L. Bushman also referred to Smith's involvement with the Methodists in his book, Joseph Smith: Rough Stone Rolling, Knopf. 2005, pp. 69-70." With Joseph's realization of himself as a prophet, the rearrangement of memory began." Rearrangement of memory? Oh really? Did not treasure seeking lead to the person he had become?

---

[37] ***Emma Hale Smith, by Linda K. Newell and Valeen T. Avery, University of Illinois Press 1994, p. 25.***

"His true history (And how do we know we can now believe this is a truer history than he already gave us?) began with his search for a church and his plea for forgiveness." Haven't we learned that Joseph Smith was indeed not searching for a church at all until he tried to join the Methodist church in 1828?

Let us stop just a moment and catch our breath! First we are asked to accept that Joseph Smith had to "rearrange" his memory. Then we are asked to accept that "treasure seeking did not lead to the person he had become". And why not? It was certainly part of his history, wasn't it? Now we are told that his "true history" began with his search for a church. Wherever did Bushman conjure up this idea? Did Joseph Smith ask the Lord anything about his search for a church in his own writing of his first vision?

Again to remind you, Richard Bushman is one of the published authors of the Joseph Smith Papers Book we are investigating.

Then Bushman nonchalantly goes on to say "It did not occur to him that without magic his family might have scoffed at his story of Moroni, as did the minister who rejected his First Vision. Magic had played its part and now could be cast aside"?

"Treasure seeking did not lead to the person he had become" has already been stated by Bushman. Can anyone actually perceive a glimmer of sense out of these contradictory statements? The very stone Joseph Smith claimed he used to translate the Book of Mormon was the same one he used to try to find buried treasure! How could Bushman then state that "treasure seeking did not lead to the person he had become"? Wasn't Joseph Smith's entire early career involved in seeking treasure buried in the earth? Weren't the gold plates allegedly buried in the earth?

Richard L. Bushman (One of the authors of the Joseph Smith Papers) in "Just the Facts Please" Volume 6 Issue 2 pp122-123 has this to offer:

"Possibility of an error"? Perhaps a possibility of many errors? Bushman's article is titled "just the facts please". So why is he ignoring the facts?

We have a conflict here between Richard L. Bushman's first story in "Just the Facts Please" and his position as editor of the Joseph Smith Papers. He gives us two different opinions. Which is the correct one? First he says that without magic his family would have scoffed at his story about Moroni (Nephi). Then he claims treasure seeking did not lead him to the person he had become. In his seeking for treasure didn't he use magic including the stone mentioned above? Isn't this one of the men who wrote the book "Joseph Smith Papers"? Keep reading.

Oliver Cowdery stated in his fourth letter to Wm W. Phelps (Page 56 Histories) "You will recollect that I mentioned the time of a religious excitement, in Palmyra and vicinity to have been in the 15th year of our brother J. Smith Jr.s age-that was an error in the type-It should have been in the 17th year."

His statement on page 53 "…and a cry-I am right – you are wrong-was introduced in their stead" has no historical documentation and in fact quite the opposite beliefs were taught at that time. So Oliver Cowdery now places the time of the first vision of Joseph Smith to have occurred in Joseph Smith's 17th year, making him 16 years old instead of 14 years old. Wouldn't this make it 1822 instead of 1820 as Joseph Smith said in the first account? Is Oliver Cowdery right in this or is Joseph Smith right saying he was 14 when it happened? We already know that Joseph Smith's original testimony of his first vision of the Lord was changed and since we know the changes were made in Oliver Cowdery's writings isn't it logical to believe that Oliver Cowdery made these changes, perhaps after going over them with Joseph Smith and perhaps making his own suggestions to Joseph Smith in making these changes?

Now we have Oliver Cowdery making seemingly incorrect statements in his letter to Wm. W. Phelps regarding the religious excitement of the times in Joseph Smith's life. When Joseph Smith was 14 (in his fifteenth year) there was no special religious revivalism taking place and while there was a rise in revivalism in 1821 it calmed down that same year and didn't resume activity until 1825. Nor was there any special revivalism in Joseph Smith's 17th year.

Oliver Cowdery states in his 3rd letter to Wm. W. Phelps (Page 53) "To profess godliness without its benign influence upon the heart, was a thing so foreign from his (Joseph Smith's) feelings, that his spirit was not at rest day nor night," This flies right in the face of what the ministers of that time were professing, "the Baptists generally in this Western Country…are of the opinion that ministers should take no thought how or what they should speak…for it is not they that speak, but the Spirit which speaketh in them. And one of the Ministers told me that I must let the Holy Ghost study my sermons for me".

So it appears the ministers of that time were not going about saying they were the only true church but encouraging their members to seek the Spirit of God and they prayed the Holy Ghost would work with them in their sermons. Does this sound like they were an "abomination" in the eyes of God? Remember from above we learned that it was Alexander Campbell who claimed to have had a revelation wherein he saw Christ and was told to join no other church as they were an abomination to God. Alexander Campbell claimed "Christ also told me, that every denomination of professing Christians had become extremely corrupt." This was published in 1824 which was 18 years prior to Joseph Smith publishing his story about having a vision of christ.

So here we are, right at the beginning of what Joseph Smith claims happened to him. He says he is confused because all the churches are claiming they are the only true church of Christ and so he has to go to the Lord in prayer to find out which one is really the true church. But this is not the fact at all. We can find none of the churches claiming they were the one and only true church of Christ and they were instead encouraging their members to seek out the spirit of the Lord. All the ministers were of the belief that they should "take no thought how or what they should speak…for it is not they that speak but the Spirit which speaketh in them."

However, we do know that many other men who claimed to have vsions of Christ in the time ear of 1811 to 1824 said that they were told all Christian churchs were corrupt and to join none of them. These were individuals and not churches making such claims. The only individual who started a church prior to Joseph Smith starting his church was Alexander Campbell who initially started as a Baptist preacher and later changed his church to the Church of Christ.

Right at the beginning Joseph Smith lays a very shaky and questionable foundation for his story.

The ministers of the area Joseph Smith resided in are historically documented as recommending that they should strive to let the "spirit" direct and guide them in their sermons. They encouraged "their members to seek the Spirit of God and they prayed the Holy Ghost would work with them in their sermons." Yet Joseph Smith would have us believe that all of these people are in error and **"I** *was* answered that I must join none of them (Christian Churches), for they were all wrong…that **all** their creeds were an abomination in His sight" (Joseph Smith History 1:19). There creeds were an "abomination in His sight?" All these people who were praying the Holy Ghost would work with them in their sermons and seeking to let the spirit direct and guide them are an "abomination in His sight"?

So God told him that he "must join none of them"? Why did he then join the Methodist church as we earlier have shown? He was told there "creeds were an 'abomination in His sight?'" What's going on here? Why does he continue to try to do just the opposite of what God tells him to do?

The statement "exhortations of the old professors, and a cry – I am right – you are wrong was introduced in their stead" appears to be a complete fabrication of Oliver Cowdery. Joseph Smith wrote his history in 1832, about three years after meeting Oliver Cowdery although it was not published in print until 1842. Then two years later his story was changed by Oliver Cowdery or perhaps by Frederick G. Williams, Warren Parrish, or Warren Cowdrey…or maybe by all of them combined. Who knows? We don't know for sure if Joseph Smith composed his history as he wrote it or if he was copying from another record. In either case his initial statements were written by him in his own handwriting, not that of Oliver Cowdery. Indeed the story we are led to believe was written by Joseph Smith and is contained in the Pearl of Great Price (a scripture of the LDS church) was in fact not written by Joseph Smith at all but rather by Oliver Cowdery (and/or friends). The story written down by Joseph Smith is different than the one written by Oliver Cowdery.

It appears that Joseph Smith's first vision was not considered of any serious importance to Joseph Smith as he allowed Oliver Cowdery to write another version of what happened as well as writing several letters to people telling yet other versions of what happened to him. Even though these later versions differed substantially from Joseph Smith's own writing of his first vision Joseph never felt it necessary to explain the differences or even admit to them. Yet from the time Joseph F. Smith became president of the Mormon Church Oct 17, 1901 the first vision became of primary importance.

Unfortunately by this time there were so many different versions of it that nobody can really sift through them accurately to show what really happened, if anything.

Now in his fourth letter to Wm. W. Phelps from Oliver Cowdery he states "In my last, published in the 3rd No. of the Advocate I apologized for the brief manner in which I should be obliged to give, in many instances, the history of this church. …but as there are, in a great house, many vessels, so in the history of a work of this magnitude, many items which would be interesting to those who follow, ***are forgotten***. In fact, I deem every manifestation of the Holy Spirit, dictating the hearts of the saints in the way of righteousness to be of importance, and this is one reason why I plead an apology," Page 54 His idea of "brief" seems vastly different than Joseph Smith's. He changes Joseph Smiths writings and elaborates in his eloquent style telling of things that Joseph Smith never said had happened to him.

Yet Cowdery writes as if Joseph Smith is talking and telling things differently than he (Joseph Smith) initially did. From all that is written about the churches of this time it definitely appears these ministers were sincerely trying to follow the spirit of the Lord in all their teachings and were not hostile to each other arguing which one was true. To claim all these churches were an "abomination" in the eyes of God is an extremely strong statement.

By many of the ministers own claims of the day they were sincerely trying to teach by the Spirit of God and under the direction of the Holy Ghost. I am led to wonder why all these individuals who were sincerely seeking God's direction were denied His personal visitation to them yet when one 14 year old boy (or was he 15? Or 16?) guilty of many sins and transgressions goes out to pray, God immediately appears to him? What of the many other men who claimed heavenly revelations, some very similar to Joseph Smith's claim? Were these men's claims an abomination also? Why then did Joseph Smith seem to copy their revelations in building his own claim to revelation?

CHAPTER 16

THE ANGEL NEPHI OR MORONI APPEARS TO JOSEPH SMITH

After three years go by with Joseph smith committing many sins and transgressions in his own handwriting (circa summer 1832) "…when I was seventeen years of age (according to Oliver Cowdery he was now 19 or 20 years of age) I called again upon the Lord". No explanation is given why he waited three years after seeing Jesus Christ to once again "call upon" him. "…and he shewed (sp) unto me a heavenly vision for behold an angel of the Lord came and stood before me and it was by night and he called me by name and he said the Lord had forgiven me my sins and he revealed unto me that in the Town of Manchester Ontario County N.Y. there was plates of gold upon which there was engravings which was engraven (sp) by Maroni & his fathers…" (Page 14) "… and thus he appeared unto me three times in one night and once on the next day and then I immediately went to the place and found where the plates was deposited as the angel of the Lord had commanded me, and straightway made three attempts to get them and then being exceedingly frightened I supposed it had been a dream or vision but when I considered I knew that it was not therefore I cried unto the Lord in the agony (agony of his soul?-agony means wretchedness, bitterness, misery, anguish, desolation, heartache grief, despair) of my soul why can I not obtain them behold the angel appeared unto me again and said unto me you have not kept the commandments of the Lord which I gave unto you therefore you cannot now obtain them for time is not yet fulfilled…" (Page 14 Histories)

Now let Oliver Cowdery get a hold of this story: (Page 57, 58 Histories) "On the evening of the 21st of September, 1823, previous to retiring to rest, our brother's mind was unusually wrought up on the subject which had so long agitated his mind-his heart was drawn out in fervent prayer, and his whole soul was so lost to every thing of a temporal nature, that earth, to him had lost its charms, and all he desired was to be prepared in heart to commune with some kind messenger who could communicate to him the desired information of his acceptance with God.

At length the family retired, and he, as usual bent his way, though in silence, where others might have rested their weary frames locked fast in sleep's embrace; but repose had fled, and accustomed slumber had spread her refreshing hand over others beside him-he continued still to pray-his heart, though once hard and obdurate, was softened, and that mind which had often flitted, like the wild bird of passage, had settled upon a determined basis not to be decoyed or driven from its purpose."

Whew! He hasn't even got to the appearance of the angel yet and already has written more than Joseph Smith wrote of the entire experience!

In this situation hours passed unnumbered-how many or how few I know not, neither is he able to inform me; but supposed it must have been eleven or twelve, (11 or 12? It would have been daylight of the next day if this is true!) and perhaps later, as the noise and bustle of the family, in retiring, had long since ceased. (It took his family 11 or 12 hours to go to bed at night?) – While continuing in prayer for a manifestation in some way that his sins were forgiven; endeavoring to exercise faith in the scriptures, on a sudden a light like that of day, only of a purer and far more glorious appearance and brightness, burst into the room. – indeed to use his own description, (There was no description initially given and we may believe Joseph Smith is giving this version to Oliver Cowdery. So he is remembering it better two or three years after he initially writes it down? Or did he not suppose it important enough to write down all that happened?) the first sight was as though the house was filled with consuming and unquenchable fire. This sudden appearance of a light so bright, as must naturally be expected, occasioned a shock or sensation, visible to the extremities of the body. It was, however, followed with a calmness and serenity of mind, and an overwhelming rapture of Joy that surpassed understanding, and in a moment a personage stood before him."

Apparently only Joseph Smith could see this light, which made it seem "the house was filled with consuming and unquenchable fire". Nobody else in his household remarked of any such manifestation occurring in the house that night. I wonder what he means by "consuming" and "unquenchable" fire? And how could he tell?

An observation comes to mind. At no time has the Lord or this angel told Joseph Smith he was to start a church or that he was to continue asking for more revelations from God. In fact Joseph Smith did not ask for any other revelations after his first vision until three years later when he felt he had to pray to God once more for the forgiveness of his sins. God is not coming to him, but rather he is going to the Lord, at his own leisure it would seem when sufficiently feeling the need to be forgiven for his sins and transgressions.

But wait! Oliver Cowdery comes to the rescue here and tells us that Christ tells Joseph Smith not to join any of the churches as they are all wrong and are an "abomination" and that he (Joseph Smith) will be used to show him the way. So did Joseph Smith forget this part of his first vision (or had writers cramp?) so Oliver Cowdery had to fill in what really happened?

Here we have a young man who commits many sins and transgressions and continues to sin even after the Lord first appears and tells him his sins are forgiven. We have no evidence that any of the ministers of the vicinity were guilty of committing sins or transgressions, yet we are asked to believe God refused to honor them with any direction or guidance and instead immediately answers the prayer of a fourteen year old boy who is guilty of committing many sins and transgressions, by personally appearing to him?

This angel (we have learned his name is Nephi and then changed to Moroni) then proceeded and gave a general account of the promises made to the fathers, and also gave a history of the aborigines of this continent (North America-<u>NOT</u> South America) and said they were literal descendants of Abraham".

Modern day genealogists and archeologists claim the Indians of North America came from Asia through Alaska and down into Canada and the United States area. What fathers does he mean? Adam? Noah? Abraham? David? Solomon? The Brother of Jared? Ether? What promises is he referring to that were made to whom? And what kind of history of the aborigines could this angel have given in this short visit? We know it must have been a short visit since this angel appeared to him two more times during this same night. Certainly not the whole Book of Mormon!? Why doesn't he tell us exactly what the history was that the angel told him about? It couldn't have taken much time and as long as he is sharing his account of the angel appearing, why couldn't he have included this history for our benefit?

The plates contain a history that Joseph Smith could translate "the same by the means of the Urim and Thummim, which were deposited for that purpose with the record." (Page 59) We are told by the historian that "A part of the book was sealed, and was not to be opened yet. The sealed part, said he, contains the same revelation which was given to John upon the isles of Patmos, and when the people of the Lord are prepared, and found worthy, then it will be unfolded unto them. (Page 59 Histories) Do you wonder why we need the "same revelation" given that had already been given by John?

The angel told Joseph Smith "God determined to leave men without excuse". Hold on just a minute here! God doesn't appear to most of us so how does God plan to leave us without excuse? This God who appears to Joseph Smith when Joseph Smith utters a simple prayer but does not appear to those of us who fast and pray for days on end and He claims to be no respecter of person now says He is determined to leave men without excuse? We can get into a vigorous discussion regarding faith and beliefs but that is not the purpose of this study but suffice it to say that what this angel said about God determining to leave men without excuse is, on the surface, not true. I realize this study is an inquiry but sometimes things get so ridiculous a statement must be made. God may not excuse man but man certainly has many excuses why he doesn't believe all that Joseph Smith claims him to say. Doesn't it appear that this angel's integrity and veracity are highly questionable?

The historian points out in footnote 87 on page 59 "A similar statement concerning visions being recorded and then sealed up appears later in the Book of Mormon; 'And when the Lord had said these words, the Lord shewed (sp) unto the brother of Jared all the inhabitants of the earth which had been, and also all that would be; and the Lord withheld them not from his sight, even unto the ends of the earth."

So God showed "all the inhabitants of the earth", past present and future. Thus God has determined to show certain individuals all the inhabitants of the earth, past present and future. The Book of Mormon then is clearly stating that predestation is the doctrine the Church should believe in. If every inhabitant of the earth, past, present and future, are available to be shown by God to a particular man it is incumbent to believe then that this knowledge must be available to God and those he shows it to. Why doesn't God show this information to all of us or at least to me? He claims he is no respecter of persons. Some people I have talked to claim God is a very good "guesser" and is able to portray his guesswork as reality but lets not talk fairy tales here (or should we?) God claims to know everything past, present and future. I believe in God and believe this is true. There is nothing God does not know. As Christ taught, not even a sparrow falls to the ground without God taking notice, and this must be true for the past, present and the future. It certainly appears God is leaving many excuses for man to question life and its purposes. Therefore predestination appears to be God's rule and there is nothing we can do to change this. Our lack of knowledge and our innate arrogance make many of us unbelievers of this true doctrine but it doesn't change the truth.

Since Joseph Smith was given the plates it would seem he was eventually able to stop sinning and transgressing the laws of God and become obedient "to the commandments of the Lord". This is no small feat for a young man who continued to sin and transgress God's laws even in the very short space of time between when the angel appeared to him and him telling him his sins were forgiven and "immediately" going straight forward to the place the plates were and even in that short time being denied getting the plates because of his sins and transgressions that he must have committed while enroute to the place the plates were buried!

Let us continue to endeavor to persevere. We are obligated to continue reading Oliver Cowdery's writing as he tells us what he believed actually happened to Joseph Smith. Page 74 he writes "but soon the vision of the heavenly messenger was renewed, instructing him to go immediately and view those things of which he had been informed, with a promise that he should obtain them if he followed the directions and went with an eye single to the glory of God".

What commandments could he have broken?

Well, here comes Oliver Cowdery to the rescue. Although the angel Nephi had told Joseph Smith about these plates and the history contained on them for the benefit of all mankind, read what Oliver Cowdery says about this. (Page 75 of History) "Remember, that he who does this work, who is thus favored of the Lord must do it with his eye single to the glory of the same, and the welfare and restoration of the scattered remnants of the house of Israel" – rush upon his mind with the quickness of electricity. Here was a struggle indeed, for when he calmly reflected upon his errand, he knew that if God did not give, he could not obtain; and again, with the thought or hope of obtaining his mind would be carried back to its former reflections of poverty, abuse, - wealthy, grandure (sp) and ease until before arriving at the place described, *this wholly occupied his desires*; and when he thought upon the fact of what was previously shown him, it was only with an assurance that he should obtain and accomplish his desires in relieving himself and friends from want."

He continues "…seemed to inspire further thoughts of gain and income from such a valuable history. Surely, thought he, every man will sieze (sp) with eagerness this knowledge, and incalculable income will be mine,[38] raise the expectations of any one of like experience, placed in similar circumstances it is sufficient to say that such were

---

[38] **This is directly contradictory to what Joseph Smith stated in his history Chapter 1 vs. 46 " "…and (he-the angel) added a caution to me, telling me that Satan would try to tempt me (in consequence of the indigent circumstances of my father's family) to get the plates for the purpose of getting rich. This he forbade me, saying that I must have no other object in view, in getting the plates, but to glorify God, and must not be influenced by any other motive that that of building his kingdom".**

his reflections during his walk of from two to three miles, the distance from his father's house to the place pointed out.

…and as I previously remarked, a fixed determination to obtain and aggrandize himself occupied his mind when he arrived at the place where the record was found.

So the angel told him to keep an "eye to the glory of God" only and Oliver Cowdery tries to tell us that Joseph Smith was thinking of how such an "incalculable income will be mine". I wonder how Oliver Cowdery knew that these were Joseph Smith's reflections on his way to get the plates?

There are such serious problems with this it boggles the mind. Was Joseph Smith interested in the plates because they were gold and he could sell them for a great amount of money? Did he forget God was using him to reveal things to mankind and that everything he was directed to do was from the Lord? Was he interested in them for selling them to someone who could interpret them and tell the history of the people of the land he was in? Remember, his job at the time was digging for money and precious metals. This is one reason Emma Hale's (JS wife) father (Isaac) didn't like him. He had paid him money to find treasure on his land and Joseph Smith had failed. He was certainly interested in money because when it turned out he couldn't sell the gold plates he then planned to sell his writing of the plates and sent representatives up into Canada to sell the copyright to the Book of Mormon. Joseph Smith listed himself as the author of this book and later changed it to claim he was a translator of the gold plates when he couldn't sell his book. Hiram Page and Oliver Cowdery went to Toronto for this purpose, but they failed entirely to sell the copyright, returning without any money. (*Comprehensive History of the Church* Vol. 1 pp. 162-66). So according to Oliver Cowdery was Joseph Smith very avaricious and selfish in his desire to find these gold plates so he could accumulate great wealth, not to follow Gods directions?

CHAPTER 17

AMERICAN INDIANS?

Now Oliver Cowdery gives us a little information allegedly taken from the gold plates and what happened to the people that this history tells us about. (Page 77) "It was not the wicked who overcame the righteous; far from this; it was the wicked against the wicked, and by the wicked the wicked were punished, - the Nephites who were once enlightened, had fallen from a more elevated standing as to favour and privilege before the Lord in consequence of the righteousness of their fathers, and now falling below, for such was actually the case, were suffered to be overcome, and the land was left to the possession of the red men, who were without intelligence, only in the affairs of their wars; and having no records, only preserving their history by tradition from father to son, lost the account of their true origin, and wandered from river to river, from hill to hill, from mountain to mountain, and from sea to sea, till the land was again peopled, in a measure by a rude, wild, revengeful, warlike and barbarous race, - such are our Indians." Many tribes of indians cultivated the land and lived on their agriculture. They were not "rude, wild, revengeful, warlike and barabarous" as Oliver Cowdery mistakenly reports them to be.

There has been great research done on the history of American Indians and nothing Oliver Cowdery says fits with this history. Initially, perhaps as late as 10,000 B.C. there was a land bridge across the Bering Sea from Russia to Alaska and the Eurasians following the animals they hunted and lived off of, crossed this land bridge into North America. There are many studies done on the history of the Indians, and indeed each of the many different tribes of Indians and nothing comes close to Oliver Cowdery's alleged history of the Indians.

CHAPTER 18

OLIVER COWDERY'S WRITINGS

The narrative continues regarding Joseph Smith's life. " Beginning with the entry for 22 September 1835, the history is based on Smith's 1835-1836 journal. Handwriting of Warren Parrish and Warren Cowdery (Misspelled – it was Cowdrey). Joseph Smith History, vol A-1 (earliest numbering), Church History Library, Salt Lake City." Page 93 of Joseph Smith Papers Vol 1 Yes, I am confused also, as it certainly sounds as if it is Joseph Smith himself writing this history but the historians make it clear it was these other gentlemen that were writing it.

Now the history takes on a new meaning. The circa Summer 1832 history was written mostly in Joseph Smith's handwriting and now other people are writing his history and changing what he had himself written.

Warren Cowdrey writes (Page 94 Histories) "Here the reader will observe, that the narrative assumes a different form. The subject of it becoming daily more and more noted, the writer deemed it proper to give a plain, simple, yet faithful narration of every important item in his every-day-occurrences."

He is like his younger brother Oliver Cowdery, a very flamboyant type of writer, using many words to literally say nothing. An example of this is his continuation taken from page 94 of Histories, "Therefore, he trusts, that to the man of God, no apology will be necessary for such a course; especially when he takes into consideration, that he writes, not so much for the benefit of his contemporaries as for that of posterity. The candid, reflecting mind will also realize, how highly we all estimate every species of intelligence or correct information we can obtain relative to the ancient Prophets & Apostles, through whom the Most-High condescended to reveal himself on the children of men. Such revelations, therefore, as may at any time be given through him will be inserted, and the characters of other men, from their necessary connexion (sp) with him, will in some instances be plainly pourtrayed (sp); but the digression from the main thread of the narrative, when short, will, the writer trusts, constitute that pleasing variety, those lights and shades, that picture of human life on which the eye rests with more pleasure. The ear, and the mind of both reader and hearer, will be relieved from that formal sameness, or tiresome monotony, that characterize a dull tale of no merit, and enable future generations, to duly appreciate the claims the subject of this narrative may have had, on his contemporaries for their implicit reliance on what he taught them."

What? Did he really say anything here? Lots of words but nothing seems to mean anything other than he seems to be saying he can insert anything he wants at any time. But why doesn't he clearly state he is a man of God? As I pointed out earlier, Oliver Cowdery changed Joseph Smith's history and early written statements to a totally different version of what Joseph Smith had experienced some 18 years earlier. It is evident that Joseph Smith agreed with Oliver Cowdery, and wouldn't this show he had written his experience erroneously initially?

Lets see now,… Joseph Smith claims that upon praying to God, the heavens were immediately opened to him and he saw the Lord but no angels. This was written in Joseph Smith's own handwriting about 14 years after it happened. Then two years later (or was it four?) Oliver Cowdery comes up with the story that when Joseph Smith went to pray to God he was immediately overcome with some strange dark power that seemed to immobilize him and after praying fervently to God this evil power was removed from him and he saw two beings appear to him, seemingly God the Father and His son Jesus Christ. Now two beings appear at the same time instead of one appearing first and then the second appearing later. Which version is correct?

Why did Joseph Smith initially state that upon praying to God, the Lord immediately appeared to him and later that he had to go through the evil force that sought to destroy him? Why did Joseph Smith say there was "a personage" that appeared to him and not state there were two personages that appeared? In the six years between these two versions, did Joseph Smith somehow gain additional memory of this event? Did he now realize there were no angels that appeared in this vision? Or many angels?

It would seem that now that Oliver Cowdery and Warren Cowdery were writing this, they took whatever leave they felt they wanted to in order to embellish and change Joseph Smith's original hand written document.

Let's think a moment about why this study is even being conducted. What is history if not a factual account of past events and people? If events are portrayed as being different than what really happened, is it history? Isn't it merely a fictional writing of someone showing their imagination? Why does Oliver Cowdery and his oldest brother feel they can change what actually happened and as Warren Cowdery says " The ear, and the mind of both reader and hearer, will be relieved from that formal sameness, or tiresome monotony, that characterize a dull tale of no merit?" Is Joseph Smith initial writing of an alleged personal visitation of Jesus Christ to him really a "tiresome monotony? Or a "dull tale of no merit?" Warren says we should be delighted to be relieved from these dull and tiresome writings. If you have read what I quoted him as saying on page 94 of Histories, I believe any sane and sound-minded individual will agree that Warren's writings are the ones that are monotonous and tiresome, not Joseph Smith's.

We are now faced with a serious dilemma. There are over 680 pages in addition to the index and prologue of The Joseph Smith Papers, Histories Volume 1. We are up to page 94 and are being told the writers will insert anything they please whenever they want to regarding the history of Joseph Smith. It would seem that Joseph Smith had these writings to review himself and you may argue that he must have agreed with these writings or he would have changed them. In reality Joseph Smith was by now busy running his church with all its problems and he may not have had time to read all the writings of the different historians he had appointed for his church. He had joined with Sydney Rigdon in moving to Kirtland, Indeed he fled from Ohio with the law after him. Rigdon had converted his congregation over to Mormonism from the church of Christ of which he was their minister. He had fled from New York where he had numerous warrants for his arrest. He directed a temple to be built in Kirtland, Ohio and was designing various temple ceremonies that would be carried out in this temple. He was sending many men on missions to various places on earth to preach the teachings of his church including the conflicting versions of his vision of Jesus Christ. He had written the Book of Mormon and was busy publishing it and trying to sell as many copies of it as he could to raise money. He started a bank and was trying to make it succeed. He had several newspapers going and had all the management problems of them to deal with. He had to keep writing (or caused to be written) many revelations he claimed God was giving him. He joined the Masons and participated actively in their rituals and had the largest Masonic Lodge in Illinois.

CHAPTER 19

THE WORD OF WISDOM

To try to appease his wife Emma at home, he claimed a revelation from God about what became known as the Word of Wisdom, which supposedly meant nobody should drink alcoholic beverages, smoke or use tobacco, or drink tea or coffee. This was given February 27, 1833, and specifically states "To be sent greeting; ***not by commandment or constraint***, but by revelation and the word of wisdom showing forth the order and will of God in the temporal salvation of all saints in the last days –" D&C 89:2 Yet in excommunicating John C. Bennett from the church, one of the charges was that he did not keep the Word of Wisdom. So what? It was not a commandment to the church until the Church made it a commandment in 1852 and Joseph Smith himself didn't abide by it either.

Brigham Young didn't keep the Word of Wisdom either. Documentary History of the Church, Volume 2 Pages 377-378 Joseph Smith says "Elder Orson Hyde, Luke S. Johnson, and Warren Parish, then presented the Presidency with three servers of glasses filled with wine, to bless. And it fell to my lot to attend to this duty, which I cheerfully discharged. It was then passed round in order, then the cake in the same order; and suffice it to say, our hearts were made glad while partaking of the bounty of earth which was presented, until we had taken our fill; and joy filled every bosom, and the countenances of old and young seemed to bloom alike with cheerfulness and smiles of youth, and an entire unison of feeling seemed to pervade the congregation." So their hearts were "made glad" partaking of wine and cake. This was Wednesday Jan. 20, 1836, about three years after the revelation stating "That inasmuch as any man drinketh wine or strong drink among you, behold it is not good, neither meet in the sight of your Father, only in assembling yourselves together to offer up your sacraments before him. And behold, this should be wine, yea, pure wine of the grape of the vine, of your own make. And again, strong drinks are not for the belly, but for the washing of your bodies."

Indeed John C. Bennett in his book
"The History of the Saints" shows many affidavits proving Joseph Smith freely imbibed of alcohol and drank wine to excess.

George Albert Smith (Journal of Discourses Volume 2 page 214) says "I know persons who apostatized because they supposed they had reasons; for instance a certain family, after having traveled a long journey, arrived in Kirtland, and the Prophet asked them to stop with him until they could find a place. Sister Emma, in the meantime, asked the old lady if she would have a cup of tea to refresh her after the fatigues of the journey, or a cup of coffee. This whole family apostatized because they were invited to take a cup of tea or coffee after the Word of Wisdom was given".

DHC Vol 7 pages 101-103 gives an account of the murder of Joseph Smith and states that wine was brought to them while in Carthage jail and it was not meant to be sacramental wine but was to be used for their comfort and enjoyment. All four men in the room partook of the wine and felt better for drinking it.

Brigham Young gave this information concerning the circumstances surrounding the coming forth of the Word of Wisdom:

When the School of the Prophets was inaugurated, one of the first revelations given by the Lord to his servant Joseph Smith was the Word of wisdom… I think I am as well acquainted with the circumstances which led to the giving of the Word of Wisdom as any man in the Church, although I was not present at the time to witness them. The first School of the Prophets was held in a small room situated over the Prophet Joseph's kitchen, in a house which belonged to Bishop Whitney, and which was attached to his store, which store probably might be about fifteen feet square. In the rear of this building was a kitchen, probably 10 x 14 feet containing rooms and pantries. Over this kitchen was situated the room in which the Prophet received revelations and in which he instructed his brethren. The Brethren came to that place for hundreds of miles to attend school in a little room no larger than 11 x 14. When they assembled together in this room after breakfast the first thing they did was to light their pipes, and while smoking, talk about the great things of the Kingdom and spit all over the room, and as soon as the pipe was out of their mouths a large chew of tobacco was then taken. Often when the Prophet entered the room to give the School instructions he would find himself in a cloud of tobacco smoke. This, and the complaints of his wife at having to clean so filthy a floor, made the Prophet think upon the matter, and he inquired of the Lord relating to the conduct of the Elders in using tobacco, and the revelation known as the Word of Wisdom was the result of his inquiry. Journal of Discourses Volume 12 pp 157-158.

It is interesting that in the revelation known as the Word of Wisdom, God says "…to be sent greeting <u>not</u> by commandment or constraint… showing forth the order and will of God in the <u>temporal salvation</u> of all saints in the last days (D&C 89:2) God is very clear in stating this is not sent as a commandment. In fact he further advises through Joseph Smith in D&C 29:34-35 "Wherefore, verily I say unto you that all things unto me are spiritual and not at any time have I given unto you a law which was temporal; neither any man, nor the children of men, neither Adam, your Father, whom I created. Behold I gave unto him that he should be an agent unto himself and I gave unto him commandment, but no temporal commandment gave I unto him, for my commandments are spiritual; they are not natural, nor temporal, neither carnal nor sensual".

So God gives 'advice' to Joseph concerning the temporal salvation of the saints by adhering to certain health guidelines. This Word of Wisdom was not considered a commandment to the Church until the 1852 conference in Salt Lake City, Utah when it was voted on by the membership in attendance. This was reported in the Millennial Star Vol. 14, No. 3 Page 35 Feb. 1, 1952. Although it is not a commandment while Joseph Smith is alive, he uses it as a reason for excommunicating individuals from his Church for not heeding the advice given therein although he himself fails to follow God's word. Doesn't it sound like he is still sinning and transgressing like he did at the start of all this? Violating the Word of Wisdom was important enough to excommunicate someone from his church, which could mean eternal damnation so why was Joseph Smith violating this Word of Wisdom himself?

"Frederick G. Williams first met Joseph Smith in the summer of 1831 but there is no evidence he began work as a scribe before 16 February 1832." Page 7, 8

CHAPTER 20

FANNIE ALGER AND POLYGAMY

Now we come to another interesting episode in Joseph Smith's life occurring either 1831 or early 1832 and involves his relationship with his housemaid, a 16 year old girl named Fannie Alger.

In explaining his sexual involvement with Fannie Alger he had to deal with the intense dislike of both his wife Emma as well as Oliver Cowdery and did he have to come up with a revelation from God telling him about Polygamy to perhaps get him excused for his behavior with Fanny Alger? In this venture he was drawing an enormous amount of opposition from both inside his church as well as from those who didn't believe in his church.

In 1872, William E. McLellin told Joseph Smith III that he repeated the rumors about Joseph being discovered with Fanny Alger in a barn, to Emma Smith, and she corroborated the stories. Todd Compton discounts McLellin's story because it contradicts the accounts of Chauncey Webb and Emma Smith's later statements on polygamy. Todd Compton was a thorough student of Joseph Smith's plural wives.

There is no legal paper record found that Joseph Smith ever married Fannie Alger, however Mosiah Hancock in the 1890s tells that his father Levi Hancock performed the wedding ceremony between Joseph Smith and Fanny Alger. We are not told where Levi Hancock ever received the authority to perform marriages and we know Joseph Smith didn't perform his first marriage ceremony until November of 1835 so there remains serious questions about the validity of such a marriage between Joseph Smith and Fanny Alger. We remain unaware of any legal recording of such a marriage.

"Mosiah Hancock wrote in the 1890s about Joseph engaging Levi Hancock, Mosiah's father, to ask Alger's parents for permission to marry. Levi Hancock was Alger's uncle and an appropriate go-between. He talked with Alger's father, then her mother, and finally to Fanny herself, and all three consented." Rough Stone Rolling page 325

The historians, as we shall shortly discover, claimed that Joseph Smith first performed a marriage ceremony in 1835 so who performed the wedding of Joseph Smith to Fanny Alger, if indeed there ever was one? Was it indeed Levi Hancock? Richard Bushman makes the statement "he (JS) felt innocent because he had married Alger". Rough Stone Rolling P 325 Now Richard Bushmen is one of the main historians listed in the front of the book Joseph Smith Papers Histories Volume 1 which we are studying. First he quotes Mosiah Hancock in what appears to be an attempt to justify Joseph Smith's relationship with Fanny Alger as a marriage relationship as stated above. Yet he has his name attached to this study, which says that the first wedding ceremony Joseph Smith ever performed was in 1835. The situation with Fanny Alger took place in either 1831, 1832 or possibly 1833.

These statements are not in accordance with one another. All statements seem to agree that the Fanny Alger story took place in either 1831, 1832 or 1833. Who performed the marriage between

Joseph Smith and Fanny Alger? It couldn't have been Joseph Smith himself as the historians have already told us clearly that he didn't perform his first wedding ceremony until 1835. Fanny Alger moved out of the area in 1836 with her parents. JS seemed very upset when Oliver Cowdery "used the doctrine of plural marriage as a license for marrying at will" Rough Stone Rolling Page 326 He (JS) seemed to feel only he had the keys of plural marriage and each individual case had to be approved by him to be both legal and approved by God.

If Joseph Smith really felt each individual case regarding plural marriage had to be approved by him, did he then feel this should apply to any other ordinances in the church such as baptism or temple ordinances? If not, why not? In 2013 the Mormon church claims over 15 million members. Even if polygamy alone was the only ordinance that must be approved by the prophet or president of the church on an individual basis, how could any man be expected to approve millions of applications for this ordinance to be performed each year?

Ann Eliza Webb Young, a divorced wife of Brigham Young, claimed Fanny's parents "considered it the highest honor to have their daughter adopted into the Prophet's family, and her mother has always claimed that (Fanny) was sealed to Joseph at that time." Ann Eliza's father, Chauncey Webb, who reportedly took Alger in when Emma learned of the marriage, said Joseph "was sealed there secretly to Fanny Alger". Rough Stone Rolling page 325

Ann Eliza could not have been an eyewitness because she was not yet born at this time but she may have heard the story from her parents who were close to the Smith's. Hers is the only testimony that Emma knew about the relationship between Alger and Smith and was furious over it.

If indeed Fanny Alger was Joseph Smith's wife, where is his support and courage in defending her when Emma became so upset with him over it? Didn't Emma know Joseph Smith had talked personally to God? If this was in 1831, Joseph Smith had not yet announced to anyone that he had a revelation from God personally to him. His first written account of such a revelation didn't occur until 1832 as we have already learned. So we must ask, if God had told Joseph Smith to enter into a plural marriage with Fanny Alger, why didn't he (JS) stand up for Fanny and defend her as a husband would be expected to do for his wife or wives? Why didn't Emma believe Joseph when he told her God had revealed the doctrine of plural wives to him? Certainly she knew him better than anyone else at that time, having lived with him as his wife. Didn't Joseph Smith tell Emma, his wife, that God had revealed this to him and he was not ashamed of God's revelations? Why did Emma cower Joseph so much? Why was he so afraid of her?

In all of this activity, he had to deal with all the complaints of the members of his church as they tried to live together and get along with each other. As Sidney Rigdon had tried living a system of United Order in his church, Joseph Smith claimed a revelation from God about this and introduced this into his church also. Woven through all of this activity Joseph Smith attempted to have sexual relations with many of his followers wives. He succeeded in some and turned some down after getting them to agree to sharing their favors with him. Some of his leaders actually left his church from his immoral behavior. (See chart at end of this report on his wives)

On Tuesday, May 8, 1838 Joseph Smith was asked a question: "Do the Mormons believe in having more wives than one?" and he answered: "No, not at the same time, but they believe that if their companion dies, they have a right to marry again." DHC Vol 3, p 28-29 Yet we have seen that Joseph Smith participated in polygamy as early as 1832 if we believe certain sources regarding Fanny Alger as shown above.

On February 19, 1854, Jedediah M. Grant, second councilor to Brigham Young, spoke in the Salt Lake Tabernacle, telling of Joseph Smiths demands for other men's wives

"When the family organization was revealed from heaven-the Patriarchal order of God, and Joseph began, on the right and on the left, to add to his family, what a quaking there was in Israel. Says one brother to another, 'Joseph says all covenants are done away, and none are binding but the new covenants; now suppose Joseph should come and say he wanted your wife, what would you say to that?' 'I would tell him to go to hell'. This was the spirit of many in the early days of this Church…"

"What would a man of God say, who felt aright, when Joseph asked him for his money? He would say, 'Yes and I wish I had more to help to build up the kingdom of God'. Of if he came and said, 'I want your wife?' O yes', he would say, 'here she is, there are plenty more'…did the Prophet Joseph want every man's wife he asked for? He did not… If such a man of God should come to me and say, "I want your gold and silver, or your wives,', I should say, 'Here they are, I wish I had more to give you. Take all I have got."
Journal of Discourses Volume 2, pp. 13-14

Orson Pratt did leave the church after refusing to let Joseph Smith engage in sexual relations with his wife as Joseph requested, stating the Lord had given her to Joseph. There is great controversy over this episode and both claims and counter claims from both sides of the story. Joseph Smith threatened Sarah Pratt that he would ruin her if she told of his proposals to engage in sexual intimacies with him but she refused anyway and Joseph Smith did his best to ruin her as he had promised. When she was asked about all the polygamous wives Joseph Smith claimed and where were the children of such unions, she pointed out that many were already married and that Dr. John C. Bennett was available to handle the single ones implying abortions were performed by Bennett (see section at end of this report for more information on John C. Bennett).

However, on February 9, 1831 (Section 42 D&C) Joseph Smith claims a revelation from God and states (Vs. 22) Thou shalt love thy wife with all thy heart, and shalt cleave unto her and none else." Again in March 1831 (D&C Section 49) Joseph claims another revelation from God and in vs. 16 states "Wherefore, it is lawful that he should have one wife, and they twain shall be one flesh, and all this that the earth might answer the end of its creation."

Why is there nothing in the Papers of Joseph Smith relating to his belief in polygamy? It is not difficult to obtain information on his beliefs on this subject so we are left to wonder why Oliver Cowdery didn't see fit to divulge what was going on in this regard. He was certainly flowery and verbose on everything else he wrote and changed much of what Joseph Smith claimed to have experienced. Yet on this subject we find him very quiet except for this:

Article on Marriage is a statement prepared by Oliver Cowdery while Joseph Smith was away on other church business. It is reported he was disturbed by this but didn't try to change anything in it at the time it was presented to and accepted by the Church.

He first states that he and the church believe in the principle of marriage as all civilized nations believe. Further, he said that all marriages in this Church of Christ of Latter-day Saints should be solemnized in apublic meeting or feast prepared for that purpose.

According to the custom of all civilized nations, marriage is regulated by law and ceremonies; You will notice he calls the name of the church Church of Christ of Latter-day Saints. I have been unable to find anywhere that the Mormon Church went by this nomenclature. From this study you will see that between 1834 and 1838 it was called the Church of the Latter-day Saints. From its inception in 1830 and until 1834 it was called the Church of Christ.

He said that it was not right to prohibit marrying out of the church but cautioned against this.

Then he proceeded to outline the actual ritual to be performed in a marriage ceremony, what is to be said, and where each husband and wife were to stand. It is interested to note that he said the ceremony was to include the statement that it was being performed by virtue of the laws of the country and authority vested in the individual performing the ceremony. From this study you may recall that only Seymour Brunson had authority to perform marriages for the Mormon church. It is not clear where Joseph Smith was ever given authority to perform marriages although he did this on different occasions.

He clarified that marriage was to be between one man and one woman putting to rest clearly the belief that homosexuality was not acceptable. Further the article claimed that since the Chruch had been accused of fornication and polygamy that they definitely did not believe in either of these activities.

It was stated that a woman should not be baptized contrary to the will of her husband, nor was it acceptable to even try to persuade a woman to leave her husband for the church.

It was read by President W. W. Phelps and accepted and adopted by a unanimous vote of the general assembly of the Church of Latter-day Saints held at Kirtland or on the 17th of August 1835 and ordered to be printed in the Doctrine and Covenants of the Church.

President Joseph Smith, Jun., and Frederick G. Williams were absent from this conference on a visit to the saints in Michigan.

Joseph Fielding Smith Doctrines of Salvation Volume 3, page 195 says that this article on marriage and this article on laws and government in general were written by Oliver Cowdery in the absence of the Prophet Joseph Smith, and the Prophet knew nothing of the action that was taken ordering them printed with the revelations. These were not revelations, never were so considered, were ordered printed in the absence of Joseph Smith, and when Joseph Smith returned from Michigan and learned what was done the Prophet was very much troubled. Orson Pratt and Joseph F. Smith were missionary companions; they traveled together. When the Prophet came back from Michigan he learned of the order made by the conference of the Church and let it go through.

What does he mean "let it go through"? It had already gone through and was considered section 101 of the Doctrine and Covenants. The Article on Marriage was made a part of the Doctrine and Covenants book of scripture even after Joseph Smith recorded his revelation as recorded in the 132nd section of the Doctrine and Covenants but eventually with the obvious conflicts between this later revelation (Sec. 132) and the Article on Marriage one had to go and so the Article on Marriage was removed from the Doctrine and Covenants entirely in 1876 and another 'revelation' was replaced as section 101. The Article on Marriage stated that one man should have only one wife and rejected the claim that the Church was being accused of polygamy and yet the 132nd section of the Doctrine and Covenants states a man can marry more than one woman which is in opposition with the Article on Marriage.

Historical Record, Vol 5, 6, 7 & 8 Book 1, Page 230 At a meeting held in Plano, Illinois, Sept. 12, 1878, Apostle Orson Pratt explained the circumstances connected with the coming forth of the revelation on plural marriage. He refuted the statement and belief of those present that Brigham Young was the author of that revelation; showed that Joseph Smith, the Prophet, had not only commenced the practice of that principle himself, and further taught it to others, before President

Young and the Twelve had returned from their missions in Europe, in 1841, but that Joseph actually received revelation upon that principle as early as 1831. He said Lyman Johnson who was very familiar with Joseph at this early date, Joseph living at his father's house, and who was also very intimate with me, having traveled on several missions together, said himself that Joseph had made known as early as 1831, that plural marriage was a correct principle. Joseph Smith said that God had revealed it to him, but that the time had not come to teach or practice it in the church, but that the time would come. To this statement Elder Pratt bore his testimony. He cited several instances of Joseph having had wives sealed to him, one at least as early as April 5, 1841, which was some time prior to the return of the Twelve from England.

From Doctrines of Salvation Vol 3. p 197 Joseph Fielding Smith says there was no doctrine of plural marriage in the church in 1835, but Orson Pratt said that the Lord did reveal to Joseph Smith, before 1835, and before 1834, and as early as 1832, the doctrine of plural marriage. The Prophet Joseph Smith revealed that to some few of the brethren, and Orson Pratt was one of them.

Joseph was commanded to take more wives and he waited until an angel with a drawn sword stood before him and declared that if he longer delayed fulfilling that command he would slay him. [39]

---

[39] ***While there is no scriptural support for this doctrine, the Mormon Church has a belief that before this world was formed a great council was held in heaven and Lucifer offered a plan for the salvation of God's children that would force everybody to obey God's commandments and therefore all be saved, but God did not accept his offer and instead wanted his children to have their free agency to obey or not to obey his commandments. Here we have Joseph Smith showing that Lucifer's plan was the one God was using by forcing him to take more than one wife.***

(Hyrum Smith, Elder Benjamin F. Johnson's letter to George S. Gibbs 1903) Has anyone ever heard of God taking a sword and destroying one of his prophets for not obeying him? Was even Judas Iscariot not destroyed for betraying Christ?

Lorenzo Snow, a prophet of the LDS Church said the Prophet Joseph Smith then explained the doctrine of plurality of wives; he said that the Lord had revealed it unto him, and commanded him to have women sealed to him as wives; that he foresaw the trouble that would follow, and sought to turn away from the commandment; that an angel from heaven then appeared before him with a drawn sword, threatening him with destruction unless he went forward and obeyed the commandment. He further said that Eliza R. Snow, had been sealed to him as his wife for time and eternity. He told Lorenzo Snow that the Lord would open the way, and he should have women sealed to him as wives.

In January 1838, Cowdery wrote his brother Warren that he and Joseph Smith had "had some conversation in which in every instance I did not fail to affirm that which I had said was strictly true. A dirty nasty filthy affair of his and Fanny Alger's was talked over in which I strictly declared that I had never deserted from the truth in the matter, and as I supposed was admitted by himself." Oliver never appeared to accept the idea of polygamy. Richard Bushman, one of the editors of the Joseph Smith Papers, wrote: "In January 1838, some months after the Algers had left Kirtland, Oliver Cowdery-one of the three witnesses to the authenticity of the Book of Mormon-wrote his brother concerning his indignation at Smith's relationship with Alger. Cowdery said he had discussed with Smith the 'dirty, nasty, filthy affair of his and Fanny Alger's…in which I strictly declared that I had never deserted from the truth in the matter, and as I supposed was admitted by himself."

As Richard Bushman (One of the authors of the History book we are studying) has noted, Smith "never denied a relationship with Alger, but insisted it was not adulterous. He wanted it on record that he had never confessed to such a sin." The best statement Smith could obtain from Cowdery was an affirmation that Smith had never acknowledged himself to have been guilty of adultery. "That," wrote Bushman, "was all Joseph wanted: an admission that he had not termed the Alger affair adulterous." All Oliver Cowdery ever granted, was that he could affirm that Smith "had never acknowledged himself to have been guilty of adultery" not that he did not actually commit adultery with Fanny Alger. A distinction without a difference.

Fanny Alger was 16 years old in 1832, born Sept 20, 1816, and was given a job as maid to help Emma Smith keep her house. Why? Couldn't Emma keep her own house? Why did she need a housemaid? Joseph Smith was 27 years old at this time (Born in 1805). Emma was born July 10, 1804 and was 28 years old at this time. Fanny Alger was reported to have been a very nice looking young girl. Joseph had been known to say "whenever I see a pretty woman I have to pray for grace".

When Emma discovered them in a barn actually in the act of sexual intercourse, she was outraged and demanded Joseph get Fanny out of their house which Joseph did. Several people reported Fanny was pregnant at this time with Joseph's child. How Oliver Cowdery learned of this is not clear, but it is clear he was well aware of it. When Oliver Cowdery was excommunicated in 1838 one of the charges against him was that he was "seeking to destroy the character of President Joseph Smith jr by falsely insinuating that he was guilty of adultry &c."

Seymour Brunson and other priesthood leaders conducting the excommunicaton trail of Oliver Cowdery did not question Oliver's claim about Joseph being sexually involved with the 16 year old girl Fanny Alger. They seemed only concerned that Oliver was seeking to destroy Joseph Smith's character. Whether he was correct or not in his statement about this matter did not become an issue in the hearing. Why not? Didn't they feel Oliver was making truthful remarks? Didn't they care? If the true remarks Oliver made appeared destructive to Joseph Smith's character, who would so construe this destruction to be such an act? Doesn't this seem rather absurd? As Paul the apostle said "Am I therefore become your enemy because I tell you the truth"? (Gal 4:16) Had Oliver become an enemy of the church because he told the truth?

Joseph would have had to claim Fanny Alger was his wife when they had sexual relations although he did not have the authority to perform marriages at that time. As is shown in this study, as late as 1836 the Church had to rely on an individual who was licensed by the state of Ohio to perform weddings. Until 1835 Seymour Brunson was the only one licensed to perform marriages in the church. There is no written or legal evidence Joseph Smith ever married Fanny Alger. Richard L. Bushman suggested Joseph involvement with Fanny Alger might have been "as early as 1831" but does not supply any documentation to explain such an early date. (Joseph Smith: *Rough Stone Rolling*, New York: Alfred A. Knopf, 2005, 323.) Pp324-326Now where does that leave Joseph Smith in this matter?

Pages 132-133 Histories Date November 24, 1835. "This evening he had an invitation to attend a wedding, at his brother Hyrum Smith's, to solemnize the rights of matrimony between Newel Knight and Lydia Goldwait. His wife and some others accompanied him. When they arrived, they found a respectable company assembled, the interview was opened by singing and prayer. President Smith then requested the bridegroom and bride, to arise and join hands, and then proceeded to make some remarks, upon the subject of marriage as follows; that it was an institution of heaven first solemnized in the garden of Eden by God himself, by the authority of the everlasting priesthood. The following is in substance the ceremony delivered on this occasion. You calling them by name you covenant to be each others companions <u>during your live</u> and discharge the duties of husband and wife in all respects to which they gave their assent. He then pronounced them husband and wife in the name of God with many blessings".

Where did Joseph Smith get the authority to perform this wedding? To have this authority it had to be granted by the state of Ohio. I am unable to find any documentation showing Joseph Smith ever received the authority to perform weddings.

Footnote 312 page 133 states "This is the first known wedding performed by Joseph Smith". So, as we shall see Joseph Smith first was given the revelation on eternal marriage in 1831, yet here at the end of the year 1835 he is said to be performing his first known wedding. And in his performance he marries them for the period "during your lives". Not forever! In other words, when one of their lives ended, so did their marriage.

Joseph Smith claimed that plural marriage was the "order of heaven" and was eternal and all marriages should be eternal marriages, and not just for this life only. Where does that leave us in the Fanny Alger situation? If he didn't perform his first wedding until Nov. 24, 1835 and only Emma Smith (and apparently Oliver Cowdery) knew Fannie Alger was having sexual relations with Joseph Smtih in 1832, then who married the two of them? Oliver Cowdery certainly didn't seem to feel they were married as he called their relationship a "dirty, filthy, nasty business". Shouldn't we be able to safely assume Oliver Cowdery did not believe marriage was a "dirty, filthy, nasty busines"?

So what else could he be referring to in regard to Joseph Smith and Fanny Alger's relationship other than it was adulterous?

Joseph Smith couldn't have performed the marriage himself as the historians make it very clear that he "didn't perform his first wedding until Nov. 24, 1835".

"It is clear they did not have the authority to perform marriages as on October 25, 1835 (5 years later) it states on page 103 footnote 199 "Brunson (Seymour)[40] who had obtained a license in Jackson County, Ohio to solemnize weddings, may have been the only Latter-day Saint with such a license at this time". Therefore just a month earlier Joseph Smith had to have Seymour Brunson perform marriages and now he suddenly performs one himself without ever claiming to obtain the proper license from the state to do this?

The following information is taken from B. H. Roberts instruction in the 5th Volume of DHC, Pages XXIX through XLVI.

The date of the heading of the Revelation on the Eternity of the Marriage Covenant, including the Plurality of wives, states the time at which the revelation was committed to writing, not the time at which the principles set forth in the revelation were first made known to the Prophet. This is evident from the written revelation itself which discloses the fact that Joseph Smith was already in the relationship of plural marrriage, as the following passage witnesses:

"And let mine handmaid, Emma Smith, receive all those that have been given unto my servant Joseph, and who are virtuous and pure before me."

There is indisputable evidence that the revelation making known this marriage law was given to the Joseph Smith as early as 1831. In that year, and thence intermittently up to 1833, the Prophet was

---

[40] **Seymour Brunson obtained a position as Justice of the Peace and in this office was able to perform marriages and other legal duties that went with this position. To have legally recognized clergy status in Ohio, one must have ordination papers from a church recognized in Ohio. In May 1830, the other Mormons from New York came to Kirtland. This small town near Cleveland became the headquarters of the Church from January 1831 to December 1837.**

engaged in a revision of the English Bible text under the inspiration of God, Sidney Rigdon mainly acting as his scribe. As he began his revision with the Old Testament, he would be dealing with the age of the Patriarchs in 1831. He was doubtless struck with the favor in which the Lord held the several Bible Patriarchs of that period, notwithstanding they had a plurality of wives.

Where is a record of Isaac having more than one wife or concubines? How many wives did father Adam have? How many wives did Joseph (Mary's husband) have? How many wives did Lehi or anyone of his descendants in the Book of Mormon have?

…it is evident that as early at least as 1835 a charge of polygamy was made against the Church Why was that the case unless the subect of "polygamy" had been discussed within the church?

…Again, in May, 1836, in Missouri, in a series of questions asked and answered through the Elder's Journal, the following occurs: "Do the Mormons believe in having more wives than one?"
To which the answer is given'
"No, not at the same time".

…All these incidents blend together and make it clearly evident that the revelation on marriage was given long before the 12th of July, 1843, doubtless as early as 1831.

In addition to these indirect evidences is the direct testimony of the late Elder Orson Pratt, or the council of the Twelve Apostles. In 1878, in company with President Joseph F. smith, Elder Pratt visited several states east of the Mississippi in the capacity of a missionary; and at Plano, Illinois, at a meeting of the so-called Reorganized 'Church of the Latter-day Saints, he was invited…to occupy the time, which he did. In his remarks, according to his own and his companion's report of the meeting –

…He explained the circumstances connected with the coming forth of the revelation on plural marriage. Refuted the statement and belief of those present that Brigham Young was the author of that revelation; showed that Joseph Smith the Prophet had not only commenced the practice himself, and taught it to others, before President Young and the Twelve had returned from their missions in Europe, in 1841, but that Joseph actually received revelations upon that principle as early as 1831. Said Lyman Johnson, who was very familiar with Joseph at this early date, Joseph living at this father's house, and who was also very intimate with me having traveled on several missions together, said that Joseph had made known early as 1831, that plural marriage was a correct principle. Joseph declared to Lyman that it is not in the Church, but that the time would come.' (What about Fannie Alger in 1832?)

Relative to committing the revelation to writing on the 12th of July, 1843, that can best be told by the man who wrote the revelations as the Prophet Joseph dictated it to him, William Clayton; and the man who copied it the day following, Joseph Kingsbury, and from which copy the revelation was afterwards printed as it now stands in the current editions of the Doctrine and Covenants. In a sworn statement before John T. Caise, a notary public in Salt Lake City, on February 16th, 1874, William Clayton said:

"On the 7th of October, 1842, in the presence of Bishop Newel K. Whitney and his wife, Elizabeth Ann, President Joseph Smith appointed me Temple Recorder, and also his private clerk, placing all records, books, papers, etc. in my care, and requiring me to take any charge of and preserve them, his closing words being, 'when I have any revelations to write, you are the one to write them'. * * * On the morning of the 12th of July, 1843, Joseph and Hyrum Smith came into the office in the upper story of the brick store, on the bank of the Mississippi river. They were talking on the subject of Plural Marriage. Hyrum said to Joseph, 'If you will write the revelation on Celestial Marriage, I will take it and read it to Emma, and I believe

I can convince her of its truth, and you will hereafter have peace'. Joseph smiled and remarked, 'You do not know Emma as well as I do'. Hyrum repeated his opinions, and further remarked 'The doctrine is so plain, I can convince any reasonable man or woman of its truth, purity, and heavenly origin,' or words to that effect.

Joseph then said 'Well, I will write the revelation and we will see'. He then requested me to get paper and prepare to write. Hyrum very urgently requested Joseph to write the revelation by means of the Urim and Thummin, but Joseph in reply, said he did not need to, for he knew the revelation perfectly from beginning to end. Did Joseph Smith still have the Urim and Thummin at this time? Wasn't it given back to the angel with the gold plates? Does the church have them today?

"Joseph and Hyrum then sat down and Joseph commenced to dictate the revelation on Celestial Marriage, and I wrote it, sentence by sentence, as he dictated. After the whole was written, Joseph asked me to read it through, slowly and carefully, which I did, and he pronounced it correct. He then remarked that there was much more that he could write on the same subject, but what was written was sufficient for the present.

"Hyrum then took the revelation to read to Emma. Joseph remained with me in the office until Hyrum returned. When he came back, Joseph asked him how he had succeeded. Hyrum replied that he had never received a more and angrier response. Joseph quietly remarked, 'I told you you did not know Emma as well as I did'. Joseph then put the revelation in his pocket, and they both left the office.

The revelation was read to several of the authorities during the day. Towards evening Bishop Newel K. Whitney asked Joseph if he had any objections to his taking a copy of the revelation; Joseph replied that he had not, and handed it to him. It was carefully copied the following day by Joseph C. Kignsbury. Two or three days after the revelation was written Joseph related to me and several others that Emma had so teased, and urgently entreated him for the privilege of destroying it, that he becanme so weary of her teasing, and to get rid of her annoyance, he told her she might destroy it and she had done so, but he had consented to her wish in this matter to pacify her, realizing that he knew the revelation perfectly, and could rewrite it at any time if necessary.

Orson Pratt, August 29, 1852, states that the revelation on plural marriage was given to Joseph Smith July 12, 1843. (J.D. 1:64

A little diversion here might be of interest. Section 132 (This is the revelation on plural marriage now being investigated), Verse 26 says in part "... and he or she shall commit any sin or transgression of the new and everlasting covenant whatever, and all manner of blasphemies...yet they shall come forth in the first resurrection, and enter into their exaltation;"

Then Verse 41 speaks about adultery "and if she be with another man, and I have not appointed unto her by the Holy anointing, she hath committed adultery and shall be destroyed".

Then in Verse 44 it says that Joseph shall have the power "to take her and give her unto him that hath not committed adultery".

It would seem to me that committing adultery would fall under the category of "any sin or transgression of the new and everlasting covenant whatever". So why does Joseph have the power to take someone and give them to someone else? Verse 45 states that Joseph has the keys and power of the priesthood. Wouldn't this mean that what he does with these keys and powers would be eternal in nature?

In verse 39 it talks about King David's situation. Now I know of nothing King David did about committing any sin against the Holy Ghost when he caused Uriah to be placed in the front lines of the army to be killed and then he committed adultery with Bathsheba. We are not specifically told that Uriah was still alive when King David had his sexual relationship with Bathsheba but that is another story. This seems to be at variance with verse 26 also where it says "any sin or transgression" category. Any sin or transgression would seem to include adultery or murder as long as the individual is not committing a sin against the Holy Ghost. Verse 27 tells us the blasphemy against the Holy Ghost...is in that ye shed innocent blood and assent unto my death, after ye have received my new and everlasting covenant". Wouldn't you think King David did not assent unto Christ's death as Christ had not even been born yet much less killed so that would only leave him guilty of shedding innocent blood. This too may be questioned as how can we know what is "innocent blood"? There are two conditions mentioned, first shedding innocent blood, and second assenting unto Christ's death. Isn't it clear that both must be met to qualify for a sin against the Holy Ghost? Even if we are to assume Uriah's blood was "innocent" we have no evidence that David ever assented to Christ's death and we can question severely the idea that Uriah's blood was innocent. He was over 8 years old and was in the army and from what we know of the military activities of Israel's army he probably killed many other enemies of Israel which would seem to make his blood far from "innocent".

Since God gave David all his wives and concubines, they were David's for eternity and there seems to be a serious question that David ever committed a sin against the Holy Ghost. Of course God can judge anyway he wishes to.

He tells us we can commit <u>any</u> sin or transgression, <u>whatever</u>! And still enter into our exaltation.

Then Orson Pratt goes on at a later date to say:

In the early rise of this Church, February, 1831, God gave a commandment to its members, recorded in the book of Covenants, wherein He says, "Thou shalt love thy wife, with all thy heart, and shalt cleave unto her and to noone else;" and then He gave a strict law againsst adultery. Joseph Smith said this, and you have, no doubt, read; but let me ask whether the Lord has the privilege and the right to vary from this law (here he is asking an impossible question – Can God break his own laws?) it was given in 1831, when the one-wife system prevailed among this people. I will tell you that the Prophet Joseph said in relation to this matter in 1831, also in 1832, the year in which the law commanding the members of this Church to cleave to one wife only was given. Joseph was then living in Portage County, in the town of Hiram, at the house of Father John Johnson. Joseph was very intimate with that family, and they were good people at that time, and enjoyed much of the Spirit of the Lord.

Joseph Smith does not answer his impossible question. Does God have the right to vary from any of his laws at any time? Are God's laws eternal and everlasting? Are they really laws? Isn't a law something firm and concrete in nature? What does JS mean when he asks if the Lord has the "privilege" to vary from his law? If it is a law how can God or anybody "vary" from it? He might use other laws to accomplish his wishes such as airplanes flying and seemingly overcoming gravity.

There are many testimonies relating to plural marriage not being practiced, nor believed in, by the Church of Jesus Christ of Latter-day Saints which is confusing after reading what has already been shown above. One example, and there are many very similar, taken from Joseph Smith on May 26th at 10:00 a.m. 1844 is as follows:
     …A man asked whether the commandment was given that a man may have seven wives; and now the new prophet has charged me with adultery. I never had any fuss with these men until that female Relief Society brought out the paper against adulterers and adulteresses.

     …Be meek and lowly, upright and pure; render good for evil. If you bring on yourselves your own destruction, I will complain. It is not right for a man to bear down his neck to the oppressor always. Be humble and patient in all circumstances of life; we shall then triumph more gloriously. What a thing it is for a man to be accused of committing adultery, and having seven wives, when I can only find one.

I am the same man, and as innocent as I was fourteen years ago; and I can prove them all perjurers. I labored with these apostates myself until I was out of all manner of patience; and then I sent my brother Hyrum, whom they virtually kicked out of doors. Joseph Smith DHC Volume 6, p. 411

Joseph Smith claims that on May 26, 1844 he was able to only find one wife. Yet he was found with Fanny Alger back in 1832 and Emma Smith made him force Fanny Alger out of their house. There are numerous testimonies that Joseph Smith married other women so what is going on here? Isn't it clear Joseph Smith had intimate relationships with Fanny Alger? Was she his wife at the time or not? He tried to say she was, without making a lot of noise about it but Oliver Cowdery was terribly upset about it as shown above. From all recorded history Fanny Alger was never Joseph Smith's wife yet he certainly violated his marriage covenant with Emma by having sex with Fanny. This last statement of Joseph Smith directly above made May 26, 1844 is made up of whole cloth. By this time he had more than seven wives, yet he tries to make us believe he only has one. Why did Joseph Smith endeavor to deceive us in this matter?

In the Book of Mormon Joseph Smith has stated, "Woe unto the liar for he shall be thrust down to hell" 2 Nephi 9:34. Hebrews 13:8 "Jesus Christ the same yesterday, today and forever." D&C 20:12 "Thereby showing that he is the same God yesterday, today and forever. Amen."

Now Paul the Apostle has clearly stated that Jesus Christ is the same all the time. Yet Joseph Smith states that God changes as he sees fit. We are faced here with a dichotomy. Two clearly opposite views yet both claiming to be part of the whole. Which one are we to believe?

As the history of Joseph Smith began at the start of this study it has been shown there are differences of what happened to Joseph Smith. It has been shown earlier, "Joseph Smith circa Summer 1832 is the only narrative of the foundational spiritual events of Joseph Smith early life that includes his own handwriting". (Page 4) With this statement being made it becomes imperative that we continue to return to this history that has been written in Joseph Smith's own handwriting. Any conflict with his own handwritten documents should be considered highly suspicious and in fact, if directly contradictory, shouldn't it be considered false? With all of the conflicts in the various versions of Joseph Smith's first vision, how do we know which one (if any) is the correct and true version? Are we being unfair to suggest we believe the version he actually wrote himself…the one that is in his own handwriting?

Emma Bidamon (Formerly Emma Smith), widow of Joseph Smith, the Prophet, died in Nauvoo, Ill April 30, 1879, Shortly afterwards an article was published in the Saints Advocate, a monthly periodical published by the Reorganized Church, at Plano, Ill., under the heading "Last Testimony of Sister Emma", in which that lady is made responsible for a statement to the effect that Joseph Smith, the Prophet, never in his lifetime taught nor practiced the principle of plural marriage.

I wonder why we are not given all of the information relating to Joseph Smith. It has already been shown that "circa Summer 1832" was the only history actually written in Joseph Smith's own handwriting. Should we then only study this history? Yet there are over 500 more pages in this first volume yet for us to peruse and study. We are only given certain papers by the authors of this work for us to study. Certainly polygamy was extremely important during Joseph Smith's life. We will consider this issue as we persevere in our study.

Eventually when Nauvoo, Illinois was established, Joseph Smith sought to be the first mayor. With everything else he was doing, where did he think he would have time to be a mayor of a city? John C. Bennett, a doctor and close friend, was elected mayor however and this sealed Bennett's doom in the church since Joseph wanted the job of mayor and so John C. Bennett was excommunicated after being accused of spiritual wife doctrine and not keeping the word of wisdom, even though the word of wisdom clearly stated it was "not by commandment or constraint". As you would guess, wasn't Joseph Smith guilty of Spiritual Wife doctrine himself and he also did he not keep the word of wisdom as he repeatedly tells us how his spirit was made glad by the fruit of the vine on numerous occasions plus other actions already mentioned herein?

He brushed off complaints from members of his church about why he continued to drink tea and coffee and smoke by simply claiming he was testing the new members testimony to be sure they were not trying to use him to get into heaven. A great deal of time and effort was made by many to make John C. Bennett appear to be a terrible scoundrel and evil person, yet nothing is said about the same sins beings committed by Joseph Smith. Indeed he was drinking wine at the time of his murder in Carthage, IL. John C. Bennett was at one time a very close friend and confidant of Joseph Smith and was made an "assistant president" of the church. Unfortunately, he desired Nancy Rigdon as his wife and Joseph Smith wanted her also. Nancy never agreed to plural marriage and refused both of these men's advances. As Joseph Smith's harem of wives grew it seemed his desire for more and more women grew also. He had already tried to get Sarah Pratt to have sexual intimacies with him and had been rejected and now Nancy Rigdon treated him the same way. It was under these circumstances we find John C. Bennett and Joseph Smith breaking up their friendship and both men accused each other of many of the same things such as breaking the word of wisdom and spiritual wife ideas.

There is nothing to indicate that sexual relations were left out of plural marriages. Noble testified that Joseph spent the night with Louisa Beaman after the wedding.

From Rough Stone Rolling p 439 we read: "The marital status of the plural wives further complicated the issue. Within fifteen months of marrying Louisa Beaman, Joseph had married eleven other women. Eight of the eleven were married to other men. All told, ten of Joseph's plural wives were married to other men at the same time. All of them went on living with their first husbands after marrying the Prophet."

Joseph Smith had over 40 wives. We are told that Sarah Pratt, Jane Law and Nancy Rigdon were very attractive women and refused to either have sexual relations with Joseph Smith, or marry him. Bushman states categorically about that "all told, ten of Joseph's plural wives were married to other men". Has law and order completely flown out the window here? How can Joseph Smith be married to a woman who is already married to someone else? Doesn't the definition of words mean the same to all of us? Isn't it clear what adultery means? Isn't it clear what bigamy or polygamy mean? How could these men allow their wives to engage sexually with Joseph Smith? Weren't these men planning on an eternal marriage with their wife? Didn't they have emotional feelings for these wives? Why did they agree to give them up for eternity and let Joseph Smith use them for his sexual purposes? Joseph Smith already had over 30 other wives already. This is far more than any of the prophets in the Bible or Book of Mormon. Why did he have to take these other women who were married and living with their husbands at the time?

Doesn't the Book of Mormon incorporate the "fullness of the Gospel"? Why doesn't it show any of the prophets in its story having more than one wife? In fact it condemns the idea of polygamy. If indeed plural wives are necessary to have the "fullness of the Gospel" why is this not indicated anywhere in the Bible or Book of Mormon? The story of Abraham and Jacob having plural wives clearly shows their wives were given to them by their first wife.

In Joseph Smith's case Emma was very bitter towards him in this regard, and as shown above actually denied he ever practiced this doctrine on her deathbed. Hyrum Smith states he tried to convince Emma about the doctrine of plural marriage but was severely rebuked by her. Emma nagged Joseph repeatedly until he told her she could destroy the written revelation on plural marriage. Doesn't this sound far from the way Abraham and Jacob's wives handled their situation?

With all of this in mind we will continue to try to follow the "history" as recorded in Joseph Smith Papers Histories Volume 1.

CHAPTER 21

THE GOLD PLATES

It is of some interest to note that the Book of Mormon was published and made available for purchase December 1829. Nothing is mentioned about how the plates were obtained, nor what disposition was made of them. There is some concern they may not have been gold at all but were made of some "ore" as is described in 1 Nephi. In the Testimony of the Prophet Joseph Smith at the beginning of the Book of Mormon he states quoting what the angel told him "he said there was a book deposited, written upon gold plates". Nephi states (1 Nephi 1:17) "Behold I make an abridgment of the record of my father, upon plates which I have made with mine own hands".

Emma Smith said she had to move them from place to place as was necessary. "Last Testimony of Sister Emma", The Saints Herald. Oct. 1, 1879, 290 Joseph Smith said they were gold and if so would have weighed over 200 pounds. Why did Emma have to move them from place to place as was necessary? What would make it "necessary"?

Martin Harris, one of the eight witnesses of the gold plates, claimed he saw them with his spiritual eyes only, not his natural eyes. He further said this was like his imagination and this applied to all of the witnesses of the plates. In other words, all of the witnesses experienced things in their imagination, not actually witnessing them with their natural eyes.

The question arises as to whether the angel Nephi (or Moroni) was correct in telling Joseph Smith these plates were made of gold. We must believe the angel, as he wouldn't have lied would he? Is it reasonable, perhaps impossible, to imagine Joseph Smith carrying home the gold plates, weighing about 200 pounds, a distance of three miles? And Emma Smith moving them from "place to place" as she cleaned her house? For such a feat of strength to have really happened it would seem that some mention would have been made about the ability to move such weight around. An average man can lift about 100 pounds but would not be able to carry such weight three miles and Joseph Smith wants us to believe he carried over 200 pounds three miles and his wife moved this weight from place to place as was needed. Nothing is mentioned about using a back pack or any other type of assistance leaving us to believe Joseph Smith simply carried these gold plates the entire three mile distance to his house. Several people have tried to estimate the weight of the gold plates to be about 60 pounds but there is no way all that gold could have only weighed 60 pounds which leads to the possibility of them not really being gold plates at all but merely some other type of metal. But didn't God call them GOLD plates? Even if they weighed 60 pounds wouldn't it still have been difficult for Joseph Smith to have carried them three miles? That is a lot of weight. Try carrying a 40 pound bag of salt for a water softener just 100 feet. Much easier if you use a back pack.

CHAPTER 22

THE THREE WITNESSES AND EIGHT WITNESSES

Now Joseph Smith tells us that God will provide three witnesses whom God will show these things, meaning the golden plates. Yet, Martin Harris clearly states he was not shown them except in his imagination (spiritual eyes) and confirmed that this was the case also with Oliver Cowdery and David Whitmer. So isn't the testimony of the three witnesses invalid? And God is specific in his revelation to Joseph Smith when he states: And to none else will I grant this power, to receive this same testimony among this generation D&C 5:11 Also in the Book of Mormon 1830 ed. 2 Nephi 27.12 and also Ether 5:2-4 it states there will be three witnesses given to testify of the record on the **gold** plates. There were to be only three witnesses and we see that these witnesses merely imagined what they were supposed to be witnessing. God says "to none else will I grant this power (that of witnessing the gold plates)". For some reason Joseph Smith decided there must be an additional eight witnesses to the plates despite God saying (2 Nephi 27:13) "And there is none other which shall view it, save it be a few according to the will of God". And God says "none other" shall view it so why does Joseph Smith get eight other people to witness it, other than the three (or as God says "save it be a few" or at least three)? But wait! The eight witnesses claim they saw the plates also and in fact state they "did handle with our hands".

Here is the testimony of the eight witnesses:

> Be it known unto all nations, kindreds, tongues, and people, unto whom this work shall come: That Joseph Smith, Jun., the translator of this work, has shewn unto us the plates of which hath been spoken, which have the appearance of gold; and as many of the leaves as the said Smith has translated we did handle with our hands; and we also saw the engravings thereon, all of which has the appearance of ancient work, and of curious workmanship. And this we bear record with words of soberness, that the said Smith has shewn unto us, for we have seen and hefted, and know of a surety that the said Smith has got the plates of which we have spoken. And we give our names unto the world, to witness unto the world that which we have seen. And we lie not, God bearing witness of it.

Here is the testimony of the three witnesses:Be it known unto all nations, kindreds, tongues, and people, unto whom this work shall come: That we, through the grace of God the Father, and our Lord Jesus Christ, have seen the plates which contain this record which is a record of the people of Nephi, and also of the Lamanites, their brethren, and also the people of Jared, who came from the tower of which hath been spoken. And we also know that they have been translated by the gift and power of God, for his voice hath declared it unto us; that we have seen the engravings which are upon the plates; and they have been shown unto us by the power of God, and nor of man. And we declare with words of soberness, that an angel of God came down from heaven, and be brought and laid before our eyes, that we beheld and saw the plates and the engravings thereon;

and we know that it is by the grace of God the Father, and our Lord Jesus Christ, that we beheld and bear record that these things are true. And it is marvelous in our eyes. Nevertheless, the voice of the Lord commanded us that we should bear record of it; wherefore, to be obedient unto the commandments of God, we bear testimony of these things. And we know that if we are faithful in Christ, we shall rid our garments of the blood of all men, and be found spotless before the judgment seat of Christ, and shall dwell with him eternally in the heavens. And the honor be to the Father, and to the Son, and to the Ho9ly Ghost, which is one God. Amen.

Oliver Cowdery
David Whitmer
Martin Harris

The eight witnesses claim they handled the gold plates. The three witnesses were not given this privilege but were shown the plates by an angel and heard the voice of the Lord commanding them to bear record of it. The eight witnesses do not claim that they were commanded to bear witness as the three witnesses were.

Section 17 of the Doctrine and Covenants is a revelation given through Joseph Smith to Oliver Cowdery, David Whitmer and Martin Harris in June 1829. It seems to be Jesus Christ giving this revelation to Joseph Smith:

Vs. 1 ..."You shall have a view of the plates, and also of the breastplate, the sword of Laban, the Urim and Thummin, which were given to the brother of Jared upon the mount, when he talked with the Lord face to face". Vs. 3 "And after that you have obtained faith, and have seen them with your eyes, you shall testify of them by the power of God".

From reading the testimony of the three witnesses, and also the eight witnesses, we can see that nowhere do they testify that they have seen "the breastplate, the sword of Laban, the Urim and Thummin" which we have just read that Jesus Christ told them they were to testify of seeing these items. See the next chapter for more on this.

Now here is an interesting statement made by David Whitmer.

An Address to All Believers in Christ, page 27 by David Whitmer:

"If you believe my testimony to the Book of Mormon, if you believe that God spake to us three witnesses by his own voice, then I tell you that in June, 1838 God spake to me again by his own voice from the heavens, and told me to separate myself from among the Latter-day Saints, for as they sought to do unto me, so should it be done unto them. In the Spring of 1838 the heads of the church and many of the members had gone deep into error and blindness. I have been striving with them for a long time to show them the errors into which they were driving and for my labors I received only persecutions."

This quote creates a quandary. If we accept Whitmer's testimony regarding his experience with the angel and the gold plates, than we must also accept his testimony that God also declared the current Mormon Church in a fallen state. To disavow the revelation he received stating that the Mormon church since 1838 has "gone deep into error and blindness" means we must hold as suspect his testimony to the Book of Mormon if we do not believe the church has "gone deep into error and blindness". He clearly states that "God spake to me again by his own voice from the heavens". If we believed him as one of the three witnesses, do we still believe him when he says God spoke to him from the heavens in 1838?

The year 1838 was momentous to Joseph Smith. John Whitmer and David Whitmer were excommunicated from the church. Joseph Smith said God told him to change the name of the church from The Church of the Latter-day Saints to the Church of Jesus Christ of Latter-day Saints. Three more official histories of Joseph Smith's first vision are published. John Whitmer refuses to give up his written documents regarding the history of the church. The Kirtland bank failed and over half of the quorum of 12 apostles left the church after losing all their money in the bank failure.

In the Doctrine and Covenants Section 5:10-14 we read "But this generation shall have my word through you; and in addition to your testimony, the testimony of three of my servants, whom I shall call and ordain, unto whom I will show these things, and they shall go forth with my words that are given through you. Yea, they shall know of a surety that these things are true, for from heaven will I declare it unto them. I will give them power that they may behold and view these things as they are; And to none else will I grant this power, to receive this same testimony among this generation in this the beginning of the rising up and the coming forth of my church out of the wilderness– clear as the moon and fair as the sun, and terrible as an army with banners"*.

Here we go again about the 'wilderness'. The footnote from page 11 is reproduced here: "Footnote #13 Wilderness is a natural environment on earth that has not been significantly modified by human activity. Joseph Smith wasn't in the wilderness at all but merely in a grove of trees on or near his house." Is the sun "fair"? And is the moon "clear"? and "terrible as an army with banners?" What does this mean? Perhaps an army with a flag representing their nation or cause? Why would an army with banners be more terrible than an army without banners?

HOW DID JOSEPH SMITH WRITE OR TRANSLATE THE GOLD PLATES?

From this actual photo of the first printing of the Book of Mormon it seems clear that Joseph Smith claimed to be the "author" of this book, and later changed this to claim he was a translator of the book.

> B. H. Roberts, a general authority and historian for the Mormon Church, expressed the idea that Joseph Smith was capable of producing the Book of Mormon himself. Joseph Smith tells the story of the golden plates and is the only source for a great deal of the story because much of it occurred at times when he was the only human witness. He told the story to his family, friends, and acquaintances and some of these provided second-hand accounts.

Mormon scholars have collaborations such as Foundation for Ancient Research and Mormon Studies. Among these studies the credibility of the plates has been, according to Bushman, a "troublesome item."

The Mormon sources constantly refer to the single most troublesome item in Joseph Smith's history, the gold plates on which the Book of Mormon was said to be written. For most modern readers, the plates are beyond belief, a phantasm, yet the Mormon sources accept them as fact." Richard N. Ostling and Joan K. Ostling, *Mormon America: The Power and the Promise (HarperSanFrancisco, 1999)* begin a chapter called "The Gold Bible" (pp. 259–77) with a question posed by liberal Mormon Brigham D. Madsen: "'Were there really gold plates and ministering angels, or was there just Joseph Smith seated at a table with his face in a hat dictating to a scribe a fictional account of the ancient inhabitants of the Americas?' Resolving that problem haunts loyal Mormons." (at p. 259).

A reputed transcript of reformed Egyptian characters, which Smith said were copied from the golden plates in 1828. The characters are not linked to any known language.

The Book of Mormon itself portrays the golden plates as a historical record, engraved by two pre-columbian prophet-historians from around the year AD 400: Mormon and his son Moroni. Mormon and Moroni, the book says, had abridged earlier historical records from other sets of metal plates. Their script, according to the book, was described as "reformed Egyptian" a language unknown to linguists or Egyptologists. The Community of Christ, however, while accepting the Book of Mormon as scripture, no longer takes an official position on the historicity of the golden plates.

> McMurray, W. Grant, "They 'Shall Blossom as the Rose': Native Americans and "the dream of zion" an address delivered February 17, 2001, accessed September 1, 2006 ("The proper use of the Book of Mormon as sacred scripture has been under wide discussion in the 1970s and beyond, in part because of long-standing questions about its historicity and in part because of perceived theological inadequacies, including matters of race and ethnicity."). At the 2007 Community of Christ World Conference, church president Stephan M. Veazey ruled a resolution to "reaffirm the Book of Mormon as a divinely inspired record" as being out of order. In so doing he stated that "while the Church affirms the Book of Mormon as scripture, and makes it available for study and use in various languages, we do not attempt to mandate the degree of belief or use. This position is in keeping with our longstanding tradition that belief in the Book of Mormon is not to be used as a test of fellowship or membership in the church." Andrew M. Shields, "Official Minutes of Business Session, Wednesday

March 28, 2007," in*2007 World Conference Thursday Bulletin*, March 29, 2007.

> Western New York was noted for its participation in a "craze for treasure hunting." Beginning as a youth in the early 1820s, Smith was periodically hired, for about $14 per month, as a <u>scryer</u>, using what were termed " in attempts to locate lost items and buried treasure. Smith›s contemporaries described his method for seeking treasure as putting the stone in a white <u>stovepipe hat</u>, putting his face over the hat to block the light, and then "seeing" the information in the reflections of the stone.

Smith did not consider himself to be a "peeper" or <u>"glass-looker,"</u> a practice he called "nonsense." Rather, Smith and his family viewed their folk magical practices as <u>spiritual gifts</u>. Although Smith later rejected his youthful treasure-hunting activities as frivolous and immaterial, he never repudiated the stones themselves nor denied their presumed power to find treasure, nor did he ever relinquish the magic culture in which he was raised <u>Bushman (2005</u>, pp. 50–51) Smith "never repudiated the stones or denied their power to find treasure. Remnants of the magical culture stayed with him to the end";

Jan Shipps, *Mormonism: The Story of a New Religious Tradition*, University of Illinois Press, p. 11. He came to view seeing with a stone in religious terms as the work of a "seer".

Smith's first stone, apparently the same one he used at least part of the time to translate the golden plates, was chocolate-colored and about the size of a chicken egg, found in a deep well he helped dig for one of his neighbors.

The statement has been made that the Urim and Thummim was on the altar in the <u>Manti</u> Temple when that building was dedicated. The

Urim and Thummim so spoken of, however, was the seer stone which was in the possession of the Prophet Joseph Smith in early days. This seer stone is currently in the possession of the Church. . The LDS Church released photographs of the stone on August 4, 2015.

Smith's contemporaries who claimed to have heard the story—both sympathetic and unsympathetic—generally agreed that Smith mentioned the following additional commandments: that Smith take the plates and leave the site where they had been buried without looking back, This commandment is described in the account of Joseph Knight, Sr., a loyal Latter Day Saint friend of Smith's (Knight 1833, p. 2), and Willard Chase, an associate of Smith's in Palmyra during the 1820s (Chase 1833, p. 242). Both Knight and Chase were treasure seekers, but while Knight remained a loyal follower until his death, Chase was a critic of Smith's by the early 1830s. Some unsympathetic listeners who allegedly heard the story from Smith or his father recalled that Smith had said the angel required him to wear "black clothes" to the place where the plates were buried, Chase (1833, p. 242) (an affidavit of Willard Chase, a non-Mormon treasure seeker who believed Smith wrongly appropriated his seer stone). Chase said he heard the story from Smith's father in 1827. Fayette Lapham, who traveled to Palmyra in 1830 to inquire about the Latter Day Saint movement and heard the story from Joseph Smith, Sr., said Smith was told to wear an "old-fashioned suit of clothes, of the same color as those worn by the angel", but Lapham did not specify what color of clothing the angel was wearing (Lapham 1870, p. 305). Chase (1833, p. 242) (affidavit of Willard Chase, relating story heard from Smith's father in 1827). A friendly but non-believing Palmyra neighbor, Lorenzo Saunders, heard the story in 1823 from Joseph Smith, and also said Smith was required to ride a black horse with a switch tail to the hill, to call for the plates by a certain name, and to "give thanks to God."

According to Smith's followers, Smith said he took the plates from the box, put them on the ground, and covered the box with the stone to protect the other treasures it contained. Knight (1833, p. 2) (account by Joseph Knight, Sr., a loyal life-long follower who had worked with Smith in treasure expeditions); Smith (1853, p. 85) (account by Smith's mother, saying this occurred on Smith's *second* visit to the hill); Salisbury (1895, p. 14) (account of Smith's sister, saying this occurred on Smith's *third* visit to the hill, but that it happened prior to their brother Alvin›s death, which was in November 1823); Cowdery (1835b, p. 197) (account by Smith's second-in-command Oliver Cowdery, stating that when Smith was looking in the box for other artifacts, he hadn't yet removed the plates).

Nevertheless, the accounts say, when Smith looked back at the ground after closing the box, the plates had once again disappeared into it. In response to his question, Smith said the angel appeared and told him he could not receive the plates because he "had been tempted of the adversary and sought the Plates to obtain riches and kept not the commandments that I should have" According to Smith's followers, Smith had also broken the angel's commandment "not to lay the plates down, or put them for a moment out of his hands", and according to a non-believer, Smith said "I had forgotten to give thanks to God" as required by the angel.

Smith said the angel instructed him to return the next year, on September 22, 1824, with the "right person": his older brother Alvin. Alvin died in November 1823, and Smith returned to the hill in 1824 to ask what he should do. Smith said he was told to return the following year (1825) with the "right person"—although the angel did not tell Smith who that person might be. But Smith determined after looking into his seer stone that the "right person" was Emma Hale, his future wife. For the visit on September 22, 1825, Smith may have attempted to bring his treasure-hunting associate Samuel T. Lawrence.

Smith said that he visited the hill "at the end of each year" for four years after the first visit in 1823, but there is no record of him being in the vicinity of Palmyra between January 1826 and January 1827 when he returned to New York from Pennsylvania with his new wife. In January 1827, Smith visited the hill and then told his parents that the angel had severely chastised him for not being "engaged enough in the work of the Lord", which may have meant that he had missed his annual visit to the hill in 1826.

Smith said that the plates were engraved in an unknown language, and he told associates that he was capable of reading and translating them. This translation took place mainly in Harmony, Pennsylvania (now *Oakland Township*), Emma's hometown, where Smith and his wife had moved in October 1827 with financial assistance from a prominent, though superstitious, Palmyra landowner Martin Harris. The translation occurred in two phases: the first, from December 1827 to June 1828, during which Smith transcribed some of the characters and then dictated 116 manuscript pages to Harris, which were lost. The second phase began sporadically in early 1829 and then in earnest in April 1829 with the arrival of Oliver Cowdery, a schoolteacher who volunteered to serve as Smith's full-time scribe. In June 1829, Smith and Cowdery moved to Fayette, New York, completing the translation early the following month.

Smith used scribes to write the words he said were a translation of the golden plates, dictating these words while peering into a stone, which he said allowed him to see the translation. Smith's translation process evolved out of his previous use of seer stones in treasure seeking. During the earliest phase of translation, Smith said he used what he called Urim and Thummim—two stones set in a frame like a set of large spectacles. Witnesses said Smith placed the Urim and Thummim in his hat while translating.

We have read that Joseph Fielding Smith claimed the Urim and Thummim was the one stone Joseph Smith used to translate the Book of Mormon. Now we are told the Urim and Thummin was an object like spectacles that were small enough to fit in a hat.

After the loss of the first 116 manuscript pages, Smith translated with a single seer stone that some sources say he had previously used in treasure seeking. Smith placed the stone in a hat, buried his face in it to eliminate all outside light, and peered into the stone to see the words of the translation. A few times during the translation, a curtain or blanket was raised between Smith and his scribe or between the living area and the area where Smith and his scribe worked. Sometimes Smith dictated to Harris from upstairs or from a different room.

Smith's translation did not require the use of the plates themselves. Though Smith said very little about the translation process, his friends and family said that as he looked into the stone the written translation of the ancient script appeared to him in English.

Smith's dictations were written down by a number of assistants including Emma Smith, Martin Harris, and Oliver Cowdery. In May 1829, after Smith had lent 116 un-duplicated manuscript pages to Harris, and Harris had lost them, Smith dictated a revelation explaining that Smith could not simply re-translate the lost pages because his opponents would attempt to see if he could "bring forth the same words again." According to Grant Palmer, Smith believed "a second transcription would be identical to the first. This confirms the view that the English text existed in some kind of unalterable, spiritual form rather than that someone had to think through difficult conceptual issues and idioms, always resulting in variants in any translation."

When Smith and Emma moved to Pennsylvania in October 1827, they transported a wooden box, which Smith said contained the plates, hidden in a barrel of beans. For a time the couple stayed in the home of Emma's father Isaac Hale; but when Smith refused to show Hale the plates, Hale banished the concealed objects from his house. Afterward, Smith told several of his associates that the plates were hidden in the nearby woods. Emma said that she remembered the plates being on a table in the house, wrapped in a linen tablecloth, which she moved from time to time when it got in the way of her chores According to Smith's mother, the plates were also stored in a trunk on Emma's bureau However, Smith did not require the physical presence of the plates in order to translate them.

In April 1828, <u>Martin Harris</u>'s wife, <u>Lucy</u>, visited Harmony with her husband and demanded to see the plates. When Smith refused to show them to her, she searched the house, grounds, and woods. As a result of Martin Harris' loss of the <u>116 pages</u> of manuscript, Smith said that between July and September 1828, the <u>angel Moroni</u> took back both the plates and the <u>Urim and Thummim</u> as a penalty for his having delivered "the manuscript into the hands of a wicked man." According to Smith›s mother, the angel returned the objects to Smith on September 22, 1828, the anniversary of the day he first received them.

In March 1829, Martin Harris visited Harmony and asked to see the plates. Smith told him that he "would go into the woods where the Book of Plates was, and that after he came back, Harris should follow his tracks in the snow, and find the Book, and examine it for himself." Harris followed these directions but could not find the plates.

In early June 1829, the unwanted attentions of locals around Harmony necessitated Smith's move to the home of <u>David Whitmer</u> and his parents in <u>Fayette, New York</u>. Smith said that during this move the plates were transported by the <u>angel Moroni</u>, who put them in the garden of the Whitmer house where Smith could recover them. The translation was completed at the Whitmer home.

After translation was complete, Smith said he returned the plates to the angel, although he did not elaborate about this experience.

According to accounts by several early Mormons, a group of Mormon leaders including Oliver Cowdery, David Whitmer, and possibly others - Young (1877, p. 38) (mentioning only Smith and Cowdery); Packer (2004, pp. 52, 55) (including David Whitmer in the list and describing Whitmer's account of the event, and citing William Horne Dame Diary, 14 January 1855, stating that Hyrum Smith was also in the group) - accompanied Smith and returned the plates to a cave inside the Hill Cumorah. There, Smith is said to have placed the plates on a table near "many wagon loads" of other ancient records, and the Sword of Laban hanging on the cave wall. According to Brigham Young's understanding, which he said he gained from Cowdery, on a later visit to the cave, the Sword of Laban was said to be unsheathed and placed over the plates, and inscribed with the words "This sword will never be sheathed again until the kingdoms of this world become the kingdom of our God and his Christ."

CHAPTER 23

NO WITNESSES TO THE SWORD OF LABAN NOR THE URIM AND THUMMIN

A s in 2 Nephi 27:13 God again states in the identical words, "And to none else will I grant this power to receive this same testimony". Here he doesn't even allow a "few" more to witness the plates. Clearly he states "to none else will I grant this power to receive this testimony".

Further in Section 17:1-3 The Lord says in a revelation through Joseph Smith to Oliver Cowdery, David Whitmer, and Martin Harris ""...if you do with full purpose of heart you shall have a view of the plates, and also of the breastplate, the sword of Laban, the Urim and Thummin, which were given to the brother of Jared upon the mount...and after that you have obtained faith, and have seen them, with your eyes, you shall testify of them by the power of God;"

The testimony of the Three Witnesses only says that they "have seen the plates" and there is nothing said about the breastplaste, the sword of Laban or the Urin and Thummin. Joseph Smith has failed to give us any explanation as to why the three witnesses did not testify about all the things the Lord said they were supposed to testify they had seen. Did they really see these things or not? Apparently not, as they testified they had seen only the plates and the engravings on the plates and that is all they testify about seeing.

Since God said "And to none else will I grant this power, to receive this same testimony among this generation" why the need of eight additional witnesses? Did God forget to make a footnote of his statement like, "and to none else (except eight other people)" etc.? He didn't give this footnote. God's statement about only a few being allowed to witness the plates would certainly be covered by the three witnesses, wouldn't it? In any event Martin Harris showed us that the testimony of the three witnesses was imaginary or spiritual and David Whitmer showed us that if we believe his testimony we must also believe God told him the church was in error and blindness. So if we accept the church, believing it was not in error and blindness, we must dismiss David Whitmer as a witness.

This, coupled with Martin Harris' imagination, leaves only Oliver Cowdery as a witness and Martin Harris included him in his statement that the witnessing of the gold plates was 'imaginary' or 'spiritual'. So now we do not have any witnesses to the gold plates except in two men's imagination, yet God said he would set up three witnesses so is God's prophecy about three men being witnesses a false prophecy?

The testimony of those who were closest to Joseph Smith state that Joseph never used the plates anyway while doing the translation. He used his seer stone in his hat to translate the Book of Mormon. The following is taken from the notes to pages l68-72 in Richard L. Bushman's Rough Stone Rolling: "…said a blanket hung between Oliver and Joseph. But Elizabeth Ann Whitmer Cowdery, who saw and heard translation 'for hours' in Fayette, said Joseph 'never had a curtain drawn between him and his scribe'.

The description of translation comes from Emma Smith, Oliver Cowdery, David Whitmer, Martin Harris, and William Smith…

Richard Howard has pointed out that early newspaper accounts of the translation make no mention of the Urim and Thummin. The first was in the Evening and Morning Star (Independence, MO). Jan 1833. Previously the instrument was called 'interpreters'.

From page 71 of Rough Stone Rolling we read "Day after day, Cowdery reported in 1834, I continued, uninterrupted, to write from his mouth, as he translated with the Urim and Thummin".

First Bushman quotes that there is no mention of the Urim and Thummin, then he quotes Cowdery stating Joseph used the Urim and Thummin. How can this be?

"Emma said she sat at the same table with Joseph, writing as he dictated, with nothing between them, and the plates wrapped in a linen cloth on the table." Page 71 Rough Stone Rolling. Doesn't it seem that the Urim and Thummin was not used in the translation process? Isn't it clear he did not use the Urim and Thummin as they merely sat on the table wrapped in a linen cloth?

As stated in the Doctrine and Covenants Section 5 "Revelation given through Joseph Smith the Prophet, at Harmony, Pennsylvania, March 1829 at the request of Martin Harris. HC 1:28-31 so isn't Joseph Smith clearly stating this section came from God?

If the plates were never used in the translation process, why the need for witnesses? And as we have learned, there were no real witnesses to the plates anyway. Only in someone's imagination.

Another thought occurs here also. Can you imagine how close the seer stone must have been in his hat to his eyes? The stone must have almost been touching his eyes wouldn't it? Sort of like he was seeing through his hat, and/or talking through his hat?

It is unclear why Richard Bushman states Joseph Smith used the Urim and Thummin to translate the gold plates when he also is very clear that Joseph Smith put the seer stone in his hat and buried his face in the hat and dictated what Oliver Cowdery wrote.

And what of statements claiming he put the Urim and Thummin in his hat with the seer stone? How big a hat did he have? He had his face in the hat and the stone in his hat, so how could he have found room for the Urim and Thummin also in his hat?

CHAPTER 24

JOSEPH SMITH HISTORY CONTINUES

C urrent Mormon doctrine on the nature of God, the priesthood, use of temples, eternal and celestial marriage (including polygamy), wearing temple garments, baptism and work for the dead, and men becoming gods is nowhere contained in the Book of Mormon. In fact the use of temple ordinances are nowhere mentioned in any of the scriptures accepted by the Church of Jesus Christ of Latter-day Saints. Nor do we find any instructions to place golden statues (idols) atop any temples yet D&C Section 20:8-9 states the Book of Mormon contains the "fullness of the gospel of Jesus Christ". By 1847 not a single one of the surviving eleven witnesses were any longer members of the Mormon church.

It is interesting that Joseph Smith claims to have revelations about what might seem to be ordinary events and makes one wonder why the Lord would have to give revelations on such seemingly minor occurrences. November 2, 1835 Monday (Page 111) The word of the Lord came thus unto him, saying, "it is not my will that my servant, Frederick should go to New York, but inasmuch as he wishes to go and visit his relatives, that he may warn them to flee the wrath to come let him go and see them, for that purpose, and let that be his only business. And behold in this thing he shall be blessed with power to overcome their prejudices. Verily thus saith the Lord, Amen".

The Lord says it is "not my will that my servant Frederick should go to New York". Then he says that since Frederick "wishes to go and visit his relatives" then "let him go and see them". So it is "not" God's will, but since Frederick "wishes" to go then it is alright to "let him to"? What about God's will?

Joseph Smith Journal 2 Nov 1835 in JSP Jn82 says that this is either Frederick G. Williams or Oliver Cowdery. Oliver Cowdery had relatives in New York but there is no record that Frederick G. Williams had any relatives in New York. He was born in Connecticut but was married in 1815 and was living in Chadron, Ohio by 1828. This revelation the authors of the Joseph Smith papers say was given Nov. 2, 1835 is not found in the current Doctrine and Covenants. Why not?

So Oliver needed to have God's permission to go visit his relatives? Or was it Frederick G. Williams?

If it was permissible to go visit his relatives "that he may warn them to flee the wrath to come", what wrath was to come? Did any wrath ever come to his relatives or the area they lived in? Why would Frederick go to New York when the Lord clearly stated "it is not my will that my servant Frederick should go to New York"? Same applies if this was Oliver Cowdery. Was this another false prophecy?

At this point the authors of this history book give many somewhat mundane stories of what Joseph Smith went through in his every day life in the area of 1835 to 1838. We are now introduced to a section titled "History Drafts 1838-Circa 1841". As I stated in the introduction, we are now presented with yet another version, or versions, of Joseph Smith's history. From June 1839 to 1841 the handwriting of this history is that of James Mulholland and Robert B.

Thompson. There are three different "drafts" that we will be dealing with covering this period of history.

"This volume was originally used for Joseph Smith's 1834-1836 history comprising 154 pages", as is stated on page 189 of the history book. We have learned that the 1834-1836 history was written by Oliver Cowdery, Warren Parrish, Warren Cowdery and Frederick G. Williams. We have seen the "flowery" pattern of Oliver and Warren Cowdery's writings expressed and seen the differences between the earlier written history by Joseph Smith himself of the events he experienced. Now we are being presented with yet another history, circa 1841. Remember, John Whitmer wrote a history of the period up to 1838 but "Whitmer was excommunicated in 1838 and declined to make his work available to the Church" (Page 193 History). We have no record of Sidney Rigdon and Joseph Smith's history although we know they created one but the authors state this history cannot be found. It would have covered the period of 1836 to 1838.

We now have Joseph Smith circa 1832 history, Oliver Cowdery's et. Al. history including the time from 1832 to 1836 which also portrayed the same earlier history already written by Joseph Smith himself in his own handwriting, John Whitmer's history which is available to read, and now we Have James Mulholland and Robert B. Thompson's writing covering the period 1839 to "about 1841" (page 192) Robert Coray's history (1841) Draft 3. From page 193 of History we read "It was in the context of these inadequate and unavailable records that Joseph Smith and Sidney Rigdon began a new history project. On 27 April 1838, they began a 'history of this Church' from the earliest period of its existence up to this date. Joseph Smith Journal 27 April 1838 in JSP, Jr. 1:260". This would be the sixth history prior to Draft 3 written by Robert Coray.

The Wentworth letter and Joshua the Jewish minister incident may be considered histories also as they contain Joseph Smith's portrayal of events that happened to start him on the road to establishing a church. These being considered we have eight histories and will soon learn of Draft No. 3 by Robert Coray making the ninth history of Joseph Smith and his visions. "Because the history produced by Joseph Smith and Sidney Rigdon in 1838 is not extant, it is impossible to know the exact relationship between that work and the extant versions of Joseph Smith's history presented here. It is <u>probable</u> however, that Draft 1 represents the resumption of the historical narrative at the point where the now lost 1838 manuscript ended. The extant draft picks up the narrative at the baptism of Joseph Smith and Oliver Cowdery and covers the publication of the Book of Mormon, the organization of the Church of Christ, and events later in 1830. The narrative covering mid-April through August 1830, much of which involved Newel Knight as either a participant or an eyewitness, is relatively detailed. It was <u>likely</u> during work on this portion of the history that, according to Joseph Smith's journal, Joseph Smith was 'assisted by Br Newel Knight'". Page 194 History

"Mulholland began his new draft of the history in the back of the volume in which the 1834-1836 history had been inscribed" (Page 195)"Mulholland's tenure as a scribe was cut short when he died on 3 November 1839, possibly the victim of a stroke". Page 195

Draft 2 Page 195 "James Mulholland…began this new draft of the history ". The authors comment on this Draft 2, "Textual evidence that the non-extant 1838 material was used when composing Draft 2 is found in the second paragraph of the latter, which situates the composition in the 'eighth year since the (1830) organization of said Church', and a later passage that gives the date of composition as the Second day of May, One thousand Eight hundred and thirty eight".

Joseph Smith caused to be written an introduction to Draft 2, which was written "not long after Joseph Smith had fled Kirtland, Ohio, for Far West, Missouri, under threat of several lawsuits". Page 195.

On January 12, 1838, "faced with a warrant for his arrest on a charge of illegal banking, Smith fled with Rigdon to Clay County, Missouri just ahead of an armed group out to capture and hold Smith for trial" leaving at night by horseback. Over half of the Quorum of the 12 Apostles accused Joseph Smith of improprieties involving his bank known as Kirtland Safety Society and left the Church over the bank failure.

Joseph Smith fled New York state with lawsuits against him there and went to Kirtland, Ohio where Sidney Rigdon had his entire congregation waiting for him to be their leader. Then with many lawsuits and warrents out for his arrest, he left Ohio and went to Missouri, where he was soon put in jail from December 1, 1838 until April 6, 1839.

On April 6, 1839, Joseph Smith was transferred to Davies County Jail in Gallatin, Missouri where a grand jury was investigating him. The grand jury was to indict them on murder, treason, burglary, arson, larceny, theft and stealing. Joseph Smith was to appeal for a change of venue to Marion County, Missouri in the northeast corner of the state near the village of Commerce, Illinois, however, the venue was changed to Boone County, Missouri.

On April 15, 1839, en route to Boone County, Joseph Smith, Hyrum Smith, Lyman Wight, Alexander McRae, and Caleb Baldwin were allowed to escape after the sheriff and three of their guards drank whiskey while the fourth guard helped them saddle their horses for the escape. They arrived in Quincy, Illinois on April 22, and from there were to regroup at Nauvoo, Illinois.

CHAPTER 25

THE NAME OF THE CHURCH

L et us pause here for a moment before we begin reviewing the
ninth history regarding Joseph Smith and the beginning of
the Church. It seems necessary to try to establish the proper
name of the Church as there is some confusion involved here.

"For thus shall my church be called in the last days, even The Church
of Jesus Christ of Latter-day Saints" (D&C 115:4). This revelation
from God is dated April 26, 1838

David Whitmer makes the following observation:

"In June, 1829, the Lord gave us the name by which we must call
the church, being the same as he gave the Nephites. We obeyed His
commandment, and called it the Church of Christ until 1834, when,
through the influence of Sydney Rigdon, the name of the church
was changed to `The Church of the Latter Day Saints,' dropping
out the name of Christ entirely, that name which we were strictly
commanded to call the church by, and which Christ by His own lips
makes so plain" (Address to All Believers in Christ, pg. 73).

A current picture is taken from the Kirtland Temple showing the name of the church at that time was "The Church of the Latter Day Saints". This still shows on the Kirtland Temple today. The name of Christ, or Jesus Christ, is totally omitted and was for a four year period from 1834 to 1838 when the current name of the church was given in section 115:4 of the Doctrine and Covenants. The hyphen in 'Latter-day' was added about a century or so later to be grammatically correct.

On 3 May 1834, Kirtland was the scene of "a Conference of the Elders of the Church of Christ" at which "a motion was made by Sidney Rigdon, and seconded by Newel K. Whitney, that this Church be known hereafter by the name of 'The Church of the Latter-day Saints.' Remarks were made by the members, after which the motion passed by unanimous vote" (*History of the Church* 2:62-63).

The Book of Mormon says that the true church must have the name of Christ in it. 3 Nephi 27:8 reads:

"And how be it my church save it be called in my name? For if a church be called in Moses' name then it be Moses' church; or if it be called in the name of a man then it be the church of a man; but if it be called in my name then it is my church, if it so be that they are built upon my gospel."

According to the Book of Mormon, Jesus Christ revealed the name of his church to the Nephite people: the " church of Christ". "And they who were baptized in the name of Jesus were called the church of Christ". 3 Nephi 26:21

Again we read in 3 Nephi 27:3-11 "And they said unto him: Lord, we will that thou wouldst tell us the name whereby we shall call this church; for there are disputations among the people concerning this matter. And the Lord said unto them; Verily, verily, I say unto you, why is it that the people should murmur and dispute because of this thing? Have they not read the scriptures, which say ye must take upon you the name of Christ, which is my name? For by this name shall ye be called at the last day; And whoso taketh upon him my name, and endureth to the end, the same shall be saved at the last day. Therefore, whatsoever ye shall do, ye shall do it in my name; Therefore ye shall call the church in my name; and ye shall call upon the Father in my name that he will bless the church for my sake. And how be it my church save it be called in my name? For it a church be called in Moses' name then it be Moses' church; or if it be called in the name of a man then it be the church of a man; but if it be called in my name then it is my church, if it so be that they are built upon my gospel. Verily I say unto you, that ye are built upon my gospel; therefore ye shall call whatsoever things ye do call, in my name; Therefore if he call upon the Father, for the church, if it be in my name, the Father will hear you; And if it so be that the church is built upon my gospel then will the Father show forth his own works in it. But if it be not built upon my gospel, and is built upon the works of men, or upon the works of the devil, verily I say unto you they have joy in their works for a season, and by and by the end cometh, and they are hewn down and cast into the fire, from whence there is no return."

If we are to use the rule mentioned above in Third Nephi 27:3-11 are we then to assume that the church the Apostle Paul addresses in 1 Thessalonians 1:1 was in a state of apostasy? After all, Paul refers to it as "the Church of the Thessalonians"! Consider also that Paul refers to the body of believers in Corinth as "the church of God which is at Corinth". (See 1 Corinthians 1:2)

It is interesting that the name of the Church was given by Sidney Rigdon and not Joseph Smith or Oliver Cowdery, the first two elders of the Church both of whom were present at this meeting. The proposition for the name change was presented by Sydney Rigdon and seconded by Newell K. Whitney. It is also interesting that David Whitmer apparently disapproved of this action yet the record from the History of the Church says the motion to change the name to The

Church of the Latter-day Saints "passed by unanimous vote". The definition of "unanimous" means all or everybody. Apparently the historian who wrote this into the History of the Church did not know what this word meant as David Whitmer said he was opposed to this renaming of the Church. We are led to believe Joseph Smith himself was the author of this series of books called "The Documentary History of the Church". If he was at this meeting and indeed made the record in the Church History, why did he not record it accurately stating David Whitmer was opposed to the change in the name of the church? And why did he instead say the vote was unanimous?

David Whitmer wrote three papers, A Proclamation published March 24, 1881, An Address to Believers in the Book of Mormon, published April 1887, and An Address to All Believers in Christ also published in 1887.

He made three statements of his beliefs. First, on Polygamy …"I do not endorse polygamy or spiritual wifeism. It is a great evil, shocking to the moral sense, and the more so because practiced in the name of religion. It is of man and not God, and is especially forbidden in the Book of Mormon itself."

Regarding the change of the name of the Church of Christ, "I do not endorse the change of the name of the church, for as the wife takes the name of her husband so should the Church of the Lamb of God, take the name of its head, even Christ himself. It is the Church of Christ."

His third statement of belief involved the office of High Priest: "As to the High Priesthood, Jesus Christ himself is the last Great High Priest, this too after the order of Melchizedek as I understand the Holy Scriptures."

Even before the Nephite disciples prayed to know how they should call the Church, "they who were baptized in the name of Jesus were called the church of Christ" (3 Nephi 26:21). D&C 20:8-9 says that "the Book of Mormon contains a record…and the fullness of the gospel of Jesus Christ". The "fullness" would certainly seem to mean all of the doctrines of Jesus Christ that were ever in His church in earlier times. There is no mention in the Book of Mormon concerning the Church of Christ of the many offices of the Priesthood such as a First Presidency, the office of Seventy, the office of deacon, the bishoprics, nor temple work or rituals such as Joseph Smith instituted in his church. We can find no mention of the Relief Society in the Book of Mormon nor of the Primary organizations, nor wearing special underwear. Perhaps these are not part of the fullness of the Gospel of Jesus Christ? And what about Polygamy? Why isn't it mentioned in the Book of Mormon? Why would Jesus instruct Joseph Smith as to the name of His Church in 1830, then change it in 1834 and again change it in 1838? Why wouldn't Jesus get it right the first time? Joseph Smith was the moderator at the conference May 3, 1834 when Sidney Rigdon made the motion to change the name to The Church of the Latter-day Saints and made no objection. Wonder why he sat quietly by after claiming to have received revelation from God in translating the Book of Mormon to the effect that if it was Christ's church it should have His name in the title? After sitting quietly by and allowing this, why then did Joseph Smith have to have a revelation four years later again changing the name of the Church?

It must have been very important for Jesus Christ to give a revelation to Joseph Smith to make this change. The question of timing makes us wonder why the changes? Also the actual changing of the name repeatedly makes us wonder why? The alleged peoples of the Book of Mormon reportedly made quite a report stating that Christ taught them clearly that the name of their church should be the Church of Christ, not the Church of Jesus Christ or the Church of the Latter-day Saints.

CHAPTER 26

BACK TO THE HISTORIES

Now the historians state on page 197 "Significant instances of anachronism are identified in the annotation of the text herein". So James Mulholland began writing the history of Joseph Smith …and copied the revelations into the history from the 1835 editions of the Doctrine and Covenants rather than from earlier versions. Many of Joseph Smith's early revelations underwent significant updating and expansion in order to suit rapidly changing circumstances after the organization of the Church of Christ in 1830, so the inclusion of the 1835 version of revelations into a narrative covering events before 1835 introduced numerous anachronisms."

The historians do not seem concerned about these "anachronisms" although they significantly change the history itself of what has already been claimed. They go on to say "Joseph Smith and his associates were dependent upon unrecorded memories for the balance of the historical account found in Draft 2. Joseph Smith used collective memory and oral recollections of fellow participants such as Newel Knight, to reconstruct the events of early church history."

Why did he have to use "collective memory"? He had already written in his own handwriting what happened to him as we have seen in Joseph Smith circa Summer 1832 history.

What is the purpose of the History Drafts 1838 Circa 1841? First Joseph Smith himself wrote his own history in his own handwriting. He gave another version of his history November 9, 1835 to a man calling himself Joshua, the Jewish Minister. (See page 115 Histories) Oliver Cowdery, Warren Parrish, Warren Cowdery and Frederick G. Williams wrote yet another version of Joseph Smith's history in 1834 to 1836. Now we are being presented with three additional histories in the "History Drafts" and yet other scribes are now involved in writing the history of Joseph Smith. This brings us to a total of nine histories all being written about the history of Joseph Smith and the Mormon Church and a lot of it is being copied from earlier accounts. The historians admit that there are "numerous anachronisms " and expansion in order to suit rapidly changing circumstances after the organization of the Church of Christ in 1830, so the inclusion of the 1835 version of revelations into a narrative covering events before 1835".

"Suit rapidly changing circumstances"? Changing history to suit "changing circumstances?" Joseph Smith and his associates were dependent upon unrecorded memories for the history in draft 2? Unrecorded memories? Joseph Smith used the "oral recollections of fellow participants" to "reconstruct the events of early church history"? What was wrong with simply using the Joseph Smith circa Summer 1832 history? Why did they have to keep changing the history? Why did there have to be "numerous anachronisms" between different versions of the histories written? Why did they have to change the name of the Church three different times? Who changed the name of the angel Nephi to the angel Moroni? And why? In Joseph Smith's lifetime it was always the angel Nephi. Since the 1855 version of the Pearl of Great Price called him the angel Nephi, we must believe it was sometime after 1855 that someone changed the name to the angel Moroni. Yet from the writings of Oliver Cowdery he claims (pretending he is Joseph Smith speaking) the angel eventually told Joseph Smith his name was Moroni.

So many questions, so few answers. It turns out there were no witnesses to the Gold Plates at all except in certain individuals imagination. Yet the Lord told Joseph Smith that he would have three witnesses and said nothing about these witnesses just imagining things. Joseph Smith didn't bother to use the gold plates to translate them into the Book of Mormon, but rather put a stone in his hat and put his face in the hat and dictated it to Oliver Cowdery and Emma Smith so why all the fuss and bother about the gold plates? He was literally 'talking through his hat'.

We have Draft 1 to begin with of the three histories mainly written by James Mulholland in 1838. Draft 2 is copied from Draft 1 and edited by the authors as they wished, written by James Mulholland and Robert B. Thompson in 1839 and Draft 3 was copied from Draft 2 and heavily edited by its author, Howard Coray in 1841.

Draft 1 begins at the time Joseph Smith and Oliver Cowdery baptize each other so our study will encompass Draft 2 and Draft 3 up until that time. Draft 2 and 3 began with birth of Joseph Smith. Draft 2 states it is beginning "now the eighth year since the organization of said Church". Draft 2 reports "My father Joseph Smith Senior, left the State of Vermont and moved to Palmyra, Ontario (now Wayne) County in the State of New York when I was in my tenth year". Draft 3 reports "When I was 10 years old" etc. Difference here of one year. Draft 2 spells Joseph Smith's sister Cathrine as Katharine and Draft 3 spells her name as Catherine.

Both draft 2 and draft 3 report an "unusual religious excitement. Commencing in the Methodist Society". We have already covered this claim earlier in this study and have shown there was no such "unusual religious excitement" as claimed in both Draft 2 and Draft

3. Draft 2 and Draft 3 however appear to be the first time Joseph Smith claims that the Lord told him all the churches were wrong and he should join none of them. In the circa summer 1832 account Joseph Smith writes that the Lord told him "the world lieth in sin at this time and none doeth good, no not one, they have turned aside from the gospel and keep not my commandments". Such a pronouncement arouses considerable suspicion of its authenticity. We are to believe there was not one single solitary individual that did good "no, not one"? Joseph Smith himself continually claimed to be sinning and transgressing the law so we know he certainly did not do good, but what about his father and mother. He said they were "goodly" parents and it seems they tried earnestly to provide and teach their large family (9 children) good things. We have shown that the ministers constantly preached to the people to seek the spirit of God and themselves prayed for the Holy Ghost to guide them in their sermons. The denominations all taught Jesus Christ was the Son of God and was crucified for the sins of the world. They preached from the Bible. Yet, Joseph Smith tells us the Lord told him they were all wrong and were an "abomination in my sight". In the Old Testament (Micah 6:8) we are told, "and what doth the Lord require of thee but to do justly and to love mercy and walk humbly with thy God". Christ repeatedly taught love and mercy and forgiveness throughout his ministry on earth. Yet we are to believe that people who taught from the Bible and those who lived simple yet productive lives were all bad? They were an "abomination" in the eyes of God? Abomination would mean bad and evil. Some other adjectives might be wickedness, depravity, prejudice, evil doers, vile, wretched, intolerable, sinister, and we could add many more words to the meaning. We have shown the various denominations were not vile, wretched, and certainly not intolerable. It has been my experience that among people who believe in God and among those who don't believe in God, we can find many good hearted people who try to live by societies rules and laws so it is difficult to believe Joseph Smith when he says there was not one that taught the commandments of God. They were teaching right from the Bible! Yet Joseph Smith claims the Lord specifically

said "none doeth good no not one" etc. Not just the ministers, but the Lord claims <u>everybody</u> was evil and an abomination in his sight.

Draft 2 reports Joseph Smith as saying his "feelings were deep and often pungent, still I kept myself aloof from all these parties though I attended their several meetings as occasion would permit". How could he keep himself "aloof" if his feelings were "often pungent"? Draft 3 uses no such terms, merely stating "my feelings were deeply interested".

A new experience is now introduced in Draft 2 and Draft 3. Joseph Smith alleges that he reported this vision to a Methodist minister. There is no evidence from any of the Methodist recordings of such an event. The authors state that he, Joseph Smith, "would have had numerous opportunities for contact with" George Lane, a Methodist minister. (Page 217 footnote 52) Now Joseph Smith has already stated that the Lord spoke to him and told him not to join any of the churches and that they were all an abomination in his sight. Why then did Joseph Smith feel he needed to confront a minister of one of these "abominations"? God essentially told him they were all wrong and to <u>avoid</u> all of them so what business did Joseph Smith have going against God's direct command to join none of them? There is no confirmation he ever did what he claims to have done. No one in his family recalls him telling of such an event.

We have already learned that Martin Harris informs us that his testimony and those other two (David Whitmer and Oliver Cowdery) were of a spiritual nature, not a real witness of physically seeing and handling the gold plates. In the trial of Joseph Smith in South Bainbridge, New York Newell Knight was examined by lawyer Seymour and asked Knight:

"Q. And are you sure it was the Devil

Answer yes sir Q. Did you see him after he was cast out of you.

A. Yes Sir. I saw him.

B. Q. Pray what did he look like

Here one of my Lawyers told the Witness that he need not answer the question. The witness replied I will answer you provided you answer me one questions to wit Do you Mr. Seymour understand the things of the spirit.

No. (Answered) Mr. Seymour. I do not pretend to such big things. Well, then (replied Knight) it would be of no use to tell you what the devil looked like, for it was a spiritual sight, and spiritually discerned and of course you would not understand it, were I to tell you of it." Page 410-411

It becomes increasingly evident that all of Joseph Smith's claims rely on them being spiritual rather than actual or real. This would explain why no one in his house was aware of the vision of Nephi (or Moroni) when he appeared in such a great light in the middle of the night. Critics hold varying opinions about the true nature of the first vision, believing it to be a dream, a hallucination, a self-deception, and intentional fabrication, or some combination of these. In fact, Alexander Campbell, a well known minister of the time, believed Joseph Smith was subject to epileptic seizures which he claimed were revelations from God.

Unfortunately Joseph Smith doesn't describe what God and Christ looked like in much detail other than saying "I saw two personages, whose brightness and glory defy all description, standing above me in the air, one of them spake unto me, calling me by name and said, pointing to the other – This is My Beloved Son, Hear Him!" Did they have beards or were they clean shaven? Did they have long hair to their shoulders or short hair? Did they look exactly alike as if they were twins? Were they wearing sandals or shoes? Were they wearing identical robes? In the Mormon Temples there is a movie depicting

God the Father and Jesus Christ and they are not identical. Both men wear beards but of different lengths. It is difficult to determine how long their hair is.

The statues of the Angel Moroni on the Mormon temples appears clean shaven. Why should we be interested in all details? There is an old proverb, "Trifles make perfection but perfection is no trifle." Paul the Apostle taught us to "prove all things, and hold fast to that which is good". Notice he said "all" things, not most things or the majority of things. Now the Bible clearly states that no man has seen God the Father in the flesh and there is a great difference in whether God the Father has indeed been seen by any human. Joseph Smith claims he saw God the Father with Jesus Christ when they appeared to him (or at least this is claimed by the historians). At first he said the Lord appeared to him but the more he thought about it the more he added to his account. He eliminated the angels that he at first claimed to be present and added one more character to his vision, i.e. God the Father. The Bible clearly tells us that no man can look upon the face of God the Father and live so it is unclear how Joseph Smith accomplished this with just a simple prayer to find out which church he should join.

Joseph Smith wrote a letter to John Wentworth in May of 1842 in which he said "I was enwrapped in a heavenly vision, and saw two glorious personages, who exactly resembled each other in features and likeness, surrounded with a brilliant light which eclipsed the sun at noon day. They told me that all religious denominations were believing in incorrect doctrines, and that none of them was acknowledged of God as His Church and kingdom; and I was expressly commanded 'to go not after them' at the same time receiving a promise that the fullness of the Gospel should at some future time be made known unto me."

Again he confirms that God told him not to go after any of these churches so the questions remains unanswered as to why he completely broke God's command and told a Methodist minister about his revelation. In this Wentworth letter we also see that he now claims he was "enwrapped in a heavenly vision". This confirms our above speculation that all of his claims were based on his imagination and not real events happening to him. Very similar to Charles Finney's revelation as stated earlier.

The story of the Wentworth letter is printed on page 492 of the "Histories". Mr. John Wentworth, Editor, and Proprietor of the "Chicago Democrat" requested information about the rise of the Mormon Church and Joseph Smith answered in a letter that became known as the "Wentworth Letter". As we read about this we will be referred back to the many "histories" already presented about the origin of the Mormon Church and Joseph Smith's visions. In this letter to John Wentworth Joseph Smith again states that "I retired to a secret place in a grove and began to call upon the Lord, while fervently engaged in supplication my mind was taken away from the object with which I was surrounded, and I was enwrapped in a (p.706) heavenly vision and saw two glorious personages who exactly resembled each other in features, and likeness, surrounded with a brilliant light which eclipsed the sun at noon-day. (Page 494)

First, the historians refer us to page 706. Page 706 of what book? Not this Histories book as it only has 686 pages so what are they referring to?

Second, the historians tell us in footnote 17 that Joseph Smith "Identified these two personages as God the Father and Jesus Christ. (Joseph Smith History Drafts 1838-ca. 1841, p. 214 herein; see also JS History, circa summer 1832 pp. 11-13 herein etc. We have already studied all these references and found that nowhere does Joseph Smith identify who these two beings are. In fact in the first personally handwritten version, Joseph Smith said he only saw the Lord. Was this Jesus Christ? Christ taught that there are Lords many so we should be told specifically who this was before we rush to a judgment. Also Joseph Smith said there was only the one personage. The idea of God the Father appearing is never specifically addressed although later versions of this vision add a second personage to the first and at one point the second personage states "this is my beloved son". Well, can this be understood to be God the Father, or simply a personage and his son?

Now, in this Wentworth Letter Joseph Smith adds more to his story about the Angel appearing to him three years later. In this reiteration Joseph Smith says his first vision occurred "when about fourteen years of age". He was born in 1805 so this would make this approximately 1819. As noted earlier in this study we come to a significant discrepancy in the time line. On page 494 the Wentworth Letter has Joseph Smith saying "On the evening of the 21st of September A.D. 1823, while I was praying unto God" etc We have learned in earlier versions that there was a space of about three years between Joseph Smith's first vision and the second vision where the angel appears to him in the night time. Now we learn it was "on the evening" and not during the night that this angel appears to him. We also see it is four years later, not three. He specifically states "this messenger proclaimed himself to be an angel of God, sent to bring the joyful tidings" and nowhere does he give his name. Yet the historians in footnote 19 on page 494 make this statement: "He previously identified the messenger as Moroni". This is incorrect. Dear Reader, you have read over eight different versions of angels appearing to Joseph Smith and have you seen anything in any of these version where this angel tells Joseph Smith his name is Moroni? We have seen many references that Joseph Smith said his name was Nephi, but not one where Joseph Smith says his name was Moroni. Currently the church has changed the revelation of his first vision to read that the angel said his name was Moroni. None of these versions tell us why he should now be depicted playing a horn of some type and is a clean-shaven individual. We won't go into this again. Personally I think he played the bass Trombone, but that has already been explored.

On Page 495 Joseph Smith states "I was also told where there was deposited some plates on which were engraven an abridgement of the records of the ancient prophets that had existed on this continent". "This Continent? Isn't it clear Joseph Smith states the Gold plates were buried in the Hill Cumorah in the state of New York? Isn't this the North American continent? Shouldn't' we be clear this record takes place on the North American continent and has nothing to do with the South American continent? Some people have made strong suggestions the people of the Book of Mormon existed on the South American continent and migrated up to New York but we can see that is not accurate from Joseph Smith's own words.

Then Joseph Smith says "through the medium of the Urim and Thummin I translated the record by the gift, and power of God". We have been over this also haven't we? Didn't he already tell us he put a stone in a hat and put his face in the hat and dictated the Book of Mormon to Oliver Cowdery and his wife Emma? Perhaps I missed the part where the historians told about Joseph Smith using the Urim and Thummin? Or Perhaps they didn't include this episode in their history book? Also did they neglect to write about Joseph Smith translating from the gold plates? Or did I just miss the parts I am asking about now?

"He goes on to say that these people of the Book of Mormon had "apostles, prophets, pastors, teachers and evangelists". He quotes page 707 but again, there is still only the 686 pages I referred to earlier so where is page 707? Where does it state that the Book of Mormon people had Pastors, Teachers, and Evangelists? In fact, where in the Mormon Church do we find any Pastors or Evangelists? Now let's not take some other office in the Mormon Church and try to say this is a Pastor or an Evangelist. I have a sign on my office wall of an ace of spades playing card and underneath it says "I call this a spade"! A Pastor is a Pastor and an Evangelist is an Evangelist, right? Originally the Mormon Church had licenses for the various

Priesthood offices and I have seen no references to any Priesthood offices such as Pastor or Evangelist.

Well Joseph Smith goes on to say "On the 6th of April 1830, the Church of Jesus Christ of Latter-Day Saints, was first organized in the town of Manchester, Ontario county, state of New York". Now, we know for a fact this isn't true, don't we? Didn't we learn it was called The Church of Christ that was organized in 1830? Didn't we learn the name was changed in 1834 to "The Church of the Latter-day Saints"? Didn't we learn the name was changed for the third time in 1838 to "The Church of Jesus Christ of Latter-day Saints?

In footnote 21 on page 496 we are presented with some serious questions on just where the Church was organized. We are told "the earliest sources place the meeting at Fayette, New York, and later Joseph Smith documents support this designation. Some later documents, including the present history, say the meeting took place at Manchester. In the Wentworth Letter Joseph Smith says it "was first organized in the town of Manchester, Ontario county, state of New York". Well, haven't we seen many other instances of Joseph Smith making incorrect statements in this study? Does it really matter whether it was Manchester or Fayette where the church was organized? Doesn't it seem important that we need to have the facts of history correct? Why else have a history?

Interestingly enough in a revelation given through Joseph Smith the Prophet at Kirtland, Ohio, September 22 and 23, 1832 HC 1:286-295 vs. 21-22 it states "And without the ordinances thereof, and the authority of the priesthood, the power of godliness is not manifest unto men in the flesh; for without this no man can see the face of God, even the Father, and live". This would conflict with several of his later versions of his first vision wherein he makes it appear that God the Father and Jesus Christ both appeared to him at the same time and this was long before he ever had the priesthood. How did Joseph Smith see the face of God without the "authority of the Priesthood" and live?

This shows that the authors do use other sources than the histories herein to endeavor to explain different situations, which is what we have done in this work also.

Footnote 132 Page 327 "David Whitmer recalled that about seventy individuals had been baptized by 6 April 1830. (Whitmer, Address to All Believers in Christ, 33)" This shows that people were baptized but not into the Church as it had not been established until 6 April 1830. It also shows that the authors of the History of Joseph Smith give credibility to David Whitmer's "Address to All Believers in Christ", and this is where David Whitmer claims the church is fallen. Was David Whitmer correct?

On page 435 footnote 226 We read: "The information to whom Joseph Smith referred" i.e. Page 433-434 "…In the neighborhood where I lived the principal instigator of which was professing to be a minister of God …this man came to understand that my father in law and his family had promised us protection and were friendly, and enquiring into the work, and knowing that if he could get him turned against me, my friends in that place would be but few, he accordingly went to visit my father in law, and told him falsehoods concerning me, of the most shameful nature, which turned the Old gentlemen and his family so much against us, that they would no longer promise us protection, nor believe our doctrine." Now continuing the footnote: "…was likely Nathaniel Lewis, brother-in-law of Isaac Hale and Uncle of Emma Smith. Lewis, a minister of the Methodist Episcopal Church, wrote in 1834 that Joseph Smith was 'not a man of truth and veracity', and that 'his general character in this part of the country, is that of an imposter, hypocrite and liar'. An accompanying statement by Lewis' son Levi asserted that Joseph Smith and Martin Harris had said adultery was not a crime and that Harris said he did not blame Smith for his (Smith's) attempt to seduce Eliza Winters, a friend of

Emma Smith. Such allegations may have been passed along to Isaac Hale, leading him to withdraw his support of Joseph Smith. (Howe, Mormonism Unvailed, 266-269).

The source referred to is "Mormonism Unvailed" which by quoting would show there is some validity according to the authors of History to this work although it is considered anti-Mormon rhetoric.

As we have not addressed the subject of Joseph Smith receiving revelations for the book Doctrine and Covenants it should be brought to the readers attention. Joseph Smith claims repeatedly that after inquiring of the Lord he receives such and such revelation. He does not say how he receives them. At first he claimed the Lord appeared to him in answer to his inquiry, then two personages with a host of angels, then God the Father and Jesus Christ with no angels, and again later Jesus Christ appeared to him alone. We are not told how he received all of the other revelations he claimed to receive. Did he use the urim and thummin? He certainly claimed to receive some of the revelations from using the urim and thummin. Did the revelation just appear to him in his mind? Did he bury his head in a hat with the seer stone and read the revelations as he did the Book of Mormon? Do you wonder how deep the hat was Joseph Smith used and how close to his eyes the seer stone would have been when he looked into the hat? Why did he need the gold plates if he used the seer stone in his hat to say what was on the plates? His comments on this subject are strangely silent.

He certainly received a lot of different revelations. Yet, once he was killed, the revelations came to an abrupt stop. Nowhere does God enlighten the people with His directions as he did through Joseph Smith. Brigham Young claimed his statements were as binding as any scripture the people had available to them and claimed one direct revelation regarding the movement of the Saints to Utah (D&C Section 136).

It would appear that Joseph Smith simply spoke the alleged revelation as being from God. Where Joseph Smith claimed to have received over 120 revelations in a period of twenty-four years, since his death there have been only 4 additions to the Doctrine and Covenants and in none of these do the Prophets involved state God revealed them directly to them. The one regarding the cessation of the principle of Polygamy states it is given for "political purposes" Official Declaration D&C. Nowhere in this statement does the Prophet claim that God has revealed to him what to say and that God has ordered them to stop practicing plural marriage. Notice this is an "Official Declaration 1" and not a "revelation". The Official Declaration 2 is dated September 30, 1978 Again this doesn't claim to be a "revelation" given from God to a prophet although the First Presidency by signature do claim "and by revelation has confirmed, that the long-Promised day has come etc…" No details are given how these three men all received this 'revelation' together nor where the "long Promised day" idea came from.

Even if we assume Declaration 1 and Declaration 2 are revelations it still seems strange that only three revelations, possibly four (including Declarations 1 and 2) if we consider the dream Joseph F. Smith has as section 138 of the D&C, have been received since the death of Joseph Smith to the present time.

Again let us review the many versions of Joseph Smith's first vision:
First, Joseph Smith circa summer 1842
Second, Joshua the Jewish Minister 1835
Third, Oliver Cowdery, Warren Parrish, Warren Cowdery and Frederick G. Williams 1834-1836
Fourth, fifth and sixth, History Drafts 1, 2 and 3 1838-1841
Seventh, Joseph Smith and Sidney Rigdon…history not extant 1836-1838
Eighth, John Whitmer…history never released. Record found in Reorganized Church
Ninth, Joseph Smith letter to John Wentworth March 1, 1842

Now we come to yet another version of the history, number ten.

On page 503 of Histories we read that in July 1843 Joseph Smith received a letter from Clyde, Williams & Co of Harrisburg, PA inviting Joseph Smith or "some other competent person" representing the Latter-day Saints to submit an "impartial account of the Rise and Progress, Faith and Practice" of the church. We are told that William W. Phelps prepared a letter in reply promising such an article would be "matured and forwarded in season to meet your anticipations". The resulting essay was published as "Latter Day Saints". Pages 506 through 516 follow recording this essay. More interesting differences result from this tenth version.

First, Joseph Smith claims now that he went from one society to another inquiring about salvation. In his earlier versions he never went to any of these other societies but read the bible and went out to pray for guidance.

Second, he says he began to "reflect upon the importance of being prepared for a future state".

Third, he now claims the different religious societies were "diametrically opposed" to one another. Haven't we shown this claim to be untrue?

Fourth, he confirms a previous version, but isn't this still in conflict with his earlier versions, wherein he claims that he was expressly commanded to "go not after them" while at the same time "receiving a promise that the fullness of the gospel should at some future time be made known unto me?"

Fifth, he says "I was informed also concerning the aboriginal inhabitants of this country, and shown who they were, and from whence they came; - a brief sketch of their origin, progress, civilization, laws, governments" etc. Why hasn't he told us about their laws and civilization and governments?

Sixth, he states that there were some "plates" deposited upon which were engraved an abridgment of the records of the ancient prophets that had existed on this continent. Notice here he omits claiming they were "gold plates" and says now they "had the appearance of gold".

Seventh, he states categorically that "through the medium of the Urim and Thummim I translated the record by the gift and power of God." But haven't we already seen he didn't use the plates to translate anything? Didn't he tell us he used a seer stone which he put in a hat and dictated what he saw in the hat? Did he ever mention using the Urim and Thummim while looking in the hat? Did he ever mention using the Urim and Thummin to translate the gold plates?

Well, we could go on but we have already seen so many different versions it is just getting tedious seeing the same mistakes over and over. The History book continues and basically ends with Orson Pratt's version of the history of Joseph Smith and the church, but he is merely repeating what he has heard and read of the other history writers and doesn't claim to have received any special revelations to reveal this history to him. In fact the historians call his version an "Interesting Account of Several Remarkable Visions and of The Late Discovery of Ancient American Records" by O. Pratt, Minister of the Gospel. The historians state "Interesting Account is not a Joseph Smith document, because Joseph Smith did not write it, assign it, or supervise its creation. However, two Joseph Smith documents in this volume, 'Church History' (pages 489-501 herein) and 'Latter Day Saints' (a later version of Church History, pages 503-516 herein), quote extensively from Pratt's pamphlet. These documents made use of Pratt's language to describe Joseph Smith's early visionary experiences and built on Pratt's summary of the church's 'faith and doctrine' for the thirteen-point statement of church beliefs that came to be known as the Articles of Faith." So this is not a Joseph Smith document? This is confirmation that the historians feel is altogether fitting and proper to introduce whatever they choose to include in a work entitled "The Joseph Smith Papers".

Added to this the many instances where the historians use words like "permit, perhaps, may be, possibly, etc." show this work seems to have some other purpose which I am unable to ascertain. Why have they made such an extensive compilation of records and used guess words like "maybe, etc." and added words and works from other documents? Why can't they simply accept the first version, which by their own words is the "only" version written by Joseph Smith's own hand? Why do they use Orson Pratt's version in this work but fail to use those documents written by Norris Stearns, Elias Smith, Alexander Campbell, Asa Wilde, Solomon Chamberlain and Charles G. finney? All of these individuals claimed to have similar revelations to those of Joseph Smith. Orson Pratt never claimed to have a single vision so doesn't it seem it would be better to quote from those men who did claim to have visions of God and Christ and angels appearing to them rather than merely an individual who quoted from earlier versions of Joseph Smith's history?

With Joseph Smith's easy access to these recorded visionary experiences of the above named men, doesn't it seem highly likely Joseph Smith simply made up his alleged vision based on his reading these other peoples written history? Even Orson Pratt claimed that during Joseph Smith's first vision a great light descended that seemed to cover all the trees and land around about him without consuming them. Does this not seem to make this vision an imaginary one? Martin Harris claimed that his vision of the gold plates and also David Whitmer's and Oliver Cowdery's were imaginary (Spiritual) and not real and Joseph Smith's first written account of his vision seems to fall in this same category. This would also be true of his visit by the angel on September 21, 1822 (later changed to 1823 by others who perhaps knew more about his personal vision than he did?) where we are told by Joseph Smith in his own handwriting that an angel appeared to him three times during this one night. Later Oliver Cowdery and others said the entire house he lived in was consumed in an intense bright light, brighter than the sun at noonday, and yet none of his family living there ever said a word about such an occurrence. Don't you think this definitely shows the occurrence was in his mind and not in reality?

It is interesting how Orson Pratt came to other conclusions regarding the history of the church and about the gold plates. He is quoted on page 532 as stating "the Lord God promised to give them America, which was a very choice land in his sight, for an inheritance… Moreover, he promised to make them a great and powerful nation, so that there should be no greater nation upon all the face of the earth". Then he continues saying these people occupied North America. Anybody ever hear of a great and powerful nation on the North American continent? We hear about Incas and Mayans but they were in South America and from what we can tell they were far from being the "greatest nation upon all the face of the earth". So do we have a false prophecy here? Can we see evidences of these people in their pyramids and other structures proving their existence? Certainly. Also we can see evidences of various different Indian cultural remains such as Mesa Verde in southwestern Colorado. If we can see these, shouldn't we be able to see remains of "the greatest nation upon all the face of the earth"? We certainly have evidences of ancient Rome, Constantinople, the great wall of China, and many other things of different civilizations in Europe, the British Isles, Asia, and Africa. Why not North America? Doesn't this appear obvious that it never happened and this is merely another false prophecy?

The Book of Mormon reportedly states that there were two groups of people, the Nephites and the Lamanites in North America. A study of the history of the American Indians will show there were many different groups of people or tribes of Indians inhabiting North America. Even a cursory study of Indian history in North America will quickly persuade the reader that there were many different tribes and cultures existing both in North America and South America. Nowhere can we find that there were only two major groups of people, especially living in North America.

He continues his version through page 546 of Histories. Following this there begins various indexes of chronology, maps and biographical sketches of different individuals and thus we come to the end of the book Page 686)

When Joseph Smith first began telling about having visions relating to heavenly beings appearing to him, he broadcast (or wrote down) what experience he had enjoyed. He first claimed that the Lord, and here we do not know exactly who the Lord is and may take the liberty of assuming he meant this was Jesus Christ, appeared to him. Later he amended this story to include a second individual who appeared along with the first and again we are not told who this being is but from his announcements we are led to believe this is God the Father he is speaking about.

As we have learned there are many different variations of what he claimed happened, although we have only one account in his own handwriting and it is very different from the many later claims made on his behalf. However, all ten accounts investigated in this Effort of Inquiry, tell us of heavenly beings appearing to Joseph Smith. After what seems to be quite a distance later in time Joseph Smith claims that John the Baptist appeared to him and Oliver Cowdery for the purpose of bestowing upon them the Aaronic Priesthood May 15, 1829 (Section 13 D&C). He makes reference in a general sense that many angels appeared to him in addition to these three appearances of heavenly messengers but does not specifically tell us of any of these occurrences. The first vision claimed to have been given to him sometime during his fourteenth or fifteenth year of life, making it about 1820 or 1821.

CHAPTER 27

THE DOCTRINE AND COVENANTS

S ection 2 claims to be an "extract from the words of the angel Moroni" September 21, 1823, but we have already learned this was not Moroni, but Nephi who appeared to him.

Section 3, 6*, 7, 11, 14*, 15* and Section 16* of the Doctrine and Covenants purports to be revelations he received through the Urim and Thummin. How did he receive revelation through the Urim and Thummin? Many Rabbi's in the Old Testament times questioned why the Urim and Thummin had to be used when a prophet was present. There is no evidence that the Urim and Thummin were ever used to translate unknown texts in biblical times. Joseph Smith used the Urim and Thummin to translate texts stating he wore them as a sort of breastplate affair and could then somehow see a particular text as written in the English language. Oliver Cowdery used them once himself to try to receive revelation from God. Section 9 of the D&C is given to caution him not to try to use them but to be a scribe for Joseph Smith and write for him. This puts these revelations in the same sphere as those revelations Joseph Smith claimed he received but does not say how he received them, giving the impression he saw them in his mind or his imagination.

Section 27 claims this revelation was given from a visit by a "heavenly messenger". Section 1, 4, 5, 8*, 9, 10, 12*, 17*, 18*, 19, 20, 21, 22, 23*, 24, 25, 26,, 28*, 29, 30, 31, 32*, 33, are revelations Joseph Smith claimed he had received but doesn't say how he received them. Those with an asterisk indicate he received the revelation through the Urim and Thummin.

Section 34 is given to Orson Pratt who is 19 years old at the time (November 4, 1830). Christ tells him, "For behold, verily, verily, I say unto you, the time is soon at hand that I shall come in a cloud with power and great glory. (8) And it shall be a great day at the time of my coming for all nations shall tremble. (9) But before that great day shall come, the sun shall be darkened, and the moon be turned into blood; and the stars shall refuse their shining, and some shall fall, and great destructions await the wicked." 183 years later this still hasn't happened, July 14, 2013. Christ's definition of "soon" must mean something different than what we mean when we use this word. Also does it make you wonder why God continues to say "verily, verily"? Isn't one verily enough? Verily means truly or really. Does God need to say "truly, truly", or "really, really"?

35, 36, 37, 38, 39, 40, 41, 42, 43*, 44, 45*, 46, are continued revelations. The asterisks indicate these revelations came after Joseph Smith asked God for an answer to a particular situation.

Section 47 John Whitmer was appointed historian for the Church March 8, 1831 but later refused to deliver up his written history.

Section 48, Another revelation to Joseph Smith but we are not told how he received it.

Section 49* March 1831 Verse 16 says "Wherefore, it is lawful that he should have one wife, and they twain shall be one flesh, and all this that the earth might answer the end of its creation;" Joseph Smith was having his sexual affair with Fanny Alger at this time.

Later he would marry other women and engage sexually with others who were married to other men claiming they were his spiritual wife. This doctrine or set of ideas was called *"Spiritual Wifery"* and was present in other religious organizations of Joseph Smith's time. And Joseph Smith denied he ever did this at a later time despite the revelations. Joseph Smith never explained how it was acceptable to break his marriage vows by having sex with other women who were married to other men by simply saying they were his spiritual wife. Does this mean if you are sealed to a woman for eternity you can do anything sexually with her in mortality? What about this very section 49 we are investigating now, stating "it is lawful that he should have one wife and they twain shall be one flesh"? Why doesn't Joseph Smith explain how it is acceptable to God for these women, already married to their husbands, to engage in sexual relations with him? Is it all right for him to break his marriage vows by simply saying the woman was his "spiritual wife"? What is a "spiritual wife"? What about these women who are married, and are now engaging in sexual relations with Joseph Smith? Aren't they breaking their marriage vows?

Sections 50* 51*, 52, 53*, 54*, 55*, 56*, 57*, 58*, 60*, 61, 62, 63*, 64, 65, 66*, 67*, 68*, are revelations received by Joseph Smith, those with the asterisk indicating they are given in response to questions asked by Joseph Smith.

Section 69 An interesting revelation requesting John Whitmer to accompany Oliver Cowdery with moneys to publish a compilation of revelations received as of November 1831. John Whitmer left the church in 1838 as did Oliver Cowdery.

Sections 70, 71, 72, 73, 74, 75, are revelations Joseph Smith received but does not tell us how he received them.

Section 76 was claimed to be a vision that both Joseph Smith and Sidney Rigdon experienced together Feb. 16, 1832. Joseph Smith says

"We, Joseph Smith, Jun. and Sidney Rigdon, <u>being in the Spirit</u> on the sixteenth day of February etc." From our study so far it appears being in "the spirit" refers to seeing things "spiritually" and not from the normal five senses and three dimensions normally given us to see things. Would this be like imagining something or fantasizing about it or perhaps dreaming?

77* This revelation apparently was seen by Joseph Smith with his spirit eyes only in March of 1832. The preface of this section says "beasts have spirits and shall dwell in eternal felicity on an immortal earth;" Further he says "and of creeping things, and of the fowls of the air" indicating all these creatures will have eternal life as well as humans through resurrection.

78, 79, 80, 81, 82, 83, 84, 85*, 86, are revelations given to Joseph Smith but again he does not tell us how he received them.

87 Revelation states, "Verily, thus saith the Lord, concerning the wars that will shortly come to pass beginning at the rebellion of South Carolina…" Note: Only one "verily" used this time. The word "shortly" turns out to be 28 years later. We are left to wonder still what the word "soon" turns out to be as it has been 183 years so far since it was given in section 34. "Soon" and "Shortly" apparently have significantly different meanings.

88, 89*, 90, 91*, 92, 93, 94, 95, 96*, 97, 98, 99, 100, 101, 102, 103, 104, 105, 106, 107, 108*, 109, are revelations Joseph claimed but doesn't say how he got them.

Section 110 This was a vision manifested to Joseph Smith and Oliver Cowdery in the temple at Kirtland, Ohio April 3, 1836 The Lord appears and then Moses appears, then Elias appears and then Elijah appears. These appearances are in connection with the dedication of the Kirtland Temple, which to this day has a title on it announcing it is made for the Church of The Latter-day Saints. It would appear

Christ neglected to change the title of his Church at this appearance even though he was appearing in a building dedicated to the Church of the Latter-Day Saints, yet two years later gave a special revelation to Joseph Smith to change the name to the Church of Jesus Christ of Latter-day Saints. Yet when He gave this revelation to Joseph Smith, he evidently neglected to have Joseph Smith change the title on His Temple from the Church of the Latter-day Saints, to the Church of Jesus Christ of Latter-day Saints. We are left to wonder why Christ didn't correct the title on his Holy Temple in 1836 when he appeared there and the other beings also appeared inside this building? Didn't he instruct Joseph smith to change the name of His church two years later to the Church of Jesus Christ of Latter-day Saints? If it was important enough to give Joseph Smith a revelation about the name of the church, why didn't he instruct him to change the name on His Temple?

Sections 111, 112, 113, 114, are revelations received by Joseph Smith and again he doesn't tell us how he received them.

Section 115 Christ gives the name of his church April 17, 1838. This is the third name given for his church, the first being The Church of Christ April 6, 1830 the second being the Church of the Latter-day Saints 1834, and now the Church of Jesus Christ of Latter-day Saints. This subject is covered earlier in this original study or inquiry.

116, 117, 118*, 119*, 120, 121, 122*, 123, 124, 125, 126, 127, 128, 129, 130, 131, 132, 133*, are revelations received by Joseph Smith, those with an asterisk indicate they are responses to questions Joseph Smith asked the Lord about certain subjects.

134 is not a revelation but a declaration of belief regarding governments and laws in general.

135 is not a revelation but a statement about the martyrdom of Joseph Smith and Hyrum Smith June 27, 1844, written by Elder John Taylor who was a witness to the events.

136 is a revelation given through Brigham Young at Winter Quarters January 14, 1847.

137 is a vision given to Joseph Smith January 21, 1836.

138 is a vision given to Joseph F. Smith in Salt Lake City, UT October 3, 1918.

Following these sections are two official declarations of the Church, the first relating to polygamy and the second relating to giving Priesthood authority to all worthy men of any race.

In summary we have 6 visions recorded in the Doctrine and Covenants other than Joseph Smith's original recording of his vision of "the Lord" in his 14th or 15th year of age which recording of this vision is not included in the Doctrine and Covenants but is recorded in the Pearl of Great Price..

We have 37 revelations given to Joseph Smith when he asked various questions of the Lord.

We have 92 revelations Joseph Smith recorded that he came up with on his own, although he claimed they were from the Lord and 5 sections not claiming to be revelations at all but stating they are the will of the Lord for a total of 140 sections of the Doctrine and Covenants.

Nowhere in these 140 sections do we see anything about a revelation regarding the Temple or Temple Endowments or temple garments.

Section 110 has the Lord appearing to accept the Kirtland Temple as being dedicated properly to Him, but does not go into any details regarding what is to transpire in His temple and as we have noted, ignored correcting the title on His Holy Temple.

Volume 5 of the Documentary History of the Church has this to say: "Wednesday May 4, 1842 I spent the day in the upper part of the store, that is in my private office (so) called because in that room I keep my sacred writings, translate ancient records, and receive revelations and in my general business office, or lodge room (that is where the Masonic fraternity meet occasionally, for want of a better place) in council with General James Adams, of Springfield, Patriarch Hyrum Smith, Bishops Newel K. Whitney and George Miller, and President Brigham Young and Elders Heber C. Kimball and Willard Richards, instructing them in the principles and order of the Priesthood, attending to washings, annointings, endowments and the communication of keys pertaining to the Aaronic Priesthood, and so on to the highest order of the Melchizedek Priesthood, setting forth the order pertaining to the Ancient of Days, and all those plans and principles by which any one is enabled to secure the fullness of those blessings which have been prepared for the Church of the First Born, and come up and abide in the presence of the Eloheim in the eternal worlds."

Notice he says nothing about what or how these activities relate to Temple Work. However this is as close as we get to him claiming to give "endowments" to others. What is the "order pertaining to the Ancient of Days?" What are "all those plans and principles by which any one is enabled to secure the fullness of those blessings etc."? Even in this account Joseph Smith fails to state that these "washings, annointings, etc." have anything to do with temple work. There seems to be no record of when these were made part of the temple procedures and who made them so.

CHAPTER 28

YET ANOTHER CHURCH?

Now Joseph Smith produces yet another name for his church, "the Church of the First Born" but he doesn't tell us anything about this Church or how it is connected to the Church of Jesus Christ of Latter-day Saints. This is in 1842 and the name of the Church of Jesus Christ of Latter-day Saints was given this name in 1838. Who or what is the "Church of the First Born"? Section 93:21-23 "And now, verily (or truly) I say unto you, (Note: Only one "verily" used here…interesting each time we read this, as if he didn't say verily, or truly, we might think he is not truly saying things unto us) I was in the beginning with the Father, and am the Firstborn; (22) And all those who are begotten through me are partakers of the glory of the same, and are the Church of the Firstborn. (23) Ye were also in the beginning with the Father; that which is Spirit, even the Spirit of truth;" O.K., so how is anyone "begotten through" Christ? You think you are confused now? Read this!

D&C 76:23-24 "For we saw him, even on the right hand of God; and we heard the voice bearing record that he is the Only Begotten of the Father (24) That by him, and through him and of him, the worlds are and were created, and the inhabitants thereof are begotten sons and daughters unto God."

Begotten – definition: (typically of a man, sometimes of a man and a woman) Bring (a child) into existence by the process of reproduction.

Now we really get confused. Jesus Christ is said to be the "only begotten of the Father". Christ tells us above that he is the "Firstborn" of God the Father. Then he tells us we were "also in the beginning with the Father" and he says the inhabitants of the worlds are "begotten sons and daughters unto God".

If Jesus Christ is the "Only Begotten" of the Father, how are we also "begotten sons and daughters unto God"? If we are begotten sons and daughters unto God, how can Christ remain the "Only Begotten?" Our definition of begotten as given above shows that begotten means bringing a child into existence by the process of reproduction.

Christ is the "Only Begotten" so was he the only one God brought into existence by the process of reproduction? God then must have been literally his father in the flesh or in mortality here on earth. So must he be the Only one that God reproduced on earth which would make Christ His Only Begotten (in mortality at least)? So God is literally the father of Jesus Christ, which can only mean his sperm and Mary's egg united to produce a child, which was Jesus Christ. Now watch all the religions start running around in tiny circles trying to tell us that begotten really means something different than our definition and etc. and also trying to tell us what God can and cannot do.

If that isn't enough to digest, how are we begotten sons and daughters unto God? If we are "begotten" wouldn't that take the word "Only" away from Christ as the "Only Begotten of the Father"?

Does this mean what it says? Are we begotten sons and daughters of God and therefore members of the Church of the Firstborn? What are the offices in this church? Are they similar to the Church of Jesus Christ of Latter-day Saints? Since Christ was the "Firstborn" does that mean the Church of Jesus Christ of Latter-day Saints is the same as the Church of the Firstborn? Christ says "those who are begotten through me" are members of the Church of the Firstborn. How are we "begotten through" Jesus Christ? He has said we were in the beginning with God as was he, so how can we be begotten through him? If we were "in the beginning with God" how can any of us be His "first born"?

Just because we take upon us his name and agree to his teachings, can this change our creation status? We have already looked at what is truth and we see we cannot change truth. It would appear that someone is trying to change the meaning of words we use but they cannot explain why they are doing this. Can God explain why he has four different names of his church, i.e. The Church of Christ, The church of the Latter- day Saints, The Church of Jesus Christ of Latter-day Saints, and now the Church of the Firstborn?

CHAPTER 29

QUESTIONS

Why does the current temple ceremonies refer to God the Father as Eloheim, yet as seen above Joseph Smith refers to "the Eloheim" which means plural Gods?

Didn't Joseph Smith have 6 direct revelations from spiritual beings about various subjects?

Didn't Joseph Smith inquire of the Lord 37 times about different questions and receive revelations from the Lord in answer to his requests?

Didn't Joseph Smith have 92 other revelations from God about such things as the Word of Wisdom, the Civil War, Thomas B. Marsh's problems with sharing the milk skimming with his neighbor?

According to the authors of the "Joseph Smith Papers" Joseph Smith received a revelation from God on November 5, 1842 giving Oliver Cowdery (or Frederick G. Williams) permission to visit their relatives in New York and this was to warn them of their impending doom, but did this ever happen?

Does it seem out of order to inquire why Joseph Smith didn't receive any detailed revelation from God about building temples and doing temple ordinances in them? Aren't temple ordinances that important compared to milk skimming of Thomas B. Marsh and appointing different men to different positions in the church and sending them on missions or giving someone permission to visit their relatives? Don't you think the temple ceremonies would be more important than the Word of Wisdom which was given "not by commandment or constraint"?

Aren't you just a little bit curious why Joseph Smith came up with the temple ceremonies just a few months after joining the Masons?

Following this, aren't you just a little bit curious as to why Joseph Smith's temple ceremonies and temple clothing so closely resembled the Masonic ordinances and clothing?

I wonder why the Mormon Church requires its members to wear temple garments as underwear outside of the temple?

Isn't it important to have this information in a revelation as all the other written revelations on various subjects?

With all the revelations and visions Joseph Smith claimed to experience is it unreasonable to feel if the temple ceremonies were needed that he would have received a direct revelation on the subject? Didn't he receive revelations about the Priesthood being restored, The name of the church, Polygamy, the United Order, The civil war, the word of wisdom, visiting relatives, etc.?

He received many revelations about minor items, He seemed to have difficulty with the name of the church Jesus wanted him to establish and it took Christ (or Joseph Smith) nine years to get the name correct and then only through another revelation on the matter. Is temple work part of Christ's church? Is temple work important to us? Are you aware that many people spend their entire time doing temple work and working on ceremonies in the temple in behalf of those who have died?

Why didn't Joseph Smith receive a revelation about temple ordinances and ceremonies and wearing temple garments as underwear? Why didn't Joseph Smith wear his temple garment-underwear when he went to Carthage jail and was killed? Didn't he have faith they would protect him?

Now why cannot a person discuss the temple ordinances and endowments outside of the temples? What is the most important and sacred thing about the gospel? Is it not Jesus Christ? It would seem that nothing can exceed the importance and sacredness of Jesus Christ. Can we talk about Jesus Christ outside the temple? Why are we being sworn to secrecy about the temple ceremonies? Is there something terrible about revealing how we shake hands or place our fingers in various places on another persons hand and wrist or giving out names for Aaronic and Melchizedek Priesthood tokens?

Is it perhaps that people can easily see the connection to the Masonic ordinances and tokens if they were able to discuss them freely with others? Is it "Let's keep it all secret and only talk about it in the temple away from the Masons and the world so they can't see we copied it all from the Masons"? Indeed Reed Durham, a very strong believer of the Mormon Church said:

"…. I suggest that enough evidence presently exists to declare that the entire institution of the political kingdom of God, including the Council of Fifty, the living constitution, the proposed flag of the kingdom, and the anointing and coronation of the king, had its genesis in connection with Masonic thoughts and ceremonies …."

A significant number of early Latter-day Saints were Masons prior to their involvement in the movement. Some of these were Brigham

Young, Heber C. Kimball, John C. Bennett, Hyrum Smith and Joseph Smith, Sr.

Joseph and Sidney [Rigdon] were inducted into formal Masonry ... on the same day..." being made "Masons on Sight" by the Illinois Grandmaster.

Joseph Smith was raised to the third degree or master mason "on sight" by Grand Master Jonas of the Grand Lodge of Illinois. This was fully within Jonas' right of office, but was a fairly rare procedure.

> Wednesday, March 16. — I was with the Masonic Lodge and rose to the sublime degree. (History of the Church, Vol.4, Ch.32, p.552)

In *The Mormon Church and Freemasonry* (2001), Terry Chateau writes:

> [The Joseph Smith family] was a Masonic family which lived by and practiced the estimable and admirable tenets of Freemasonry. The father, Joseph Smith, Sr., was a documented member in upstate New York. He was raised to the degree of Master Mason on May 7, 1818 in Ontario Lodge No. 23 of Canandaigua, New York. An older son, Hyrum Smith, was a member of Mount Moriah Lodge No. 112, Palmyra New York.

The relationship between Mormonism and Freemasonry began early in the life of Joseph Smith, Jr. as his older brother and his father were masons. By the 1840s Smith and other prominent Mormons were Masons and founded a lodge in Nauvoo, Illinois in March of 1842. Soon after joining the Masons, Joseph Smith introduced a new ceremony which he called the "Endowment" which included a number of symbolic elements that were identical with the Masons.

In researching the Bible and Book of Mormon and Pearl of Great Price and the Doctrine and Covenants, there is no record of God ever denying his people from being able to read His words written down by his prophets as Joseph Smith claimed God instructed him to do in hiding the gold plates. This was a first!

Why did God tell Joseph Smith to hide the plates and the urim and thummim? Doesn't the Mormon Church have the urim and thummin today in its possession? Why won't they show it to us? What is all this about hiding things from the people God wants to have believe in him and follow him? Isn't God able to protect the plates from being stolen by other people? In the Book of Mormon God instructed Nephi to kill Laban so he could obtain his sword and records on plates that Laban was said to possess. Didn't God send death and pestilence upon the Egyptians to get them to release the children of Israel from captivity? Why couldn't he have done the same to Laban to get the plates to Lehi? Why didn't Joseph Smith realize God could protect the gold plates from any misadventures without Joseph having to keep them hidden?

So many questions, so few answers. No record of Joseph Smith ever spending much time with his children or expressing any desire for more children. He never said he wanted more wives so he could have more children. Certainly he realized if any of the women got pregnant that were married to other men he would not be able to spend time with them as they grew up. Is it very difficult to ask why he wanted so many women? If not for children, then….?

The following pages may be considered appendix items regarding various subjects referred to above in this work.

JOHN COOK BENNETT

John C. Bennett was the first mayor of Nauvoo, Illinois and a prominent member of the Mormon Church. He was a medical doctor and surgeon of high renown and well respected in the medical profession of many states in addition to Illinois and also well known and respected by many ministers of various religions of the time. He was recognized by the Governor of Illinois who held him in high regard and appointed him to be a Justice of the Peace in addition to his duties as Mayor of Nauvoo and legally held offices of Major-General and Quarter-Master-General of Illinois. He was elected Chancellor of the University of the City of Nauvoo and was appointed Master in Chancery for Hancock County which incorporated Nauvoo. He was baptized into the Mormon church in Sept. or Oct. of 1840. The Mormon Church respected him highly and many excellent articles were written about him and published in the Times and Seasons (the Mormon Church newspaper). He even garnered praise for his lobbying efforts on behalf of the Mormons from the young Abraham Lincoln. At one time he was assistant President of the Mormon church and was appointed to the first presidency of the church by Joseph Smith. He was involved in a quarrel with Joseph Smith in 1842 and was disfellowshipped from the church May 11, 1842 and withdrew his membership from the church May 17, 1842. The quarrel was never discussed in detail and the parting was apparently mutual and friendly. Since Bennett and Joseph Smith were so intimately acquainted it is speculated that

Smith was afraid of what Bennett might reveal about him which is why he didn't try to cut him off from the church sooner as he had received written confirmation from George Miller, Hyrum Smith and William Law that Bennett had misused his current wife and was continually committing adultery.

Although he was accused of "spiritual wifery" how was this any different than what Joseph Smith was doing with Fanny Alger and other women as we have already studied? Did he really (verily) commit adultery with other women as he was accused of? How was this different than what Joseph Smith was doing and had been doing with other women also?

Something eventually went wrong as he and Joseph Smith soon became bitter enemies. Joseph Smith accused him of adultery and teaching a form of polygamy he called "spiritual wifery" and also accusing him of not following the word of wisdom which caused Bennett's separation from the church to become permanent having him excommunicated June 21, 1842. It is unclear why Joseph Smith had him excommunicated when he had already agreed to Bennett's request to have his name removed from the membership of the church.

July 1842 - Bennett's Accusations Against Joseph Smith

1. That Bennett's disfellowshipment notice of May 11, 1842 signed by John E Page, William Smith and Lyman Wright was a forgery because these three men were not in Nauvoo at that time. All three were away on official church errands.
2. That Joseph Smith attempted to seduce Miss Nancy Rigdon, the eldest and single daughter of Sidney Rigdon.
3. That Joseph Smith sold valuable property to Willard Richards, N.K. Whitney, and others prior to declaring bankruptcy thus violating the bankruptcy law of the state.

4. That Joseph Smith, Brigham Young, and four others were initiated, passed and raised before the installation of the Masonic Lodge, which was against Masonic regulations.

5. That Joseph Smith introduced a new degree of masonry, called "Order Lodge", in which a part of the obligation says, "I furthermore promise and swear, that I will never touch a daughter of Adam, unless she is given me of the Lord," so as to accord with Smith's licentious practices.

6. That Bennett's affidavit, sworn on May 17, and his statement, signed on May 19 before the city council, were made under duress. Joseph Smith had threatened to kill him if he didn't sign it.

7. That Joseph Smith ordered Orrin Porter Rockwell to shoot former Governor of Missouri, Lilburn W. Boggs.

There are at least two testimonies about John C. Bennett, one by Andrew Jensen the Mormon church historian and the other by Brigham Young.

Both are completely false and coming from such supposed honorable men it is clear the story of John C. Bennett has two sides to it. Bennett died at 64 and is buried in Polk City, Iowa not in California as both Jensen and Young state. His grave is situated in a beautiful spot atop a hill overlooking a tranquil lake. His tombstone is one of the largest in the cemetery. A flag honoring his service as a surgeon in the Union army sits beside his grave. It is reported that he was well respected by his Polk City neighbors and was "well-off" when he died. He was known in Iowa for practicing medicine, breeding chickens, and cattle and promoting anti-slavery issues.

PROBLEMS WITH JOSEPH SMITH

We have learned that Oliver Cowdery and Emma Smith were very unhappy with Joseph Smith for his involvement with 16 year old Fannie Alger. Cowdery termed it "a dirty nasty filthy business" and eventually left the church over this among other things. We know Joseph Smith violated the word of wisdom until the day he died. He was not wearing temple garments at the time of his death. He killed two people and seriously wounded another at Carthage jail where he was killed himself. There were perhaps 45 women married to him. We know he tried to have sex with other married women but failed in some of these attempts, particularly with Sarah Pratt who left the church over his behavior and later he apparently lied about her and accused her of false actions to try to defend his reputation. He had her accused of being a lover of John C. Bennett to try to ruin her reputation.

"Mr. Lewis also testified that "that he saw him (Smith) intoxicated at three different times while he was composing the Book of Mormon, and also that he has heard Smith, when driving oxen, use language of the greatest profanity." History of the Saints Page 84.

He engaged in spiritual wife doctrine. Further he attempted to seduce Sarah Pratt according to her testimony, while she was married to Orson Pratt at the time. Both Orson and Sarah left the church because of this incident, although Orson returned to the church at a later time. Sara Pratt never rejoined the church. As pointed out earlier, whether he committed adultery or not is a definition (really a distinction without a difference) he tried to make to explain his extra marital affair with Fanny Alger.

Joseph Smith tried to get Nancy Rigdon as a plural wife but she refused. John C. Bennett also tried for the same woman and also failed.

"Levi Lewis states that, he has 'been acquainted with Joseph Smith, Jr., and Martin Harris, and that he has heard them both say, adultery was no crime. Harris said he did not blame Smith, for his (Smith's) attempt to seduce Eliza Winters, etc." History of the Saints Page 84

Did he bear false witness against others? Didn't he testify falsely about Sarah Pratt's reputation, trying to protect himself from her telling of his attempts to get her to engage in sexual relations with him?

He killed two people and seriously wounded a third in the Carthage Jail when a group of people stormed the prison. DHC 5:110-111 Hadn't he already claimed he had a vision of heaven? Was he really a believer and follower of Christ? Did Christ try to kill or hurt anyone when they came for him at the end of his life?

"On August 27, 1842 (DHC Vol 5 p 135) Joseph Smith says "God said, 'thou shalt not kill', at another time he said "thou shalt utterly destroy." This is the principle on which the government of heaven is conducted by revelation adapted to the circumstances in which the children of the kingdom are placed. Whatever God required is right, no matter what it is…" Isn't he teaching that God's commandments can be changed at any time as "adapted to the circumstances" of any situation?

Did he steal from others after agreeing to share whatever he found in the ground? He promised Josiah Stowell a share in anything he found in the ground. In late 1825 Josiah Stowell, a well to do farmer from South Bainbridge, chenanga County, New York who had been searching for a lost Spanish mine near Harmony Township, Susquehanna County, Pennsylvania with another seer, traveled to Manchester to hire Smith on account of having heard that he possessed certain keys by which he could discern things invisible to the natural eye.

Upon Joseph Smith's claim to have found gold plates, he refused to share these with Josiah Stowell, literally stealing from Stowell by breaking his word with him. Did he really find gold plates? If he did, why wouldn't he share with Stowell as he promised?

"Joseph Smith, Jr., and others went to Canada in September 1842. …He took money, in Canada, from a man by the name of Lawrence, and promised him a farm, when he arrived at Kirtland'; but when he arrived Joseph was among the missing, and no farm for him. He took nine hundred dollars from Lawrence". History of the Saints Page 86

William Smith (Joseph's brother) told Joseph if he did not give him some money he would tell where the Book of Mormon came from, and Joseph accordingly gave him what he wanted. History of the Saints page 87

Isaac Hale stated, "The manner in which he pretended to read and interpret, was the same as when he looked for the money-diggers, with the stone in his hat, and his hat over his face, while the Book of Plates was at the same time hid in the woods". History of the Saints Page 82.

The Times and Seasons was the official church newspaper. In volume 5, no. 3 February 1, 1844 page 423 quote "As we have lately been credibly informed, that an Elder of the church of Jesus Christ of Latter-day Saints by the name of Hiram Brown, has been preaching Polygamy, and other false and corrupt doctrines in the county of

Lapeer, State of Michigan. With all the evidence we have shown here it is difficult to refute that Joseph Smith practiced polygamy and indeed with the wives shown herein. How can the church newspaper call "Polygamy, a false and corrupt doctrine"? Their leader was practicing it at the time this article was written!

DHC Volume 6 page 411 shows Joseph Smith saying "What a thing it is for a man to be accused of committing adultery, and having seven wives, when I can only find one." How can he say this after admitting to having a sexual affair with Fanny Alger? How can he further state he did not have any adulterous relationships with any women? These statements were made in 1844. and he had many wives according to various testimonies. i.e What about Lucinda Harris?

He prophesied that there would be 3 witnesses to the Gold Plates, the urim and thummin and the sword of Laban yet we can find no record of this ever happening. He never even had one witness to the urim and thummin and plates of Laban or sword of Laban as God commanded this was to be done.

None of the 3 witnesses, nor the 8 witnesses remained in the church by 1847.

Joseph Smith didn't wear his temple garments all the time.

DID JOSEPH SMITH MAKE FALSE PROPHECIES?

Did he make false prophecies? On November 5, 1842 he claimed to have a revelation from God giving Oliver Cowdery (or was it Frederick G. Williams?) permission to go to New York to warn his relatives of the impending doom he was about to send upon that part of the world. Was there any doom that came upon that area?

In his (John Whitmer's) history he states: "Joseph and Sidney went to the several churches preaching and prophesying wherever they went, and greatly strengthened the churches that were built unto the Lord. Joseph prophesied saying: God is about to destroy <u>this generation</u>, and Christ will descend from heaven in power and great glory, with all the holy angels with him, to take vengeance upon the wicked, and they that know not God." [41]

---

[41] *God is going to take vengeance upon the wicked and those that know not God? This is the same God that loves all of us? Innocent people that have never heard about God will now suffer his vengeance? The definition of vengeance is "punishment inflicted or retribution exacted for an injury or offense". Those people who "know not God" would be those that haven't heard about him or his commandments, rules, etc. Joseph Smith tells us God will punish them for not hearing about him?*

It is very clear from historical facts that the generation living at that time (1831) was never destroyed, nor do we have any record of "Christ descending from heaven in power and great glory with all the holy angels with him".

Wilford Woodruff, who remained in the Church and became the fourth President, confirmed the fact that Joseph Smith claimed to have a revelation concerning the bank. Under the date of January 6, 1837, he recorded the following in his journal: "I also herd [sic] President Joseph Smith, jr., declare in the presence of F. Williams, D. Whitmer, S. Smith, W. Parrish, and others in the Deposit office that HE HAD RECEIVED THAT MORNING THE WORD OF THE LORD UPON THE SUBJECT OF THE KIRTLAND SAFETY SOCIETY. He was alone in a room by himself and he had not only [heard] the voice of the Spirit upon the Subject but even an AUDIBLE VOICE. He did not tell us at that time what the Lord said upon the subject but remarked that if we would give heed to the commandments the Lord had given this morning all would be well." ("Wilford Woodruff's Journal," January 6, 1837, as quoted in Conflict at Kirtland, page 296)

He predicted his bank of Kirtland, Ohio would become the greatest bank in the world. Warren Parrish, a KSSABC officer who later left the LDS church, claimed that Smith had prophesied that KSSABC "shall become the greatest of all institutions on EARTH." 1837.

It totally and completely failed within a year of his (Joseph Smith) making this prophecy.

He predicted that Missouri would be the place God would set up His kingdom on earth. Did this ever happen? Instead wasn't it Salt Lake City, Utah?

The United Order was to be an everlasting order:

Originally, the United Order was intended to be "an everlasting order for the benefit of my church, and for the salvation of men until I come". In practice, however, the Order was relatively short-lived during the life of Joseph Smith, Jr.

Doctrine & Covenants Section 1:17 Wherefore, I the Lord, knowing the calamity which should come upon the inhabitants of the earth"... The Lord knew of a calamity that "should come upon the inhabitants of the earth"?

Was there ever a great calamity that ever came upon the inhabitants of the earth? Even the World Wars that occurred almost a century to a century and a half later did not destroy as many people as did the black plague of 1348 to 1350.

"And I prophesy in the name of the Lord God of Israel, unless the United States redress the wrongs committed upon the Saints in Missouri and punish the crimes committed by her officers that in a few years the government will be utterly overthrown and wasted and there will not be so much as a potsherd left" (DHC Volume 5 p 394 1843)

The United States government has not been overthrown and wasted. It has certainly been more than "a few years" since that prophecy was made and the United States has not ever redressed the wrongs committed upon the saints in Missouri, nor punished the officers of Missouri.

According to the authors of the "Joseph Smith Papers" Joseph Smith received a revelation from God on November 5, 1842 giving Oliver Cowdery (or Frederick G. Williams) permission to visit their relatives in New York and this was to warn them of their impending doom.

There is no evidence there was any doom that came upon his relatives.

In the 87th Section of the Doctrine and Covenants Joseph Smith predicts that "wars will shortly come to pass, beginning at the rebellion of South Carolina". This was prophesied on December 25, 1832.

Doctrine and Covenants Section 87 is dated December 25, 1832, but it did not appear in the 1833 Book of Commandments *or in any edition of the* D. & C. *or other LDS scripture until after the Civil War began. It was printed in the 1851* P. of G. P. *in England and in* The Seer *by Orson Pratt in 1854, but neither of those were considered as scripture then. If this was really a prophecy from God, why did the LDS wait 30 years until after the Civil War started before including it in the* D. & C.? *Any good U.S. history book will help to put it into perspective. On July 14, 1832, (five and a half months before Smith's prophecy), Congress passed a tariff act which South Carolina declared null and void. Because tensions were high, President Andrew Jackson put the U.S. army on alert and the United States expected war in 1832. The LDS* Evening and Morning Star *and many other U.S. newspapers reported that information before Smith's prophecy. When things calmed down, and the war didn't begin in 1832 as expected, Smith's revelation was not published in the* D. & C. *until after the Civil War began in 1861.*

Doctrine and Covenants. 84:1-5, is a revelation given to Joseph Smith in September, 1832, in Kirtland, Ohio according to the heading. It says the New Jerusalem and its temple are to be built by the Mormons then living in western Missouri, "for verily this generation shall not all pass away until an house shall be built unto the Lord."

Neither the temple nor the city have yet been built, but the generation alive in 1832 has died and passed away.

Doctrine and Covenants Section 111 was given to Joseph Smith on August 6, 1836, while he was in Salem, Massachusetts according to the heading. In verses 2-4, the Lord said, "I have much treasure in this city for *you*... I will give this city into your hands... and its wealth pertaining to gold and silver shall be *yours*."

*The only recorded time that Smith was in Salem, MA was in 1836 when he was there about a month and received this revelation (*D.H.C. *Vol. 2, pp. 464-466). There is no record of the city of Salem, Massachusetts, or of its wealth pertaining to gold and silver being given to Smith before his death in 1844.*

Doctrine and Covenants section 112 claims to be a "Revelation given through Joseph Smith to Thomas B. Marsh at Kirtland, Ohio, July 23, 1837." Verse 1 begins, "Verily, thus saith the Lord unto you my servant Thomas..." while verse 6 says, "I the Lord have a great work for thee to do..." Verse 7 states, "thou art chosen..." and verse 11 says, "I know thy heart..." Verse 16 declares, "Thomas, thou art the man I have chosen to hold the Keys of my Kingdom, as pertaining to the twelve..." Marsh was President of the Twelve at the time of the revelation.

Marsh was an apostate only 15 months later on October 24, 1838 (D.H.C., Vol 3, pp. 166-167). The "Lord" who gave this revelation to Joseph Smith either did not know Marsh's heart as He claimed, or perhaps Marsh could do the work of the Lord as an apostate from the LDS Church?.

Doctrine & Covenants Section 124 was revealed to Joseph Smith in Nauvoo, Illinois on January 19, 1841 according to the heading. The introduction says that "the saints are commanded to build both a house for the entertainment of strangers and a temple in Nauvoo." Verse 1 begins, "Verily thus saith the Lord..." Verses 31-33 continues, "But I commanded you, all ye my saints, to build a house (temple) unto me; and I grant unto you a sufficient time to build a house unto me; and during this time your baptisms shall be acceptable unto me... But if ye do not these things at the end of the appointment, ye shall be rejected as a church, with your dead, saith the Lord your God."

Eleven months later on Dec. 13, 1841, the twelve apostles wrote an epistle to the LDS people saying, "The building of the Temple of the Lord in the city of Nauvoo, is occupying the first place in the exertions and prayers of many of the Saints at the present time, knowing, as they do, that if this building is not completed speedily, 'we shall be rejected as a Church with our dead;' for the Lord our God hath spoken it." This epistle was signed by nine of the twelve apostles (*D.H.C.* Vol. 4, pp. 472-475). Three of those apostles later became Presidents of the LDS Church. Brigham Young was one of those three.

Brigham Young later said concerning the temple in Nauvoo, "they got it nearly completed before it was burned, but the saints did not enjoy it" (J. of D. Vol. 18, pp. 303-304). Notice that the Lord gave enough time to complete the Nauvoo temple and if the LDS failed to complete it, they would be rejected as a church. The LDS Apostles understood and quoted this prophecy. Yet, Brigham Young admitted that the Nauvoo temple was never completed. Therefore, was this a false prophecy or have the LDS been rejected by the Lord.?

Joseph Smith declared, "And now I am prepared to say by the Authority of Jesus Christ, that not many years shall pass away before the United States shall present such a scene of bloodshed as has not a parallel in the history of our nation; pestilence, hail, famine, and earthquake will sweep the wicked of this generation from off the face of the land, to open and prepare the way for the return of the lost tribes of Israel from the North Country. The people of the Lord, those who have complied with the requirements of the new covenant, have already commenced gathering together to Zion, which is in the state of Missouri... therefore, 'Fear God, and give glory to Him, for the hour of His judgment is come'. Repent ye, repent ye, and embrace the everlasting covenant, and flee to Zion, before the overflowing scourge overtake you, for there are those now living upon the earth whose eyes shall not be closed in death until they see all these things which I have spoken, fulfilled" (*D.H.C.*, Vol. I, pp. 315-316).

This prophecy was dated January 4, 1833. All those living in 1833 are dead, but none of Smith's prophecy has been fulfilled except that there was bloodshed in the United States... which was predicted by the secular press before Smith's prophecy. But, pestilence, hail, famine and earthquakes did not sweep the wicked who lived in 1833 off of the face of the land, nor did the "lost tribes of Israel" return from the North country. And, the gathering that began in Missouri was aborted by the LDS.

Oliver B. Huntington, a devout LDS contemporary of Joseph Smith, said that Smith taught, "The *inhabitants of the moon* are more of a uniform size than the inhabitants of the earth, being six feet in height. They dress very much like the Quaker style and are quite general in style or fashion of dress. They live to be very old; coming generally; near a thousand years. This is the description of them as given by Joseph (Smith) the Seer, and he could see whatever he asked the Father in the name of Jesus to see" (*Journal of Oliver B. Huntington,* Vol. II, p. 166).

That is not what the astronauts found when they went to the moon.

President Brigham Young not only taught the moon was inhabited, but the SUN as well. In a sermon delivered in the Tabernacle in Salt Lake City, President Young made this comment: "Who can tell us of the inhabitants of this little planet that shines of an evening, called the moon?...when you inquire about the inhabitants of that sphere you find that the most learned are as ignorant in regard to them as the ignorant of their fellows. So it is in regard to the inhabitants of the sun. Do you think it is inhabited?

I rather think it is. Do you think there is any life there? No question of it; it was not made in vain." (*Journal of Discourses*, vol. 13, p. 271)

ANY EVIDENCE OLD OR NEW TESTAMENT PROPHETS HAD MANY WIVES?

J oseph Smith claimed he was curious why the old testament prophets had many wives and asked God about it and received the revelation on plural marriage. The old testament prophets did not have many wives. Abraham had one wife, Isaac had one wife and Jacob had two wives. Abraham had one intimate relationship with Hagar, Sarah's handmaid and produced a son Ishmael. Isaac only had one wife and no handmaids. Jacob was tricked into marrying two daughters of Laban, his mother's brother and they each had one handmaid that produced twelve sons and one daughter.

There are no other old testament prophets that had plural wives so what is Joseph Smith trying to tell us here? From Abraham and Jacob we see they had handmaids that produced children for the prophets. Where are the children Joseph Smith produced through what wives? The Bible tells us plainly what happened. Why doesn't Joseph Smith tell us plainly also?

King David and King Solomon of Old Testament times committed adultery even with them having many wives, and David caused Uriah to be killed in battle by putting him in the very front line of the army. It is recorded in the bible that David killed Uriah the

Hittite. Solomon claimed over 1,000 wives and concubines[42] and yet had to commit adultery with the Queen of Sheba, a reported black woman from Ethiopia. In 2 Samuel 3:2-5 "And unto David were sons born in Hebron; and his firstborn was Amnon, of Ahinoam the Jezreelitess; (3) And his second, Chiteab, of Abigail, the wife of Nabal the Carmelite, and the third, Absolom, the son of Maacah the daughter of Talmai King of Geshur; (4) and the fourth, Adonijah, the son of Haggith; and the fifth, Shephatiah the son of Abital; (5) and the sixth, Ithream, by Eglah David's wife. There were born to David in Hebron."

We see that David had these six wives listed above but we know he also was married to Michal, daughter of Saul, king of Israel and then to Bathsheba. So the total wives David had were eight. Bear in mind here, David was no prophet. Nathan was the prophet of the Lord at that time.

The bible tells us Abraham had one wife and one concubine. His son Isaac had one wife and his grandson Jacob had two wives and two concubines. Abraham and Jacob had more than one wife but what a far cry from Joseph Smith having 48 wives. Only Solomon indulged

---

[42] ***1 Kings 11:3 And he had seven hundred wives, princesses, and three hundred concubines and his wives turned away his heart. Solomon's tolerance of his wives pagan religions led to terrible sins against God. 1 Kings 11:4-9 states, For it came to pass, when Solomon was old that his wives turned away his heart after other gods; and his heart was not perfect with the Lord his God as was the heart of David his father, For Solomon went after Ashoreth the goddess of the Zionians, and after Milcom the abomination of the Ammonites, and Solomon did evil in the sight of the LORD and went not fully after the LORD, as did David his father. Then Solomon built a high place for Chemosh, the abomination of the children of Ammon, and likewise did he for all his foreign wives, which burnt incense and sacrificed unto their gods, and the LORD was angry with Solomon.***

in this type of extreme polygamy and as it says in the Bible, "and the Lord was angry with Solomon".

Nowhere in the Bible do we find that polygamy was a special "rite" of their religious beliefs. Indeed, Abraham was involved sexually with Sarah and her handmaid Hagar and had two sons, Ishmael by Hagar and Isaac by Sarah, and Sarah specifically gave Hagar to Abraham since she was unable to conceive a son for him, not because Abraham wanted another wife or additional sexual unions with a woman other than his wife. Now Abraham married Keturah after Sarah died and had children by her but she was not a polygamous wife to Abraham.

Jacob was tricked by his uncle Laban into marrying Leah, his oldest daughter after promising Jacob he could marry Rachel and Jacob served Laban another seven years in addition to the first seven he served to marry Leah, so he could marry Rachel. He was not marrying Leah because of any belief in polygamy. When Rachel saw Leah was bearing sons to Jacob she was devastated and pleaded with Jacob to take Bilhah and "go in unto her, and she shall bear upon my knees, that I may also have children by her". (Genesis 30:3-4) This was clearly not Jacob wanting another woman. When Leah saw this, and realized she was past child bearing, she also sent her handmaid in to Jacob "and Zilpah Leah's maid bare Jacob a son" (Genesis 30:12)

This is a very far cry from Joseph Smith marrying one woman after another and trying to get other men's wives to have sexual relations with him. Nowhere do we find he was trying to have more children by all these women he was having sex with. Is their any record anywhere in the Bible or Book of Mormon of anyone marrying another man's wife at the same time as she is married to another man like Joseph Smith did?

Instead we find Joseph Smith having sexual relations with Fanny Alger without Emma's knowledge and certainly without her permission. Nowhere do we find Emma Smith giving women to Joseph Smith to have sex with him in order to have children as Sarah and Leah and Rachel did with their husbands.

We have studied the Fanny Alger situation at some length. While Bushman states that Joseph Smith admitted to sexual relations with Fanny Alger, he denied any adulterous activities but we have seen that neither he, nor any Mormon except Seymour Brunson (Page 81 above) had authority to perform marriages and Joseph Smith's first marriage that he performed was in November 1835 yet his affair with Fanny Alger was in 1832. Even Bushman can find no record that Joseph Smith wanted to have sexual relations with Fanny Alger to have children by her. Oliver Cowdery appears to have been outraged by Joseph Smith's actions with Fanny Alger.

Lucinda Harris is shown as the third wife of Joseph Smith. She was originally married to William Morgan, a prominent Mason. William Morgan set about to write a book exposing all of the Masons rituals and secrets but he was kidnapped and his body later found by the Niagara River in New York. It was believed the Mason's killed him for exposing their secret rituals. Lucinda then married George Harris and in the fall of 1834 they both joined the Mormon Church.

The date of the marriage between Joseph Smith and Lucinda is uncertain. Sarah Pratt was a friend of Lucinda's and she indicated that the wedding occurred sometime during Joseph's stay in Missouri after fleeing from Ohio with the law after him. This would have been late in the year 1838. After marrying Joseph, Lucinda continued to live with George. This was typical of Joseph's other polyandrous unions. It is uncertain if Lucinda's first husband, George, was aware of the marriage.

Unrest in Missouri forced Joseph Smith to flee to Illinois. From Nauvoo, Joseph wrote to Lucinda and George, that he had selected a lot for them, "just across the street from my own". Shortly thereafter, Lucinda and George moved from Far West Missouri to Nauvoo.

Bigamy is the condition of having two wives or two husbands at the same time. The second marriage to someone who is already legally married is void and may be annulled, while there is no effect on the first marriage. A person who knowingly commits bigamy is guilty of a crime,

There is simply no way to ignore the fact that Joseph Smith was guilty of bigamy by the laws of our land and our society. He may have inferred that God directed polygamy to increase the population of his church but nowhere in any scripture is bigamy permitted or condoned. We may search endlessly in the bible to find a place where God required polygamy to be practiced to increase the population and we have also shown in this study that there are actually more males than females in our world.

JOSEPH SMITH ORDERS DESTRUCTION OF NAUVOO EXPOSITOR

As "Acting Associate Justice" in Nauvoo, George presided over the city council meeting on June 10, 1844 when the claims of the dissenting newspaper, the "Nauvoo Expositor" were discussed. The minutes of the meeting record: "Alderman Harris spoke from the chair, and expressed his feelings that the press ought to be demolished". The city council passed a resolution that directed the destruction of the press. Joseph Smith was soon arrested for abetting this destruction (Indeed it was he that ordered it) and he was later killed in Carthage jail on June 27th 1844 while awaiting trial for his actions in this matter.

Lucinda Harris eventually divorced George and according to one biographer she joined the (Catholic) sisters of charity and at the breaking out of the civil war, was acting in that capacity in the hospitals at Memphis Tennessee…"

THE MASONS

It is uncertain whether Joseph Smith was killed by the Masons for revealing their secrets, as William Butler had been, or if he was killed for destroying the Nauvoo Expositor press machines. Perhaps both reasons were in play at the time. It seems obvious that when Joseph Smith was killed he was in the act of crying out "O Lord my God…" This is the first part of the Masons plea for help and assistance, the entire plea is "O Lord my God, is there no help for the widows son?" He must have felt those trying to kill him were Masons since he was invoking the Mason's plea for help.

In 1842 Smith became a Master Mason as indicated in the History of the Church.

Tuesday, March 15 (1842) – "I officiated as grand chaplain at the installation of the Nauvoo Lodge of Free Masons, at the grove near the Temple. Grand Master Jonas, of Columbus, being present, a large number of people assembled on the occasion. The day was exceedingly fine; all things were done in order, and universal satisfaction was manifested. In the evening I received the first degree in Freemasonry in the Nauvoo Lodge, assembled in my general business office. (History of the Church, by Joseph Smith, Deseret Book, 12978 Vol. 4, Ch. 32. p 550-1)

Apparently there was earlier dealings with the Masons, as John Whitmer recorded in his history referred to earlier in this study, "John Murdock and others held a meeting in the city of Cleveland, Ohio, in the Masonic Hall by the request of some of the citizens of said city.

The influence of Freemasonry in Mormon Temples is expressed well by LDS historian Dr. Reed Durham. Dr. Durham provides a number of parallels between the two. He gives these as evidence for Masonry's clear influence on Mormonism.

> "I am convinced that in the study of Masonry lies a pivotal key to further understanding Joseph Smith and the Church. . . . Masonry in the Church had its origin prior to the time Joseph Smith became a Mason .... It commenced in Joseph's home when his older brother became a Mason. Hyrum received the first three degrees of Masonry in Mount Moriah Lodge No. 112 of Palmyra, New York, at about the same time that Joseph was being initiated into the presence of God . . The many parallels found between early Mormonism and the Masonry of that day are substantial..."

I have tried to demonstrate the Masonic influences upon Joseph in the early Church history, before his formal membership in Masonry. Let's look at a few of these influences of Masonry that Joseph Smith seemed to copy. There is absolutely no question in my mind that the Mormon ceremony which came to be known as the Endowment, introduced by Joseph Smith to Mormon Masons, came directly from Masonry. The similarities between the two ceremonies, the Masons and the Mormons, are so apparent and overwhelming that some dependent relationship cannot be denied.

It also seems obvious that the Nauvoo Temple architecture was also Masonically influenced. Indeed, it might appear that there was an intentional attempt to use Masonic symbols.

Another development in the Nauvoo Church stemming from the association with the Masons, was the creation of the Female Relief Society. This organization was the Prophet's intentional attempt to expand Masonry to include the women of the Church. The fact that the Relief Society was organized in the Masonic Lodge room, and only one day after Masonry was given to the men, was not happenstance .... included in the actual vocabulary of Joseph Smith's counsel and instructions to the sisters were such words as: ancient orders, examinations, degrees, candidates, secrets, lodges, rules, signs, tokens, order of the priesthood, and keys; all indicating that the Society's orientation possessed Masonic overtones.

There is enough evidence in existence presently to declare that the entire institution of the political kingdom of God, including the Council of Fifty, the living constitution, the proposed flag of the kingdom, and the anointing and coronation of the king, had its beginnings with Masonic thoughts and ceremonies. Can anyone deny the Masonic influence on Joseph Smith and the Church after his personal Masonic membership?

WILLIAM LAW

SECOND COUNSELOR IN CHURCH PRESIDENCY TO JOSEPH SMITH, JR.

W illiam and Jane Law were members of the Church of Jesus Christ of Latter-day Saints until sometime in 1843. William was the editor and founding father of the newspaper called the Nauvoo Expositor.

William Law was perhaps the most credible and important person to have left the hierarchy of the LDS church since Oliver Cowdery.

William Law was born in Northern Ireland in 1809 and his family migrated to western Pennsylvania about ten years later. He migrated to Canada near Toronto where he met and married his wife Jane. They joined the LDS Church in 1836 in Toronto, then moved to Nauvoo in 1839. In January 1841 William was placed as second counselor to Joseph Smith in the first presidency of the church. He served in this capacity until January 1844 and by April both he and Jane were excommunicated from the church.

He spent the rest of his life in Apple River, Illinois and Shulsburg, Wisconsin, where he was a medical doctor. He died in 1892.

The laws left Nauvoo, Illinois because he felt Joseph Smith ordered the death of his enemies. He believed that Joseph Smith ordered the assassination of Governor Lilburn W. Boggs of Missouri.

Thomas Carlin, Governor of Illinois, wrote Joseph Smith a letter saying that it was common knowledge that he "had prophesized that Boggs should die a violent death." John C. Bennett, assistant President of the church, wrote "In 1841, Joseph prophesized that Lilburn W. Boggs, now ex-Governor of Missouri, should die by violent hands within one year.

George M. Hinkle, in a June letter to Smith added, "Denying your having prophesized the violent death of Boggs won't do, too many people have heard you, myself among the rest.

Just prior to the attempted assassination of the ex-governor, John C. Bennett said, "I was then on terms of close intimacy with Joseph Smith and asked him where Porter Rockwell had gone? 'Gone" said he, 'Gone to fulfill prophecy.' " Second counselor in the first presidency of the church, William Law, said Joseph had personally told him that he had sent Rockwell to assassinate Boggs. Law declared, "Let me tell you that Joseph Smith told me the fact himself. The words were substantially like this, 'I sent Rockwell to kill Boggs, but he missed him. It was a failure; he wounded him instead of sending him to Hell.'"

Thus two members closely associated with Smith in the first presidency of the church report their first hand conversations with Smith about the Boggs assassination.

It is well documented that Joseph Smith had many plural wives. Probably because of these activities Emma Smith was not happy in her marriage with Joseph. William Clayton who was Smith's personal secretary, recorded a conversation in his journal on this date that Joseph Smith had with his wife. He (Joseph Smith) knew that she

(Emma) was disposed to be revenged on him (Smith) for some things. Emma thought that if he would indulge himself, she would too.

Joseph Jackson supported William Clayton's private entry. Jackson said that Joseph told him; "Emma wanted William Law for a spiritual husband, and she urged as a reason that as he had so many spiritual wives she thought it but fair that she should at least have one man... and that she wanted Law." Whether Josseph Jackson made this all up or not cannot be proven. A major problem with believing Jackson in this instance is that later in her life Emma denied that Joseph Smith ever practiced polygamy and even though this can be proven false it still stands that she made such a claim and in so doing it seems to show she would never have wanted William Law as a second husband.

Joseph Jackson may have been less than honest in his reporting things. His expose about Joseph Smith was similar to that of John C. Bennett's.

Still, according to Jackson, William Law refused this sexual offer although Joseph and Emma both tried to persuade Jane Law of the correctness of the doctrine, but she refused to believe it to be of God.

William Law wrote in his diary on May 13, 1844, that Smith had lately endeavored to seduce my wife but had found her a virtuous woman who refused his advances. Alexander Neibaur, a close friend of Joseph Smith, recorded that when Mr. Law came home one evening, he inquired who had been there while he was gone. Brother Joseph came by his wife replied. William Law then demanded what had transpired. Mrs. Law then told him that Joseph wanted her to be married to him as a spiritual wife.

Joseph Jackson said much the same when he wrote that it was 'shortly after the 15th of January 1844 that Joseph informed me in conversation that he had been endeavoring for some two months to get Mrs. William Law for a spiritual wife. He said that he had used every argument in his power to convince her of the correctness of his doctrine, but could not succeed. Smith shared this information, according to Jackson, because Smith wanted Law 'removed. Jackson said that shortly after January 15th: Again we must remember that Jackson's comments may have been seriously wrong.

One Sunday morning, Joseph and I had a long talk concerning Law, in which he avowed, not for the first time, however, his determination to put Law out of the way, for he had become dangerous to the church of Jesus Christ of Latter Day Saints, and that it was the will of God that he should be removed. He, however, wished to proceed in such a manner that he would be able to get Law's wife.

By January 1, 1844, it is clear from William's diary that the Laws had rejected Smith's proposal. So it is not surprising that on January 8th, Law is dropped as a counselor in the first presidency and on April 18th, the Laws were excommunicated from the church. The recordings of Joseph Jackson, while historical, leave one wondering a great deal about them and why he would record such erroneous behavior. Was there some truth to his recordings or even perhaps was all of it correct?

Five weeks before the Laws left the church, Joseph Smith established a secret organization on March 11, 1844, called the council of Fifty, sometimes spelled backward for secrecy purposes. Other designations identifying the group were Council of the Kingdom, and The Living Constitution. This theocratic-political kingdom or body of men met a number of times in Nauvoo and later in Utah until the 1880s. Joseph Smith was anointed their first king in 1844, Brigham Young in 1847, and John Taylor in 1884. The goal of this theocracy was world government. They believed they would govern and rule the earth during the millennial reign of Christ.

It was in this organization that Joseph Smith had himself set up as a candidate for the presidency of the United States.

When William Clayton, a member of the Council of Fifty wrote in his journal on April 11, 1844, that 'President Joseph was voted our Prophet, Priest and King with loud Hosannas.' The Laws and others were thunderstruck. William Law wrote in his diary four days later, 'Conference is over, and some of the most blasphemous doctrines have been taught by Joseph Smith and others ever heard of such as… that Joseph Smith is a god to this generation, that secret meetings are all legal and right and that the Kingdom must be set up after the manner of a Kingdom (and of course have a king).'

On May 10, 1844, William Law wrote in a "prospectus" prior to his publishing the Nauvoo Expositor, that it is "a sacred duty…to advocate unmitigated disobedience to political revelations, and to censure and decry gross moral imperfections wherever found, either in the plebeian, patrician or self-constituted monarch'. When the first and only issue of the Expositor was published June 7, 1844, Law strongly voiced his disdain for uniting church and state, of allowing the church temporal control over his life. He declared, "We will not acknowledge any man as king or law-giver to the church; for Christ is our only king and law-giver."

The Laws also learned from this April 11, 1844 meeting that Joseph Smith was not only anointed a king over the earth but that he was "a God to this generation". Brigham Young also taught that Smith is our "Prophet Seer Revelator and God". Young delineated some of Smith's responsibilities as a God and declared that if you "ever pass into the heavenly courts, it will be by the consent of the Prophet Joseph. If you ever pass through the gates into the Holy City, you will do so upon his certificate that you are worthy to pass. No man or woman in this dispensation will ever enter into the Celestial Kingdom of God without the consent of Joseph Smith…He also rules in the spirit-world and he rules their triumphantly…He reigns there as supreme a being in his sphere, capacity, and calling, as God does in heaven."

During the last two years of Joseph Smith's life, William and Jane Law said they had first hand experience of Joseph Smith breaking at least six of the Ten Commandments and many of the teachings in the Sermon on the Mount. Law wrote:

The gospel of Jesus Christ, as we find it recorded in the Scriptures of the Old and New Testament in which we most firmly believe, and upon which we base our hopes of eternal salvation, does not admit of murder, false swearing, lying, stealing, robbing, defrauding, polygamy, adultery, fornication, and blasphemy. And yet those evils have been introduced into the Church at Nauvoo, by Joseph Smith and others, for the purpose of accomplishing their base designs. We have always disapproved such things and opposed them both privately and publicly, and for our opposition to them, we were driven from our homes in Nauvoo.

Thus the Laws indicted Joseph Smith with: blasphemy or using God's name in vain, committing murder, committing adultery, stealing and robbing from the gentiles, bearing false witness, and coveting the wives of other men (Ex. 20:3-17). In William's final diary entry, he wrote that Smith, "Was one of the false prophets spoken of by Christ who would come in sheep's clothing but inwardly be a ravelling [ravening] wolf. His works proved it [Matt. 7: 15-16].... He claimed to be a god, whereas he was only a servant of the Devil, and as such met his fate."

Forty three years later, his views on Joseph Smith and Mormonism had not softened. He wrote, "The great mistake of my life was my having anything to do with Mormonism. I feel it to be a deep disgrace and never speak of it when I can avoid it; for over forty years I have been almost entirely silent on the subject."

KIRTLAND SAFETY SOCIETY Anti-Bank

O rganized in 1836 and reorganized January 2, 1837. It's preamble stated:

> ...for the promotion of our temporal interests, and for the better management of our different occupations, which consist in agriculture, mechanical arts, and merchandising.

By November 1837 the bank had entirely failed and closed. Joseph Smith was fined for running an illegal bank.

By the end of 1836 many recent Mormon converts had gathered in Missouri and Ohio. Kirtland itself increased from approximately 1,000 people in 1830 to 3,000 in 1836. This population growth contributed partly to a rapid land price increase between 1832 and 1837.

The average price per acre of land sold in Kirtland rose from approximately $7.00 in 1832 to $44.00 in 1837, only to fall back to $17.50 in 1839 (Ludlow p. 283). General inflation during this period accounted for between 25 and 40 percent of the price increase. Although the LDS church held considerable real estate, estimated at approximately $60,000, it also needed liquidity to repay outstanding loans. The credit needs of the church, growing population and ongoing land transactions required a local bank.

LDS apostle Orson Hyde went to the Ohio legislature to request a bank charter while Oliver Cowdery went to Philadelphia and acquired plates to print notes for the proposed Kirtland Safety Society bank. On January 2, Hyde returned to Kirtland emptyhanded. He had been unable to persuade any legislator to sponsor a bill giving KSS a bank charter. LDS church president and prophet Joseph Smith Jr. attributed the lack of sponsorship to discrimination against the Mormons.

Utilizing outside legal counsel, the Kirtland Safety Society Anti-Banking Company (KSSABC) was formed under revised articles on. January 2, 1837 as a joint stock company to serve as a quasi-banking institution. Quasi-banks operated as banks (sometimes in conjunction with other business activities) although they had no formal bank charter. These corporate institutions were not uncommon in Ohio at the time as banking regulations were limited. Whigs went so far as to encourage businesses to operate as quasi-banks.

"Anti" and "ing" were engraved before and after "Bank"- in smaller typeface on the printing plates Cowdery had previously purchased in Philadelphia. Subscribers and organizers of the KSSABC were members of the Kirtland community (merchants, farmers, etc.) many of whom became shareholders of the company. Sidney Rigdon served as the KSSABC chairman and president. Warren Parrish as signatory, secretary and teller Joseph Smith was cashier.

The proposed capitalization of the "anti-bank" greatly exceeded the resources that were available from its backers, as noted by historian, Robert Kent Fielding:

As projected, there was never the slightest chance that the Kirtland Safety Society anti-Bank-ing Company could succeed. Its organizers launched a gigantic company capitalized at four million dollars, while the entire capitalization of all the banks in the state of Ohio was only nine and one third million. The members, to be sure, pledged themselves to redeem the notes and bound themselves individually by their agreement under the penal sum of one hundred thousand dollars. But there was no transfer of property deeds, no power of attorney, no legal pains and penalties.

On May 10, 1837 in New York, every chartered bank stopped payment in specie (gold and silver coinage), leaving banks and local institutions like the KSS holding notes without adequate liquid assets. Within two months the failures in New York alone aggregated nearly $100,000,000 in value. Out of the eight hundred and fifty banks in the United States, three hundred and forty-three closed entirely, sixty-two failed partially. Smaller, privately held financial institutions, like the KSS, also failed in droves. The panic was followed by a five year depression, characterized by ongoing failures of banks and financial institutions and record unemployment levels.

In February 1837, at the behest of Newell, Samuel D. Rounds swore a writ against Smith and Rigdon for illegal banking and issuing unauthorized bank paper. At a hearing in March, this trial was postponed until autumn. Eventually Rounds voluntarily dropped all of the cases in his suit except those against Smith and Rigdon. Although Smith's only official capacity for KSSABC was cashier, other officers and parties with equal or greater responsibility were absolved from the suit. KSSABC continued issuing notes through June, but eventually failed due to insolvency, as most of the KSSABC reserves were tied up in land rather than silver as some erroneously believed.

Smith transferred all of his holdings to Oliver Granger and J. Carter in June and resigned from the KSSABC in July. Parrish and Frederick G. Williams assumed management of the KSSABC until the bank closed its doors in November of 1837 with about $100,000 in unresolved debt. Smith appointed Granger as his agent to clear up his Kirtland affairs, as Smith was named in seventeen lawsuits with claims totalling $30,206.44 over debts incurred in the failure of the KSSABC. Four of these suits were settled, three were voluntarily abandoned by the plaintiffs, and ten more resulted in judgments against Joseph Smith. According to LDS scholars, The LDS church also raised and put up $38,000 in bail money for Smith at the Geauga County Court which was to be held to satisfy any judgment that might be ajudicatedThe against Smith.

On July 28, Smith, Rigdon and <u>Thomas B. Marsh</u> headed to <u>Upper Canada</u> on church business and returned in late August. On September 27, Smith and Rigdon departed Kirtland for Missouri. They arrived about one month later, spent about two weeks in Missouri on Church business and returned to Kirtland on December 10. In their absence, in October, they were fined $1,000 for operating an illegal bank. However according to Dale W. Adams, professor of agricultural economics at Ohio State University, other, larger quasi-banks had been operating in Ohio longer than KSSABC and were not being prosecuted. After a warrant was issued for Smith's arrest on a charge of banking fraud, Joseph Smith and Sidney Rigdon fled Kirtland for Missouri on the night of January 12, 1838 on horseback just ahead of a mob intent on putting them in jail.

Among KSSABC's misfortunes, Smith also accused Parrish of embezzling $25,000 from KSSABC. In June Joseph Smith tried to get a search warrant, but was denied. He wanted this warrant to confirm his suspicions against Parrish. It is interesting that Joseph Smith didn't receive a revelation from God about Parrish embezzling money from the bank as he received revelations on many other very minor transactions. Also it may be worth noting that Warren Parrish was one who made up a version of Joseph Smith's history. If we believe his history, should we not believe he did not embezzle any money either?

Shortly before his resignation, Joseph Smith also took out a $1,225 loan from a different bank to try to help keep KSSABC solvent.

Many of The Quorum of Twelve Apostles, Warren F. Parrish, Thomas B. Marsh, William E. McLellin, Luke S. Johnson, John F. Boynten, Lyma E. Johnson, John E. Page and Lyman Wight, accused Smith of improprieties in the banking scandal, and LDS Apostle Heber C. Kimball later said that the bank's failure was so shattering that afterwards "there were not twenty persons on earth that would declare that Joseph Smith was a prophet of God." Warren Parrish, a KSSABC officer who later left the LDS church, claimed that Smith had prophesied that KSSABC "shall become the greatest of all institutions on earth." 1837. Wilford Woodruff records that Smith had a revelation on the topic, but declined to share it, saying only that "if we would give heed to the commandments the Lord had given this morning all would be well." Then Woodruff expressed his own hopes that the KSSABC will "become the greatest of all institutions on earth." Since Joseph Smith claimed he did have a revelation on the topic of the KSSABC, does it not follow that if Parrish had embezzled money from the bank, Smith would have received a revelation on this?

On January 12, 1838, faced with a warrant for his arrest on a charge of illegal banking, Joseph Smith fled with Sidney Rigdon to Clay County, Missouri just ahead of an armed group out to capture and hold Smith for trial. Smith and Rigdon were both acquainted with not only conflict and violent mobbing they experienced together in Pennsylvania and New York, but with fleeing from the law. According to Smith, they left "to escape mob violence, which was about to burst upon us under the color of legal process to cover the hellish designs of our enemies." Brigham Young left Kirtland for Missouri weeks earlier on December 22 to avoid the dissidents who were angry with Young and threatened him because of his persistent public defense of Smith's innocence. Most of those who remained committed to the church moved to join the main body of the LDS in Missouri.

One of the tangible connections from this episode to the present are the notes that were printed at the time. Some church leaders encouraged people to hold onto these notes as they said that someday they would have value again. While the notes never regained their face value, by the late 19th century they had become collector's items. A Kirtland Safety Society note bearing Joseph Smith's signature can be quite valuable; for example, in an auction in March 2006, a $100 note sold for $11,500.

Warren Parrish, who had been an officer in the bank and had left the Church, made this statement: "I have listened to him [i.e. Smith] with feelings of no ordinary kind, when he declared that the audible voice of God, instructed him to establish a banking-anti banking institution, who like Aaron's rod shall swallow up all other banks and grow and flourish and spread from the rivers to the ends of the earth, and survive when all others should be laid in ruins." (Painesville Republican, February 22, 1838, as quoted in Conflict at Kirtland, page 297)

Wilford Woodruff, who remained in the Church and became the fourth President, confirmed the fact that Joseph Smith claimed to have a revelation concerning the bank. Under the date of January 6, 1837, he recorded the following in his journal: "I also herd [sic] President Joseph Smith, jr., declare in the presence of F. Williams, D. Whitmer, S. Smith, W. Parrish, and others in the Deposit office that he had received that morning the word of the Lord upon the subject of the Kirtland Safety Society. He was alone in a room by himself and he had not only [heard] the voice of the Spirit upon the Subject but even an audible voice. He did not tell us at that time what the Lord said upon the subject but remarked that if we would give heed to the commandments the Lord had given this morning all would be well." ("Wilford Woodruff's Journal," January 6, 1837, as quoted in Conflict at Kirtland, page 296)

William Parrish, secretary for Joseph and cashier of the bank for a short time, wrote in 1838:

"I have been astonished to hear him declare that we had $60,000 in specie in our vaults and $600,000 at our command, when we had not to exceed $6,000 and could not command any more; also that we had but about ten thousand dollars of our bills in circulation when he, as cashier of that institution, knew that there was at least $150,000." (Letter to Zion's Watchman, published March 24, 1838. Cyrus Smalling also wrote that Joseph had collected only $6,000 in specie. See E. G. Lee, The Mormons, or Knavery Exposed, p. 14)

Right from the start, the bank had been operated illegally and Joseph Smith was eventually ordered by the courts to pay the standard $1,000 penalty as well as court costs (see Chardon, Ohio, courthouse, Vol. U, p. 362). The dissolution of the bank and the catastrophic effects it held for those that trusted Joseph's word resulted in widespread disillusionment with the prophet. Under accusations of fraud, Joseph threatened to excommunicate any Saint who brought suit against a brother in the church.

As Heber Kimball put it, during this time "there were not twenty persons on earth that would declare that Joseph Smith was a prophet of God." (Sermon delivered September 28, 1856. Journal of Discourses, Vol. 4, p. 105)

To prevent his creditors from hounding him to his new home in Nauvoo, Illinois, Smith declared legal bankruptcy, but not before transferring many of his assets to his wives, children, friends, and associates--some 105 people in all. (In 1844, the year of Smith's death, these transfers were declared fraudulent and illegal.) Indeed, this was a charge made by John C. Bennett against Joseph Smith in refuting the Mormon Church's action against him in his excommunication trial. It was, and still is, illegal to sell off assets a person may have prior to filing for bankruptcy. Obviously this would be very fraudulent to debtors especially after already losing whatever money was owed to them prior to a bankruptcy filing.

LIST OF SOME OF JOSEPH SMITH'S WIVES

According to LDS Historian Andrew Jenson, Joseph Smith had at least twenty-seven wives in 1844 (see Andrew Jenson, Historical Records 6 May 1887 pp 233-234. Fawn M. Brodie published the names of forty-nine alleged wives of Joseph Smith (No Man Knows My History pp 335-336). Todd Compton lists Joseph's wives as thirty-three with an additional eight "possible wives" increasing the number of alleged wives to forty-one (Sacred Loneliness, The Plural Wives of Joseph Smith, Signature Books 1997 4,6,8). Joseph Smith invited Nancy Rigdon, nineteen-year-old daughter of his close friend and counselor, Sidney Rigdon, to meet him at the home of Orson Hyde. Upon her arrival Smith greeted her, ushered her into a private room, then locked the door. After swearing her to secrecy, wrote George W. Robinson, Smith announced his affection for her for several years, and wished that she should be his...the Lord was well pleased with this matter...here was no sin in it whatever...but, if she had any scruples of conscience about the matter, he would marry her privately. Incredulous, Nancy countered that if she ever got married she would marry a single man or none at all. Grabbing her bonnet, she ordered the door opened or she would raise the neighbors. She then stormed out of the Hyde-Richards residence. The next day, Smith wrote Nancy a letter, where he justified his advances, saying " That which is wrong under one circumstance, may be, and often is, right under another. ... Whatever God requires is right, no matter what it is, although we may not see the reason thereof till long after the events transpire. ... even things which might be considered abominable to all who understand the order of heaven only in part, but which in reality were right because God gave and sanctioned by special revelation." This is his first written statement of theocratic ethics.

PLACE: Nauvoo, IL SOURCE: Official History of the Church, Vol. 5, p.134-136, Sidney Rigdon Biography by Richard S. Van Wagoner, p.295

What in the world is Joseph Smith talking about here? What is right under one circumstance may be and often is wrong under another circumstance? Why do we even have laws and commandments then? And who is to interpret when God requires something of us, it is either right or wrong? Doesn't this seem to usher in total chaos?

And what of God's repeated statements that He is the same yesterday, today, and forever?

Doesn't this seem to be giving Joseph Smith the right to arbitrarily do anything he wants to do? He can simply claim his actions are what God has directed and even thought they may seem wrong, they are right under his own circumstances. It is easy to understand Nancy Rigdon's astonishment at Joseph Smith's attempt to marry her as a plural wife under these circumstances.

POLYGAMY DEMOGRAPHICALLY DOUBTFUL

An interesting observation made and published in the Salt Lake Tribune Thursday, December 6, 1984 is reproduced hereafter:

PROVO, (AP) -, Mormon women who fret about the possibility of having to share their husbands in the hereafter may be able to rest easier says a Brigham Young University Sociologist and author of a study of "celestial demographics."

Dr. Tim Heaton, an assistant professor at the church-owned school, undertook the unlikely study as a way of illustrating there are misconception s among some Mormons about life after death.

"For some time people have taught, though I've never held it as a Mormon doctrine myself, that polygamy would be very common after death." Said Heaton, whose study shows plural marriage in the hereafter – based on earthbound demographics and church doctrine – would be difficult at best.

Members of the Church of Jesus Christ of Latter-day Saints believe everyone who has lived on Earth will be judged according to their deeds and assigned to one of three kingdoms of glory, the highest being the Celestial Kingdom, which in turn has three levels, or degrees.

Only those "exalted" to the highest degree of the Celestial Kingdom will be allowed to retain their earthly spouses, or, in the case of men, acquire additional ones, according to church doctrine.

Heaton said he also used as a "given" a statement by Mormon Church apostle Bruce R. McConkie that all children who die before the age of 8 – considered the Mormon age of accountability – automatically are placed in the highest level of the Celestial Kingdom.

"Personally, I think we don't know a lot about what will happen in the heavens, and that was really the underlying point of the study", Heaton said Wednesday.

For example, a statistical analysis of world demographics shows there automatically would be more men than women in the Celestial Kingdom, because of the 70 billion people believed to have been born, the sex ration at birth is 104 males per 100 females. And 47 percent of males and 44 percent of females die before age 8.

"It follows that 46 percent of the earth's population are automatically exalted", Heaton said.

Consequently, many more women than men who survive past age 8 would need to be exalted in order for there to be a balanced sex ratio in the Celestial Kingdom because about 1.7 billion more men than women have died in their first eight years, Heaton said.

He said the sex ratio places limits on marriage patterns. If all 19.2 billion women and none of the 18.9 billion men who have survived past age 8 were exalted, there would barely be two women per man.

"One would need an extremely favorable image of women to believe in the possibility of universal polygamy", Heaton said. "If 20 percent of the men who survive past age 8 are exalted, universal polygamy will be demographically impossible."

However, if none of the women who survive to age 9 are exalted, and all of the men are, women may face the task of keeping two men in eternal bliss. He said.

"Perhaps Eliza Snow's rhetorical question, "In the heavens are parents single?" requires more serious consideration," he said, referring to the lyrics of a popular Mormon Hymn.

Heaton, a life-long Mormon who has some polygamist ancestors, said he did not do the study as a matter of whimsy, But, he added, "I would say we come to the same conclusions that most Mormons would not anticipate which is the funny part.

"I'm not positive my results are correct," he said.

The study's results, published earlier this year in the quarterly Dialogue an independent journal of Mormon thought, also would be jarring to American Mromons who believe they will be in the majority in the Celestial Kingdom, Heaton said.

If every baptized member of the Mormon church were exalted, he said, the church would be contributing as many people to the Celestial Kingdom as the Soviet Union, based on that country's infant mortality rate, while 10 times as many would come from African nations and 30 times as many from Asian countries.

"A study of ethnic and racial composition of the Celestial inhabitants would quickly eradicate notions about the inferiority of blacks, Asians, or residents of the so-called heathen nations," Heaton said.

He said that "judging from present and projected populations of non-Caucasian nations," Jews, Christians, and Nephites – an ancient civilization described in the Book of Mormon – "will constitute a small minority of the heavenly host." (End of article)

Since the Mormon Church has deleted the "blood oaths" from their temple ceremonies, the remaining endowments and covenants seem harmless to others in our society. The false prophecies made by Joseph Smith also seem harmless to others that don't believe in him anyway. Brigham Young is certainly the one who kept the Mormon Church alive and growing to its present state. The Reorganized Church of Jesus Christ of Latter-day Saints or as it is now known, the Community of Christ, has an estimated 10,000 members and there is nothing of a negative nature manifested from them either. All of the adulterous and sinful sexual involvements Joseph Smith entered into will be sorted out by God and I believe justice will eventually prevail with those being deceived and hurt by his activities will be made whole by God.

BOOK OF HYRUM

From the Book of Hiram, pp 443-444 we read: #18 "Born in a Protestant land, we are of that faith; if we had opened our eyes to the light under the shadows of St. Peter's at Rome, we should have been devout Romanists; born in the Jewish quarter of Aleppo, we should have condemned Christ as an imposter; in Constantinople, we should have cried: 'Allah il Allah – God is great, and Mahomet is his Prophet.' Birthplace and education give us our faith.

#19 …Not one in ten thousand knows anything about the proofs of his faith. We believe what we are taught; and those are most fanatical who know least of the evidences on which their creed is based.

#20. What is truth to me is not truth to another. The same arguments and evidences that convince one mind, make no impression on another; this difference is in men at their birth. No man is entitled positively to assert that he is right, where other men, equally intelligent and equally well informed, hold directly the opposite opinion. Each thinks it impossible for the other to be sincere; and each, as to that, is equally in error. 'What is truth?' was a profound question, the most suggestive one ever put to man…"

#22."Here is a man, superior to myself in intellect and learning, and yet he sincerely believes what seems to me too absurd to merit confutation; and I cannot conceive, and sincerely do not believe, that he is both sane and honest; and yet, he is both. His reason is as perfect as mine, and he is as honest as I am…Our dreams are realities while they last."

#23. "When men entertain opinions diametrically opposed to each other, and each is honest, who shall decide which hath the truth, and how can either say with certainty that he hath it? We know not what is the truth.

#24. "That we ourselves believe and feel absolutely certain that our own belief is true, is in reality, not the slightest proof of the fact, seem it never so certain and incapable of doubt to us."

#26. "It is no merit in a man to have a particular faith, excellent and sound and philosophic as it may be. It is no more a merit than his prejudices and his passions."

#27. "Therefore she teaches her votaries that toleration is one of the chief duties of every good Mason."

#29. "It inculcates a generous love for all mankind, it matters not of what religious creed."

This Masonic teaching is incorporated in the Holy Bible also:

Romans 14:1-8 Him that is weak in the faith, receive ye, but not to doubtful disputations. (2) For one believeth that he may eat all things: another, who is weak eateth herbs. (3) Let not him that eateth despise him that eateth not; and let not him which eateth not judge him that eateth; for God hath received him. (4) Who art thou that judgest another man's servant? To his own master he standeth or falleth. Yea, he shall be holden up: for God is able to make him stand. (5) One man esteemeth one day above another; another esteemeth every day alike. Let every man be fully persuaded in his own mind. (6) He that regardeth the day, regardeth it unto the Lord; and he that regardeth not the day, to the Lord he doth not regard it. He that eateth, eateth to the Lord, for he giveth God thanks; and he that eateth not, to the Lord he eateth not, and giveth God thanks. (7) For none of us liveth to himself and no man dieth to himself. (8) For whether we live, we live to the Lord; and whether we die, we die unto the Lord: whether we live therefore, or die, we are the Lord's.

DID JOSEPH SMITH BREAK ANY OF THE 10 COMMANDMENTS?

The Laws accused Joseph Smith with: blasphemy or using God's name in vain, committing murder, committing adultery, stealing and robbing from the gentiles, bearing false witness, and coveting the wives of other men (Ex. 20:3-17). William Law wrote in his diary four days later, 'Conference is over, and some of the most blasphemous doctrines have been taught by Joseph Smith and others ever heard of such as…that Joseph Smith is a god to this generation,

John C. Bennett also accused Joseph Smith of breaking many of the 10 commandments.

Commandment #1: Thou Shalt have no other Gods before me!

Joseph Smith essentially created another god - a god that was once a man. His god is much more similar to the gods of Greek mythology than to the Hebrew God . Could it be a counterfeit god? In fact, Smith talked about more than just one God, and the fact that humans are thought to have the opportunity to become gods themselves, in LDS theology, is a clear departure from the monotheistic Judeo-Christian understanding of the Godhead. As shown above, William Law stated that Joseph Smith claimed to be a god to this generation.

In the King Follet sermon Joseph Smith claimed: "God himself was once as we are now, and is an exalted man, and sits enthroned in yonder heavens! That is the great secret."

"No man or woman in this dispensation will ever enter into the Celestial Kingdom of God without the consent of Joseph Smith... every man and woman must have the certificate of Joseph Smith, junior, as a passport to their entrance into the mansion where God and Christ are... [Joseph Smith] reigns there as supreme a being in his sphere, capacity, and calling, as God does in heaven. Many will exclaim - "Oh, that is very disagreeable! It is preposterous! We cannot bear the thought!" But it is true." Brigham Young, Journal of Discourses, volume 7, p 289. Do you really think so?

Commandment No. 5 "Thou shalt honor thy father and thy mother etc. ..." Did he dishonor his wife's parents by eloping with Emma Smith after being told specifically by Isaac Hale that he would not approve of his marrying Emma at that time because he was a stranger and appeared to be a ne-er do well?

Commandment No. 6 "Thou shalt not murder"

In Carthage jail just before he was killed, he shot and killed two other people and seriously wounded a third man he was attempting to kill. Prior to this it is claimed he ordered the killing of Governor Lilburn Boggs of Missouri but his agent, Orin Porter Rockwell, missed and only wounded him seriously.

Commandment No. 7 "Thou shalt not commit adultery"

We have shown repeatedly how Joseph Smith broke this commandment, starting with Fanny Alger along with his repeated attempts on Sarah Pratt and Nancy Rigdon to engage with him in sexual intimacies. The date of the marriage between Joseph and Lucinda Harris is uncertain. Sarah Pratt thought the wedding occurred when Joseph was in Missouri. After marrying Joseph Smith, Luncinda continued to live with her husband George. This was typical of Joseph's other polyandrous unions. It is uncertain if Luncinda's first husband, George, was aware of the marriage.

Commandment No. 8 "Thou shalt not steal"

Our study has revealed how he stole from his associates in his early career of treasure seeking, and also from Lawrence in Canada where he promised him land but never gave it to him when he came to Nauvoo.

Commandment No. 9 "Thou shalt not bear false witness against thy neighbor."

Clearly from all the different versions of his first vision we ask if he broke this commandment? Also from his story about finding gold plates and hiding them from anyone so nobody could see them, after telling Peter Ingersoll he only found white sand which he put in bags and claimed they were gold plates. When was he telling the truth about finding gold plates? When was he telling the truth about polygamy? When he claimed he never practiced it or preached it? Or when he was living in polygamy with many other women?

Commandment No. 10 "Thou shalt not covet"

Did he covet Orson Pratt's wife Sarah, and other men's wives as well, as shown above? He certainly coveted Nancy Rigdon although he failed to seduce her after trying his best. Wasn't he a married man at the same time?

Out of the 10 commandments, he appears to have broken at least 7 of them. We see the golden idol of Moroni on many of the Mormon church temples so that would seem to mean the second commandment about not having idols seems being broken even to this day.

That leaves only the third and fourth commandment of not taking the name of the Lord God in vain and it is very subjective whether Joseph Smith did this or not. If all of his many revelations were figments of his imagination he certainly is guilty of violating this third commandment. The fourth commandment is to remember the Sabbath day to keep it holy and trying to show his activities on the Sabbath day seem more like a muck raking expedition of which we are not trying to do in this study although doesn't it appear likely Joseph Smith broke all 10 of the 10 commandments in his lifetime?

ACCOUNT OF OLIVER COWDERY'S EXCOMMUNICATION

Seymour Brunson brought the following charges against Oliver Cowdery April 12, 1838:

First – For persecuting the brethren by urging on vexatious law suits against them, and thus distressing the innocent.

Second – For seeking to destroy the character of President Joseph Smith, Jr., by falsely insinuating that he was guilty of adultery.

Third – For treating the Church with contempt by not attending meetings.

Fourth – For virtually denying the faith by declaring that he would not be governed by any ecclesiastical authority or revelations whatever, in his temporal affairs.

Fifth – For selling his lands in Jackson county, contrary to the revelations.

Sixth – For writing and sending an insulting letter to President Thomas B. Marsh, while the latter was on the High Council, attending to the duties of his office as President of the Council, and by insulting the High Council with the contents of said letter.

Seventh – For leaving his calling to which God had appointed him by revelation, for the sake of filthy lucre, and turning to the practice of law.

Eighth – For disgracing the Church by being connected in the bogus business, as common report says.

Ninth – For dishonestly retaining notes after they had been paid; and finally, for leaving and forsaking the cause of God, and returning to the beggarly elements of the world, and neglecting his high and holy calling, according to his profession.

The Bishop and High Council assembled at the Bishop's office, April 12, 1838. After the organization of the Council, the above charges of the 11th instant were read, also a letter from Oliver Cowdery, as will be found record in the Church record of the city of Far West, Book A. The 1st, 2nd, 3rd, 7th, 8th, and 9th charges were sustained. The 4th and 5th charges were rejected, and the 6th was withdrawn. Consequently he (Oliver Cowdery) was considered no longer a member of the Church of the Latter-day Saints. Also voted by the High Council that Oliver Cowdery be no longer a committee to select locations for the gathering of the Saints.

Oliver Cowdery did not attend this hearing but wrote a letter endeavoring to explain his feelings and opinions on the charges brought against him. His letter to the High Council is printed below in its entirety:

Far West, Missouri, April 12, 1838

Dear Sir: (Rev. Edward Partridge, Bishop of the Church of Latter-day Saints)

I received your note of the 9th inst., on the day of its date, containing a copy of nine charges preferred before yourself and Council against me, by Elder Seymour Brunson.

I could have wished that those charges might have been deferred until after my interview with President Smith; but as they are not, I must waive the anticipated pleasure, with which I had flattered myself, of an understanding on those points, which are grounds of different opinions on some church regulations, and others which personally interest myself.

The fifth charge reads as follows: 'For selling his lands in Jackson County,' I acknowledge to be true, and believe that a large majority of this Church have already spent their judgment on that act, and pronounced it sufficient to warrant a disfellowship; and also that you have concurred its correctness, consequently, have no good reason for supposing you would give any decision contrary.

Now, sir, the lands in our country are allodial in the strictest construction of that term, and have not the least shadow of feudal tenures attached to them, consequently, they may be disposed of by deeds of conveyance without the consent or even approbation of a superior.

The fourth charge is in the following words, 'For virtually denying the faith by declaring that he would not be governed by any ecclesiastical authority nor revelation whatever in his temporal affairs.'

With regard to this I think I am warranted in saying, the judgment is also passed, as on the matter of the fifth charge, consequently, I have no disposition to contend with the Council; this charge covers simply the doctrine of the fifth, and if I were to be controlled by other than my own judgment, in a compulsory manner, in my temporal interests, of course, could not buy or sell without the consent of some real or supposed authority. Whether that clause contains the precise words, I am not certain - I think however they were these: 'I will not be influenced, governed, or controlled in my temporal interests by any ecclesiastical authority or pretended revelation whatever, contrary to my own judgment.'

Such being still my opinion, shall only remark that the three great principles of English liberty, as laid down in the books, are "the right of personal security, the right of personal liberty, and the right of private property." My venerable ancestor was among the little band, who landed on the rocks of Plymouth in 1620 - with him he brought those maxims, and a body of those laws which were the result and experience of many centuries, on the basis of which now stands our great and happy government; and they are so interwoven in my nature, have so long been inculcated into my mind by a liberal and intelligent ancestry that I am wholly unwilling to exchange them for anything less liberal, less benevolent, or less free.

The very principle of which I conceive to be couched in an attempt to set up a kind of petty government, controlled and dictated by ecclesiastical influence, in the midst of this national and state government. You will, no doubt, say this is not correct; but the bare notice of these charges, over which you assume the right to decide, is, in my opinion, a direct attempt to make the secular power subservient to Church direction - to the correctness of which I cannot in conscience subscribe - I believe the principle never did fail to produce anarchy and confusion.

This attempt to control me in my temporal interests, I conceive to be a disposition to take from me a portion of my Constitutional privileges and inherent right - I only, respectfully, ask leave, therefore, to withdraw from a society assuming they have such right.

So far as relates to the other seven charges, I shall lay them carefully away, and take such a course with regard to them, as I may feel bound by my honor, to answer to my rising posterity.

I beg you, sir, to take no view of the foregoing remarks, other than my belief in the outward government of this Church. I do not charge you, or any other person, who differs with me on these points, of not being sincere; but such a difference does exist, which I sincerely regret.

With considerations of the highest respect, I am, your obedient servant,

OLIVER COWDERY

It is interesting to observe that the Lord in a revelation to Joseph Smith March 20, 1839 Section 121 D&C HC 3:289-300 stated: vs 41-44 No power or influence can or ought to be maintained by virtue of the priesthood, only by persuasion, by long-suffering, by gentleness and meekness, and by love unfeigned; By kindness, and pure knowledge, which shall greatly enlarge the soul without hypocrisy, and without guile. Reproving betimes with sharpness, when moved upon by the Holy Ghost; and then showing forth afterwards an increase of love toward him whom thou hast reproved, lest he esteem thee to be his enemy; that he may know that they faithfulness is stronger than the cords of death. There is no record of Joseph Smith or any others in the Mormon Church ever "showing forth an increase of love" toward Oliver Cowdery or any other person they excommunicated from their church. Was this (Section 121 of the D&C) just an idle piece of meaningless talk? Oliver Cowdery eventually came back and rejoined the Mormon Church on his own in 1848 but those that excommunicated him never "showed forth an increase of love" towards him as God allegedly told us we must do after "reproving betimes with sharpness". The same may be said of many of those that Joseph Smith excommunicated from his church. We are led to ask why this is?

PRIESTHOOD

RESTORATION OF THE MELCHIZEDEK PRIESTHOOD.

The Prophet Joseph, in a communication to the Church, under date of September 6, 1842 *[more than 12 years after the event supposedly occurred]*, makes allusion to the possible appearance by Peter, James and John in the course of a review of the great things God had revealed to him. He said: "And again, what do we hear? Glad tidings from Cumorah. Moroni *(We covered this earlier in this report – someone has evidently inserted the name Moroni for Nephi in this revelation)*, an angel from heaven, declaring the fulfillment of the prophets--the book to be revealed. A voice of the Lord in the wilderness of Fayette, Seneca county, declaring the three witnesses to bear record of the book. The voice of Michael on the banks of the Susquehanna, detecting the devil when he appeared as an angel of light.

The voice of Peter, James and John in the wilderness between Harmony, Susquehanna county, and Colesville, Broome county, on the Susquehanna river, declaring themselves as possessing the keys of the kingdom, and of the Dispensation of the Fullness of Times." (Doctrine and Covenants, sec. cxxviii: 20.) Anything mentioned here about the Melchizedek Priesthood by name?

In one of the early revelations given to the Prophet Joseph, the Lord makes most direct reference to the restoration of the higher

Priesthood through the ministration of Peter, James and John. The subject matter of the revelation is the Sacrament of the Lord's supper; and in the course of it the Lord promises to "drink of the fruit of the vine" with His servants on earth to whom the revelation is addressed; "and with Moroni (Nephi?), * * * and also Michael, or Adam, the father of all, * * * and also with Peter, and James, and John, whom I have sent unto you, by whom I have ordained you and confirmed you to be Apostles, and special witnesses of my name, and bear the keys of your ministry, and of the same things which I revealed unto them; unto whom I have committed the keys of my kingdom, and a dispensation of the gospel for the last times; and for the fullness of times." (Doctrine and Covenants, sec. xxvii).

As this is quoted time and time again it should be noted that nowhere is the Melchizedek Priesthood mentioned, only that they are "ordained to be Apostles and special witnesses of my name".

This revelation was given some time early in August, 1830, but only the first four verses were written at that time. The rest of it was written in September of that year. If these revelations were indeed received in 1830 as B.H. Roberts says, they were not written until after 1833 as they didn't appear in the 1833 Book of Commandments in a form including any mention of Peter, James, & John. These two allusions--the one by the Prophet and the other by the Lord--to the restoration of the Melchizedek Priesthood not only make clear the fact that the Melchizedek Priesthood was restored in accordance with the promise of John the Baptist when conferring the Aaronic Priesthood, but they make it possible to fix upon the place where, and approximately the time when, the event occurred.

Undoubtedly the place where the ordination was performed was on the banks of the Susquehanna river, in the wilderness between Colesville, in Broome county, New York, and Harmony, in Susquehanna county, Pennsylvania; for it is there the Prophet says the voice of Peter, James and John was heard declaring themselves as "possessing the keys of the kingdom, and of the Dispensation of the Fullness of Times;" for which appearing and declaration there is no other occasion than the ordination of Oliver and Joseph to the Melchizedek Priesthood in fulfillment of the promises made by John the Baptist. The time at which the ordination took place was evidently between the 15th of May, 1829, and August, 1830 *[although this was not written until after 1833].* The last named date is the one under which the Lord so definitely referred to the circumstance of having sent Peter, James and John to ordain Joseph and others to be Apostles, even special witnesses of His name, and unto whom He had committed the keys of the kingdom. Hence the time of the ordination must have been between those two dates.

From information contained in other revelations, however, this period within which the Melchizedek Priesthood is claimed to be restored may be considerably reduced. In April, 1830, a revelation was given concerning the organization and government of the Church, and in that revelation the Lord said: "Which commandments [i.e. to organize the Church] were given to Joseph Smith, Jr., who was called of God and ordained an apostle of Jesus Christ to be the first Elder of this Church; and to Oliver Cowdery, who was also called of God, an Apostle of Jesus Christ, to be the second Elder of this Church, and ordained under his hand." (Doctrine and Covenants, sec. xx: 2, 3.) For unknown reasons this was not included in the 1833 Book of Commandments. This reference to the ordination of these men to the office of apostle, (Not the Melchizedek Priesthood) reduces the time of their ordination to the period between the 15th of May, 1829, and April 6, 1830.

But the time within which the ordination took place may be still further reduced. In a revelation bearing the date of June, 1829, making known the calling of the Twelve Apostles in these last days, and addressed to Oliver Cowdery and David Whitmer, the Lord said: "I speak unto you, even as unto Paul mine Apostle, for you are called even with that same calling with which he was called." As this could scarcely be said of men who had not been ordained to the same holy apostleship as that held by Paul, and consequently to the Melchizedek Priesthood, the conclusion is reasonable that the ordination promised by John the Baptist, doubtless occurred some time between May 15, 1829, and the expiration of the month of June of that same year 1829.

From the testimony of Oliver Cowdery, On the occasion of his returning to the Church at Kanesville, Iowa, in the fall of 1848, 18 years after the alledged visitation occurred, after an absence of eleven years from the body of the Saints, in the course of the public address which he then delivered, he said: "I was present with Joseph when an holy angel from God came down from heaven and conferred on us, or restored, the lesser or Aaronic Priesthood, and said to us, at the same time, that it should remain upon the earth while the earth stands. I was also present with Joseph when the higher or Melchizedek Priesthood was conferred by the holy angel from on high. This Priesthood, we then conferred on each other by the will and commandment of God." (History of the Church, Vol. 1, p. 40 footnote) This doesn't agree with Joseph Smith's revelation found in section 128:20 of the Doctrine and Covenants. Joseph Smith did not mention the Melchizedek Priesthood as Oliver Cowdery here does. This reminds us of how Oliver Cowdery changed the story of Joseph Smith's first vision. He has a history of changing Joseph Smith's comments to actually disagree with Joseph smith himself in his circa Summer 1832 hand written version of his first vision.

Doesn't it seem a bit strange that what would have been one of the most miraculous events in the history of Oliver Cowdery's life (Peter, James, & John appearing) is recollected as being "conferred by the Holy Angel"? Oliver doesn't seem to even remember that there were three personages there and that they were the very same Peter, James, and John of the New Testament. He also doesn't seem to remember that the angel that restored the Aaronic Priesthood was the one and only John the Baptist.

"This matter of 'Priesthood,' since the days of Sydney Rigdon, has been the great hobby and stumbling-block of the Latter Day Saints. Priesthood means authority; and authority is the word we should use. I do not think the word priesthood is mentioned in the New Covenant of the Book of Mormon. Authority is the word we used for the first two years in the church--until Sydney Rigdon's days in Ohio. This matter of the two orders of priesthood in the Church of Christ, and lineal priesthood of the old law being in the church, all originated in the mind of Sydney Rigdon. He explained these things to Brother Joseph in his way, out of the old Scriptures, and got Joseph to inquire, etc. He would inquire, and as mouthpiece speak out the revelations just as they had it fixed up in their hearts....according to the desires of the heart, the inspiration comes, but it may be the spirit of man that gives it.... This is the way the High Priests and the 'priesthood' as you have it, was introduced into the Church of Christ *almost two years after* its beginning--and after we had baptized and confirmed about two thousand souls into the church." (An Address To All Believers In Christ, by David Whitmer p. 64)

"You have changed the revelations from the way they were first given and as they are today in the Book of Commandments, to support the error of Brother Joseph in taking upon himself the office of Seer to the church. You have changed the revelations to support the error of high priests. You have changed the revelations to support the error of a President of the high priesthood, high counselors, etc. You have altered the revelations to support you in going beyond the plain teachings of Christ in the new covenant part of the Book of Mormon." (An Address To All Believers In Christ, p. 49)

"The important details that are missing from the 'full history' of 1834 are likewise missing from the Book of Commandments in 1833. The student would expect to find all the particulars of the Restoration in this first treasured set of 65 revelations, the dates of which encompassed the bestowals of the two Priesthoods, but they are conspicuously absent... The notable revelations on Priesthood in the Doctrine and Covenants before referred to, Sections 2 and 13, are missing, and Chapter 28 gives no hint of the Restoration which, if actual, had been known for four years. More than four hundred words were added to this revelation of August, 1829 in Section 27 of the Doctrine and Covenants, the additions made to include the names of heavenly visitors and two separate ordinations. The Book of Commandments gives the duties of Elders, Priests, Teachers, and Deacons and refers to Joseph's apostolic calling but there is no mention of Melchezedek Priesthood, High Priesthood, Seventies, High Priests, nor High Councilors. These words were later inserted into the revelation on Church organization and government of April, 1830, making it appear that they were known at that date, but they do not appear in the original, Chapter 24 of the Book of Commandments three years later. Similar interpolations were made in the revelations known as Sections 42 and 68." (Problems in Mormon Text, by La Mar Petersen, pp. 7-8)

Joseph Smith said, "It was the privilege of every **Elder** present to be ordained to the High Priesthood." (Far West Record, 25 Oct. 1931 - more than two years after the "High Priesthood" was supposedly restored)

"A general conference was called and . . . the Lord made manifest to Joseph that it was necessary that such of the elders as were considered worthy, should be ordained to the high priesthood." (John Whitmer's History, Chapter VII., June 3, 1831)

"The Melchizedek priesthood was then (June 4, 1831) for the first time introduced, and conferred on several of the elders." (John Corrill, *Brief History of the Church of Christ of Latter Day Saints*, 1839, Chapter 10) This shows that the Church of Christ when organized and established by Joseph Smith in 1830 did not have the Melchizedek Priesthood.

"here (June 1831) for the first time I saw the Melchizedek priesthood introduced into the Church" (Apostle Lyman Wight to Wilford

Woodruff, 24 Aug. 1857, Lyman Wight Letterbook, RLDS archives (the original letter is in LDS archives) Again we have confirmation that the Melchizedek Priesthood was not part of the original beginning of the Church of Christ in April of 1830.

"Several were then selected by revelation, through President Smith, and ordained to the High Priesthood after the order of the Son of God, which is after the order of Melchizedek. This was the first occasion in which this priesthood had been revealed and conferred upon the Elders * in this dispensation, although the office of an Elder is the same in a certain degree, but not in the fullness. On this occasion I was ordained to this holy ordinance and calling by President Smith." (Apostle Parley P. Pratt in Chapter 10 of his autobiography) More confirmation that the Melchizedek Priesthood was not in the Church of Christ at its beginning.

"...the authority of the Melchizedek Priesthood was manifested and conferred for the first time upon several of the Elders." (History of the Church) Vol. 1, pages 175-176)

A footnote on page 176 says: *"A misapprehension has arisen in the minds of some respecting the statement 'The authority of the Melchizedek Priesthood was manifested and conferred for the first time upon several of the Elders.' It has been supposed that this passage meant that the higher or Melchizedek Priesthood was now for the first time conferred upon men in this dispensation"* – Let's read again from page 176 "This was the first occasion in which this priesthood had been revealed <u>and conferred</u> upon the Elders in this dispensation" – Why shouldn't it be 'supposed'? Isn't the wording identical in each statement? The revelation regarding Peter, James and John states "by whom I have ordained you and confirmed you to be Apostles". Nothing is said about the Melchizedek Priesthood being conferred upon them. Section 128:20 says ***There were elders then that did not have the Melchizedek Priesthood?**

The voice of Peter, James and John in the wilderness between Harmony, Susquehanna county and Colesville, Broome county, on the Susquehanna river, declaring themselves as possessing the keys of the kingdom, and of the dispensation of the fullness of times!" Again, nothing about the Melchizedek Priesthood by name is mentioned here either.

First it says that this was the "first occasion in which this priesthood (Melchizedek) had been revealed ***and conferred"***. Now the author of the History of the Church Volume 1 says "this of course is an error". Where does he come up with this? Can't we believe what Joseph Smith claimed he received as a revelation from God? And isn't Joseph Smith the author of the church history?

"there was a time when this (LDS) Church was governed by the Lesser Priesthood" (Apostle Orson Pratt)

"...neither did I ever hear of such a thing as an angel ordaining them until I got into Ohio about the year 1834--or later. Oliver stated to me in Joseph's presence that they had baptized each other--seeking by that to fulfill the command. And after our arrival at fathers sometime in June 1829, Joseph ordained Oliver to be an Elder, and Oliver ordained Joseph to be an Elder in the Church of Christ." -- David Whitmer, David Whitmer Interviews, page 154.

Apostle William E. McLellin said "I never heard one word of John the Baptist, or of Peter, James, and John's visit and ordination till I was told some years after while in Ohio"

SIDNEY RIGDON

Few Mormons know the story of Sidney Rigdon. This is the case despite the fact that he influenced Mormonism between 1831 and 1839 more than perhaps anyone--including Joseph Smith. Such doctrines, policies, and key portions of Mormon history like the current two-tiered priesthood structure, moving to Kirtland, temple building, the belief of an immanent second coming in early Mormonism, the Joseph Smith "translation" of the Bible and portions of the Pearl of Great Price, the Word of Wisdom, the United Order, a First Presidency, a salary for some church leaders, the name of the church and the term "Latter-day Saint", the *Lectures on Faith*, a new Jerusalem and Zion in Jackson County, Zion's Camp, and settling in Nauvoo were all due in large part (or exclusively) to Sidney Rigdon. It is very safe to say that Mormonism would be a very different religion today were it not for Sidney Rigdon's influence. He delivered nearly every significant Mormon sermon in the 1830s.

Rigdon was Smith's spokesman. If something needed to be said, Rigdon was a far more likely source than Smith. When visiting other areas of the country or entertaining visitors at home, non-Mormons, who didn't know about Joseph Smith, thought that Rigdon was the leader of the church. In many ways, he was. Although the revelations came through Joseph Smith, Rigdon's finger prints and influence are all over them (and the early changes the 'revelations' underwent).

So why is Rigdon a forgotten source in the LDS Church? The answer can be found in the succession crisis that took place after Smith's death. The history was re-written, modified, and the emphasis changed. About the only story currently told in the LDS church about Rigdon deals with the transfiguration of Brigham Young-an event which never even occurred.

Another significant factor to Rigdon's demise in the eyes of Utah Mormons was the conflict between his daughter and Joseph Smith. Nancy Rigdon, Sidney's daughter, tried to be seduced by Joseph Smith when Smith was actively acquiring new wives. Nancy refused Smith's attempts and word leaked out to others (although Nancy and Sidney kept the issue private). The documentation for this event is abundant including a letter by Joseph Smith to Nancy, which was included in the official History of the Church. In order to make Joseph look good, many leaders of the church attempted to make Nancy look like the promiscuous one. Although Sidney reconciled with Smith, other polygamous church leaders never forgave Rigdon for not accepting and encouraging polygamy.

Rigdon and Smith left Kirtland in order to escape creditors, lawsuits, and possible jail time. The Missouri situation was more complex. Poor judgments were made on both sides which ultimately lead to the Boggs' Extermination Order and Rigdon and others spending time in jail. It also led to the unfortunate death of many Mormons and non-Mormons. Rigdon's "Salt Sermon" and 4th of July speech were two catalysts to the problems that arose. After Brigham Young excommunicated Rigdon, Elder Orson Hyde stated that Rigdon was the "cause of our troubles in Missouri". This is only partially true. Hyde and the others conveniently forgot to mention that Joseph Smith sanctioned both of Rigdon's speeches. Smith had the church's own publication entitled the *Elder's Journal* print one of the speeches and encouraged all church members to purchase a copy and read it. When the "Gentiles" and former Mormons saw and heard what Rigdon said, and experienced the effects of the Mormon aggressions, the troubles heated up. Rigdon's speech included a "war of extermination, for we will follow them, till the last drop of their blood is spilled or else they will have to exterminate us" which led to Apostle Parley P. Pratt's killing of a militiaman and severely wounding another. Boggs responded with the "Extermination Order" and Pratt, Rigdon, Smith and others did jail time before eventually escaping. The anti-Mormons were more brutal in their revenge, however, and eighteen Mormons were murdered at Haun's Mill.

Van Wagoner captures Rigdon's eccentricies (which isn't too difficult to do). He was a man caught up with religion and an immediate second coming of Jesus, which never occurred. He had a mental disorder throughout his life, which caused his personality to swing from one end of the spectrum to the other. His religious excess left a permanent mark on Mormonism. It's difficult to tell if the religious fanatics are the way they are because of the influence of religion or if religions are the way they are because of fanatics.

Sidney Rigdon is wrongly accused for many things. For example, during the succession crisis Brigham Young made much of Rigdon's July 4, 1838 speech as the incipient cause of the Saints' Missouri troubles. You may recall that the speech introduced the word "extermination" into that volatile period, later used infamously by Gov. Boggs. The speech ended with Rigdon exclaiming "We this day proclaim ourselves free, with a purpose and determination, that never can be broken, no never! No never! NO NEVER!" After the speech, which had been carefully prepared and pre-approved by Joseph Smith, the Prophet led the congregation in the Hosanna Shout. Yet, Brigham Young re-wrote this little episode to one in which Rigdon was the villain inciting the Missourians to riot.

Always believing his entire life was his absolute conviction that the Second Coming was imminent, and that he would be alive to see it. That conviction was undoubtedly shared by most members of the church - they really believed that they were engaged in the last gathering prior to the end of time.

Joseph Smith tried to get the Nauvoo postmaster position away from Sidney. Sidney Rigdon continued to report heavenly visions, in the spirit of 76, and other revelations in which God instructed Sidney's followers to support his material needs. But for his connection to Mormonism, I think most contemporary Mormons would be inclined to dismiss Sidney as a ..... "kook."

In the late 1820s a fiery young minister in western Ohio converted nearly 1,000 proselytes to the Reformed Baptist Movement. As these schismatics organized themselves into the new Disciples of Christ church, the Reverend Sidney Rigdon was already aligning himself with another, more radical movement, the Latter-day Saints, where he quickly became the LDS prophet's principal advisor and spokesman. He served Joseph Smith loyally for the next fourteen years, even through a brief spat over the prophet's romantic interest in his teenage daughter.

Next to Smith, Rigdon was the most influential early Mormon. He brought in Reformed Baptist teachings into Latter-day Saint theology, wrote the canonized Lectures on Faith, championed communalism and isolationism, and delivered many of the most significant early sermons, including the famous Salt Sermon and the Ohio temple dedicatory address.

Following Smith's death, Sidney Rigdon parted company with Brigham Young to lead his own group of some 500 secessionist Mormons in Pennsylvania. Rigdon's following gradually dwindled, as the one-time orator took to wandering the streets, taunting indifferent passersby with God's word. He was later recruited by another Mormon faction. Although he refused to meet with them, he agreed to be their prophet and send revelations by mail. Before long he had directed them to settle far-off Iowa and Manitoba, among other things. At his death, his followers numbered in the hundreds, and today they number about 10,000, mostly in Pennsylvania.

Van Wagoner details the evolving story of the alleged transfiguration of Brigham Young into Joseph Smith. Van Wagoner uses the original diaries of the people in attendance at the meeting on August 8, 1844 providing evidence that those there neglected to note the miracle that occurred before their eyes, but later in life the Utah Mormons (including many that weren't even in attendance) describe the transfiguration they supposedly witnessed first hand in great detail. This is a wonderful illustration of how many of the religious myths were/are started. The nice thing about Mormonism is that it is a recent enough religion that by studying it you can see how the myths in basically all religions are formulated.

The new *Ensign* (Aug. 96) has another piece of history falsification. I refer to the article starting on p. 22 about succession in the presidency.

Sidney Rigdon was called on a mission by Joseph Smith, and in doing so fulfilled a revelation that Joseph Smith himself had earlier made. Apostle Orson Hyde said that Joseph Smith had a specific revelation in spring of 1844 commanding Rigdon to go to Pennsylvania.

Apologists criticize Sidney Rigdon for his "lack of loyalty to the Prophet", and cite the 1843 conference [from the heavily revised by Brigham Young *Documentary History of the Church*] where Joseph Smith supposedly wanted him released. They conveniently neglect to mention the heartwarming and complete reconciliation that Sidney Rigdon and Joseph Smith had just a month or so later, which bond was never again broken. They neglect to point out that Sidney Rigdon was subsequently admitted to the Anointed Quorum and the Council of 50, and chosen to be Joseph Smith's vice-presidential running mate, hardly the marks of Joseph Smith having lost faith in him.

Samuel Taylor, in 1989, notes that the contemporary account [of the 1843 conference] in the *Times and Seasons*, the Church paper at Nauvoo [at the time],... says, that President Joseph Smith arose and satisfactorily explained to the congregation the supposed treacherous correspondence with ex-Governor Carlin, which totally removed suspicion from Elder Sidney Rigdon, and from every other person. He expressed his entire willingness to have Sidney Rigdon keep his station. In other words, Smith didn't want Rigdon released, but Brigham Young, later, made it look in the official records as if he did to shore up his claim to the presidency. This was not the first time Brigham Young falsified records in an effort to show the church was always right under his tenure.

Brigham Young and Andrew Jensen (the Church Historian) both claimed John C. Bennett lived a life of misery and suffering in California and died a pauper in disgrace in California. As shown in this study, this is totally incorrect as John C. Bennett died in Iowa, a well respected doctor in his community and has a large headstone on his grave lauding him as a doctor and good member of society in Iowa.

From Brigham Young and Andrew Jensen both testifying so falsely, doesn't it make you wonder about other statements and deeds these men did?

JOSEPH SMITH

The following is taken from Whitney R. Cross' book, The Burned Over District pp 146-150

Mormonism has usually been described as a frontier religion. But study of the circumstances of its origins and its continuing appeal in the area which bred it suggests a different view. The church did not rise during the pioneering era of western New York. Its early recruits came from many sects, but invariably from the longest settled neighborhoods of the region. Joseph's peregrination during the period when he was pregnant with the new religion were always eastward, not westward, from his Manchester home. The first congregations of the church formed at Manchester, Fayette in Seneca County, and Colesville in Broome County. These facts together with the realization of Mormonism's dependence on current excitements and upon myths and doctrines built by the passage of time into the locality's very fabric, demonstrate that the Church of the Saints was not a frontier phenomenon in origin.

Nor did it expand through an appeal to frontiersmen. The far greater gathering of converts from this area came during the region's riper maturity, after Zion itself had removed to the West. And the recruits enlisted here and elsewhere in the East by returning missionaries far outnumbered those gained in areas of the Middle West where Mormon headquarters chanced from time to time to be located. These propositions could best be supported by the church's publication of missionary journals, if they exist in the official archives. Even without that evidence, however, they can be adequately documented from scattered references of orthodox sources to Mormon proselytizing and from an analysis of the nativity figures in the Utah Territorial Census of 1860.

Trial held before justice of the peace in Bainbridge, Chenango County, New York, March 20, 1826 finds Joseph Smith guilty of being a disorderly person and an imposter. The pro-Mormon historians seem to feel that the records showing these facts cannot be used since they were moved from where they were found and so could not then be proved to not have been altered. They do not deny there are records showing this trial There are three other historians, Mr. Stanley Ivins, Mr. Dale L. Morgan and Miss Helen L. Fairbank who confirm the trial and verdict.

From the testimony of Isaac Hale, Josiah Stowell and Peter Ingersoll does it not appear that Joseph Smith was certainly an imposter and a disorderly person according to actual court records of that date and time?

In the body of this report much has been written about Joseph Smith and together with this appendix we may get a fairly accurate portrait of who he really was and how others perceived him.

THE BOOK OF MORMON

Joseph Smith Jr. said that when he was seventeen years of age (this is questionable as he first said he was in his 15th year making him 14, and then later Oliver Cowdery changed it to read that he was in his 17th year – Anybody's guess?) an angel of God named Moroni (again, anybody's guess?...He repeatedly said the angel's name was Nephi but after he died, the records all were changed to read it was Moroni) appeared to him and said that a collection of ancient writings, engraved on gold plates by ancient prophets, was buried in a nearby hill called Comorra in Wayne County, New York. The writings described a people whom God had led from Jerusalem to the Western Hemisphere 600 years before the birth of Christ. According to the narrative, Moroni was the last prophet among these people and had buried the record, which God had promised to bring forth in the latter days. Smith stated that he was instructed by Moroni to meet at the hill annually each September 22 to receive further instructions and that four years after the initial visit, in 1827 he was finally allowed to take the plates and was directed to translate them into English.

Smith's first published description of the plates said the plates "had the appearance of gold", and were described by Martin Harris, one of Smith's early scribes, to be "fastened together in the shape of a book by wires." Smith called the engraved writings on the plates "reformed Egyptian". In addition to Smith's account regarding the plates, eleven others signed affidavits that they persoanlly saw the golden plates and in some cases handled them. All eleven left the Mormon Church by 1847.

Smith enlisted the help of his neighbor, Martin Harris as a scribe during his initial work on the text. Harris mortgaged his farm to underwrite the printing of the Book of Mormon much to the displeasure of his wife, Lucy. She persuaded Martin to have Joseph Smith lend him the current pages that had been translated. Smith reluctantly acceded to Harris' requests. Lucy Harris is thought to have stolen the first 116 pages. After the loss, Smith recorded that he had lost the ability to translate, and that Moroni had taken back the plates to be returned only after Smith repented. Smith later stated that God allowed him to resume translation, but directed that he begin translating another part of the plates. In 1829 with the assistance of Oliver Cowdery the Book of Mormon was completed in a remarkably short time (April-June 1829). The Book of Mormon went on sale at the bookstore of E.B. Grandin on March 26, 1830.

Critics of the Book of Mormon claim that it was fabricated by Smith and that portions of it were plagiarized from various works available to him. Works that have been suggested as sources include the King Jame Bible, The Wonder of Nature, View of the Hebrews, and an unpujblished manuscript written by Solomon Spalding.

Joseph Smith claimed he found gold plates from which he translated them into the Book of Mormon. He then proceeded to claim nobody was allowed to see these plates except three witnesses, one of which later makes us either believe his testimony which includes admitting the Mormon Church has been rejected by God or that his original testimony was false.

David Whitmer later said:

"If you believe my testimony to the Book of Mormon, if you believe that God spake to us three witnesses by his own voice, then I tell you that in June, 1838 God spake to me again by his own voice from the heavens, and told me to separate myself from among the Latter-day Saints, for as they sought to do unto me, so should it be done unto them. In the Spring of 1838 the heads of the church and many of the members had gone deep into error and blindness. I have been striving with them for a long time to show them the errors into which they were driving and for my labors I received only persecutions."

An Address to All Believers in Christ, page 27 by David Whitmer.

About the gold plates…why do you think Joseph Smith wouldn't let anybody see them? Do you believe God would tell him to keep them secret? Did Moses keep the plates with God's ten commandments written on them a secret from the Israelites? Did the Nephite prophets in the Book of Mormon ever keep their writings on the plates secret from the people? Were the plates containing the history of the Jaredites in Book of Mormon ever kept secret so the people couldn't see them? Peter Ingersoll tells us that Joseph Smith never had any gold plates, but only bags of white sand, which he refused to show to anybody and told others they were gold plates. This would certainly be a good reason Joseph Smith refused to show them to anyone.

There is no record of anyone witnessing the Urim and Thummin. Joseph Smith's mother, Lucy Mack Smith, came close when she said she saw them through a thin cloth that was covering them. Yet in D&C 17:1-3 Joseph Smith claims that God tells him" "Behold, I say unto you, that you must rely upon my word, which if you do with full purpose of heart, you shall have a view of the plates, and also of the breastplate, the sword of Laban, the Urim and Thummim, which were given to the brother of Jared upon the mount when he talked with the Lord face to face… (Vs. 3) And after that you have obtained faith, and have seen them with your eyes, you shall testify of them by the power of God":

Where is the testimony of anyone ever seeing the Urim and Thummin? Or the sword of Laban or the breastplate?

2 Corinthians 13:1 tells us that "in the mouth of two or three witnesses shall every word be established".

There is no evidence any of the Book of Mormon was ever translated from the gold plates. The initial publishing of the Book of Mormon claims Joseph Smith is the author, not the translator. It was later changed to show him as the translator after he first tried to sell the copyright for the Book of Mormon in Canada and failed to do so.

"...the Prophet possessed a Seer Stone, by which he was enabled to translate as well as with the Urim and Thummim, and for convenience he sometimes used the Seer Stone. Martin said further that the Seer Stone differed in appearance entirely from the Urim and Thummim that was obtained with the plates, which were two clear stones set in two rims, very much resembling spectacles, only they were larger.

The Seer Stone referred to here was a chocolate-colored, somewhat egg-shaped stone which the Prophet found while digging a well in company with his brother Hyrum, for a Mr. Clark Chase, near Palmyra, N. Y. It possessed the qualities of Urim and Thummim, since by means of it—as described above—as well as by means of the Interpreters found with the Nephite record, Joseph was able to translate the characters engraven on the plates.

Roberts says "for convenience" Joseph Smith "sometimes" used the seer stone. After his first attempt at translating the gold plates and losing the translation to Martin Harris there is no record of him ever using the gold plates again to translate from. From then on he used the Seer Stone in his hat. So where did Roberts come up with his statement that Joseph Smith "sometimes" used the seer stone? Didn't he use it all the time?

Smith's father-in-law, Isaac Hale, said that the "manner in which he pretended to read and interpret was the same as when he looked for the money-diggers, with the stone in his hat, and his hat over his face, while the Book of Plates were at the same time hid in the woods!" (Hale 1834. p. 265).

It seems that Joseph Smith didn't need the gold plates to write his book of Mormon. With the help of Oliver Cowdery and his (Cowdery's) flowery manner of multiplying words as most lawyers seem able to do, Joseph Smtih produced the book of Mormon in a matter of a few months in 1829. All evidence suggests that he did not need any of the assistance the angel Nephi (or Moroni) gave him since he wrote the Book of Mormon with his face in his hat claiming he could see what was necessary to be written down with the aid of the brown stone he placed in his hat. According to his father in law Isaac Hale this was the same manner he used when searching for buried treasure before his claim of finding gold plates.

His initial claim was that he obtained the plates in 1827 and it appears he worked on translating the plates for two years and lost them when Martin Harris gave the translations to his wife. He seems to have been terribly frightened when this happened and was greatly worried that he could not again write the same things down that he had already claimed was his translation of the 116 pages lost and came up with the story that God did not want this 116 pages re-written after all. Why not? Was God afraid also that Joseph Smith could not translate the plates again in the same manner he claimed he already had done? If his "enemies" truly could try to alter his initial writing, so what? How could they prove he had written that part anyway? And even if his "enemies" had the 116 pages why could they not have published them anyway and altered them any way they wished? Why would they have to wait and see if he tried to translate them again and then come forth with their 'altered' version?

Was Joseph involved in treasure digging? Yes he was. Evidence suggests that Joseph quit the money-digging business as he began his work on the Book of Mormon. According to Martin Harris the angel Moroni once told Joseph that "'...he must quit the company of the money-diggers. That there were wicked men among them. He must have no more to do with them'" (Bushman, 74.)

ISAAC HALE

Affidavit of Isaac Hale, father-in-law of Joseph Smith, Jr., given at Harmony Township, Susquehanna County, Pennsylvania on 20 March 1834

S ource: "Mormonism," *Susquehanna Register, and Northern Pennsylvanian* 9 (1 May 1834):1, Montrose, Pennsylvania, emphasis omitted. Paragraphs are shortened for easier reading.

I first became acquainted with Joseph Smith, Jr. in November, 1825. He was at that time in the employ of a set of men who were called "money-diggers;" and his occupation was that of seeing, or pretending to see by means of a stone placed in his hat, and his hat closed over his face. In this way he pretended to discover minerals and hidden treasure. His appearance at this time, was that of a careless young man - not very well educated, and very saucy and insolent to his father.

Smith, and his father, with several other 'money-diggers' boarded at my house while they were employed in digging for a mine that they supposed had been opened and worked by the Spaniards, many years since. Young Smith gave the 'money-diggers' great encouragement, at first, but when they had arrived in digging, to near the place where he had stated an immense treasure would be found - he said the enchantment was so powerful that he could not see. They then became discouraged, and soon after dispersed. This took place about the 17th of November, 1825; and one of the company gave me his note for $12.68 for his board, which furniture &c. to this place. He then returned to Palmyra, and soon after, Alva, agreeable to the arrangement, went up and returned with Smith and his family.

Soon after this, I was informed they had brought a wonderful book of Plates down with them. I was shown a box in which it is said they were contained, which had, to all appearances, been used as a glass box of the common sized window-glass. I was allowed to feel the weight of the box, and they gave me to understand, that the book of plates was then in the box - into which, however, I was not allowed to look and see for myself.

After these occurrences, young Smith made several visits at my house, and he at length asked my consent to his marrying my daughter Emma. This I refused, and gave him my reasons for so doing; some of which were, that he was a stranger, and followed a business that I could not approve; he then left the place. Not long after this, he returned, and while I was absent from home, carried off my daughter, into the state of New York, where they were married without my approbation or consent.

After they had arrived at Palmyra [Manchester] N.Y., Emma wrote to me inquiring whether she could have her property, consisting of clothing, furniture, cows, &c. I replied that her property was safe, and at her disposal. In short time they returned, bringing with them a Peter Ingersoll, and subsequently came to the conclusion that they would move out, and resided upon a place near my residence.

Smith stated to me, that he had given up what he called "glass-looking," and that he expected to work hard for a living, and was willing to do so. He also made arrangements with my son Alva Hale, to go to Palmyra, and move his (Smith's) belongings.

I inquired of Joseph Smith Jr., who was to be the first who would be allowed to see the Book of Plates? He said it was a young child. After this, I became dissatisfied, and informed him that if there was any thing in my house of that description, which I could not be allowed to see, he must take it away; if he did not, I was determined to see it. After that, the Plates were said to be hid in the woods.

About this time, Martin Harris made his appearance upon the stage; and Smith began to interpret the characters or hieroglyphics which he said were engraven upon the plates, while Harris wrote down the interpretation. It was said, that Harris wrote down one hundred and sixteen pages, and lost them.

Soon after this happened, Martin Harris informed me that he must have a greater witness, and said that he had talked with Joseph about it - Joseph informed him that he could not, or durst not show him the plates, but that he (Joseph) would go into the woods where the Book of Plates was, and that after he came back, Harris should follow his track in the snow, and find the Book, and examine it for himself. Harris informed me afterwards, that he followed Smith's directions, and could not find the Plates, and was still dissatisfied.

The next day after this happened, I went to the house where Joseph Smith Jr., lived, and where he and Harris were engaged in their translation of the Book. Each of them had a written piece of paper which they were comparing, and some of the words were "my servant seeketh a greater witness, but no greater witness can be given him." There was also something said about "three that were to see the thing" - meaning I supposed, the Book of Plates, and that "if the three did not go exactly according to orders, the thing would be taken from them." I enquired whose words they were, and was informed by Joseph or Emma, (I rather think it was the former) that they were the words of Jesus Christ. I told them then, that I considered the whole of it a delusion, and advised them to abandon it.

The manner in which he pretended to read and interpret, was the same as when he looked for the money-diggers, with the stone in his hat, and his hat over his face, while the Book of Plates were at the same time in the woods!

After this, Martin Harris went away, and Oliver Cowdery came and wrote for Smith, while he interpreted as above described. This is the same Oliver Cowdery, whose name may be found in the Book of Mormon. Cowdery continued as scribe for Smith until the Book of Mormon was completed as I supposed, and understood.

Joseph Smith Jr. resided near me for some time after this, and I had a good opportunity of becoming acquainted with him, and somewhat acquainted with his associates, and I conscientiously believe from the facts I have detailed, and from many other circumstances, which I do not deem it necessary to relate, that the whole "Book of Mormon" (so called) is a silly fabrication of falsehood and wickedness, got up for speculation, and with a design to dupe the credulous and unwary - and in order that its fabricators might live upon the spoils of those who swallowed the deception.

ISAAC HALE.

Affirmed to and subscribed before me, March 20th, 1834.

CHARLES DIMON, Justice. [of the] Peace.

PETER INGERSOLL

Peter Ingersoll Statement on Joseph Smith, Jr.

Palmyra, Wayne Co. N. Y. Dec. 2d, 1833.

I, Peter Ingersoll, first became acquainted with the family of Joseph Smith, Sen. in the year of our Lord, 1822. -- I lived in the neighborhood of said family, until about 1830; during which time the following facts came under my observation.

The general employment of the family, was digging for money. I had frequent invitations to join the company, but always declined being one of their number. They used various arguments to induce me to accept of their invitations. I was once ploughing near the house of Joseph Smith, Sen. about noon, he requested me to walk with him a short distance from his house, for the purpose of seeing whether a mineral rod would work in my hand, saying at the same time he was confident it would. As my oxen were eating, and being myself at leisure, I accepted the invitation. -- When we arrived near the place at which he thought there was money, he cut a small witch hazle bush and gave me direction how to hold it. He then went off some rods, and told me to say to the rod, "work to the money," which I did, in an audible voice. He rebuked me severely for speaking it loud, and said it must be spoken in a whisper. This was rare sport for me. While the old man was standing off some rods, throwing himself into various shapes, I told him the rod did not work. He seemed much surprised at this, and said he thought he saw it move in my hand. It was now time for me to return to my labor. On my return, I picked up a small stone and was carelessly tossing it from one hand to the other. Said he, (looking very earnestly) what are you going to do with that stone? Throw it at the birds, I replied. No, said the old man, it is of great worth; and upon this I gave it to him. Now, says he, if you only knew the value there is back of my house (and pointing to a place near) -- *there,* exclaimed he, is one chest of gold and another of silver. He then put the stone which I had given him, into his hat, and stooping forward, he bowed and made sundry maneuvers, quite similar to those of a stool pigeon. At length he took down his hat, and being very much exhausted, said, in a faint voice, "if you knew what I had seen, you would believe." To see the old man thus try to impose upon me, I confess, rather had a tendency to excite contempt than pity. Yet I thought it best to conceal my feelings, preferring to appear the dupe of my credulity, than to expose myself to his resentment. His son Alvin then went through with the same performance, which was equally disgusting. Another time, the said Joseph, Sen. told me that the best time for digging money, was, in the heat of summer, when the heat of the sun caused the chests of money to rise near the top of the ground. You notice, said he, the large stones on the top of the ground -- we call them rocks, and they truly appear so, but they are, in fact, most of them chests of money raised by the heat of the sun. At another time, he told me that the ancient inhabitants of this country used camels instead of horses. For proof of this fact, he stated that in a certain hill on the farm of Mr. Cuyler, there was a cave containing an immense value of gold and silver, stands of arms, also, a saddle for a camel, hanging on a peg at one side of the cave. I asked him, of what kind of wood the peg was. He could not tell, but said it had become similar to stone or iron. The old man at last laid a plan which he thought would accomplish his design. His cows and mine had been gone for some time, and were not to be found, notwithstanding our diligent search for them. Day after day was spent in fruitless search, until at length he proposed to find them by his art of divination. So he took his stand near the corner of his house, with a small stick in his hand, and made several strange and peculiar motions, and then said he could go directly to the cows. So he started off, and went into the woods about one hundred rods distant and found the lost cows. But on finding out the secret of the mystery, Harrison had found the cows, and drove them to the above named place, and milked them. So that this stratagem turned out rather more to his profit that it did to my edification. -- The old man finding that all his efforts to make me a money digger, had proved abortive, at length ceased his importunities. One circumstance, however, I will mention before leaving him. Some time before young Joseph found, or pretended to find, the gold plates, the old man told me that in Canada, there had been a book found, in a hollow tree, that gave an account of the first settlement of this country before it was discovered by Columbus.

In the month of August, 1827, I was hired by Joseph Smith, Jr. to go to Pennsylvania, to move his wife's household furniture up to Manchester, where his wife then was. When we arrived at Mr. Hale's, in Harmony, Pa. from which place he had taken his wife, a scene presented itself, truly affecting. His father-in-law (Mr. Hale) addressed Joseph, in a flood of tears: "You have stolen my daughter and married her. I had much rather have followed her to her grave. You spend your time in digging for money -- pretend to see in a stone, and thus try to deceive people." Joseph wept, and acknowledged he could not see in a stone now, nor never could; and that his former pretensions in that respect, were all false. He then promised to give up his old habits of digging for money and looking into stones. Mr. Hale told Joseph, if he would move to Pennsylvania and work for a living, he would assist him in getting into business. Joseph acceded to this proposition. I then returned with Joseph and his wife to Manchester. One circumstance occurred on the road, worthy of notice, and I believe this is the only instance where Jo ever exhibited true yankee wit. On our journey to Pennsylvania, we could not make the exact change at the toll gate near Ithaca. Joseph told the gate tender, that he would "hand" him the toll on his return, as he was coming back in a few days. On our return, Joseph tendered to him 25 cents, the toll being 12 1/2. He did not recognize Smith, so he accordingly gave him back the 12 1/2 cents. After we had passed the gate, I asked him if he did not agree to pay double gatage on our return? No, said he, I agreed to *"hand"* it to him, and I did, but he handed it back again.

Joseph told me on his return, that he intended to keep the promise which he had made to his father-in-law; but, said he, it will be hard for me, for they will all oppose, as they want me to look in the stone for them to dig money: and in fact it was as he predicted. They urged him, day after day, to resume his old practice of looking in the stone. -- He seemed much perplexed as to the course he should pursue. In this dilemma, he made me his confidant and told me what daily transpired in the family of Smiths. One day he came, and greeted me with a joyful countenance. -- Upon asking the cause of his unusual happiness, he replied in the following language: "As I was passing, yesterday, across the woods, after a heavy shower of rain, I found, in a hollow, some beautiful white sand, that had been washed up by the water. I took off my frock, and tied up several quarts of it, and then went home. On my entering the house, I found the family at the table eating dinner. They were all anxious to know the contents of my frock. At that moment, I happened to think of what I had heard about a history found in Canada, called the golden Bible; so I very gravely told them it was the golden Bible. To my surprise, they were credulous enough to believe what I said. Accordingly I told them that I had received a commandment to let no one see it, for, says I, no man can see it with the naked eye and live.*[43] However, I offered to take out the book and show it to them, but they refused to see it, and left the room." Now, said Joe, "I have got the damned fools fixed, and will carry out the fun." Notwithstanding, he told me he had no such book, and believed there never was any such book, yet, he told me that he actually went to Willard Chase, to get him to make a chest, in which he might deposit his golden Bible. But, as Chase would not

---

[43] * *How did HE get to see these "plates" with the 'naked' eye then?*

do it, he made a box himself, of clap-boards, and put it into a pillow case, and allowed people only to lift it, and feel of it through the case.

In the fall of 1827, Joseph wanted to go to Pennsylvania. His brother-in-law had come to assist him in moving, but he himself was out of money. He wished to borrow the money of me, and he presented Mr. Hale as security. I told him in case he could obtain assistance from no other source, I would let him have some money. Joseph then went to Palmyra; and, said he, I there met that dam fool, Martin Harris, and told him that I had a command to ask the first honest man I met with, for fifty dollars in money, and he would let me have it. I saw at once, said Jo, that it took his notion, for he promptly gave me the fifty.

Joseph thought this sum was sufficient to bear his expenses to Pennsylvania. So he immediately started off, and since that time I have not been much in his society. While the Smiths were living at Waterloo, William visited my neighborhood, and upon my inquiry how they came on, he replied, "we do better there than here; we were too well known here to do much.

PETER INGERSOLL.

State of New York, Wayne County, ss:

I certify, that on this 9th day of December, 1833, personally appeared before me the above named Peter Ingersoll, to me known, and made oath, according to law, to the truth of the above statement.

TH. P. BALDWIN,
Judge of Wayne County Court.

JOSEPH SMITH SR.

Joseph Smith, Sr.'s dream

According to Lucy Mack Smith, Joseph Smith, Senior, the father of the Prophet, had the following dream in 1811 when the family was living in Lebanon, New Hampshire. Joseph Smith, Junior, would have been 5 years old at the time.

> I thought...I was traveling in an open, desolate field, which appeared to be very barren. As I was thus traveling, the thought suddenly came into my mind that I had better stop and reflect upon what I was doing, before I went any further. So I asked myself, "What motive can I have in traveling here, and what place can this be?" My guide, who was by my side, as before, said, "This is the desolate world; but travel on." The road was so broad and barren that I wondered why I should travel in it; for, said I to myself, "Broad is the road, and wide is the gate that leads to death, and many there be that walk therein; but narrow is the way, and straight is the gate that leads to everlasting' life, and few there be that go in thereat."

> Traveling a short distance farther, I came to a narrow path. This path I entered, and, when I had traveled a little way in it, I beheld a beautiful stream of water, which ran from the east to the west. Of this stream I could see neither the source nor

yet the termination; but as far as my eyes could extend I could see a rope running along the bank of it, about as high as a man could reach, and beyond me was a low, but very pleasant valley, in which stood a tree such as I had never seen before. It was exceedingly handsome, insomuch that I looked upon it with wonder and admiration. Its beautiful branches spread themselves somewhat like an umbrella, and it bore a kind of fruit, in shape much like a chestnut bur, and as white as snow, or, if possible whiter. I gazed upon the same with considerable interest, and as I was doing so the burs or shells commenced opening and shedding their particles, or the fruit which they contained, which was of dazzling whiteness. I drew near and began to eat of it, and I found it delicious beyond description. As I was eating, I said in my heart, "I can not eat this alone, I must bring my wife and children, that they may partake with me." Accordingly, I went and brought my family, which consisted of a wife and seven children, and we all commenced eating, and praising God for this blessing. We were exceedingly happy, insomuch that our joy could not easily be expressed.

While thus engaged, I beheld a spacious building standing opposite the valley which we were in, and it appeared to reach to the very heavens. It was full of doors and windows, and they were filled with people, who were very finely dressed. When these people observed us in the low valley, under the tree, they pointed the finger of scorn at us, and treated us with all manner of disrespect and contempt. But their contumely we utterly disregarded.

I presently turned to my guide, and inquired of him the meaning of the fruit that was so delicious. He told me it was the pure love of God, shed abroad in the hearts of all those who love him, and keep his commandments. He then commanded me to go and bring the rest of my children. I told him that we were all there. "No," he replied, "look yonder, you have two more, and you must bring them also." Upon raising my eyes, I saw two small children, standing some distance off. I immediately went to them, and brought them to the tree; upon which they commenced eating with the rest, and we all rejoiced together. The more we ate, the more we seemed to desire, until we even got down upon our knees, and scooped it up, eating it by double handfuls.

After feasting in this manner a short time, I asked my guide what was the meaning of the spacious building which I saw. He replied, "It is Babylon, it is Babylon, and it must fall. The people in the doors and windows are the inhabitants thereof, who scorn and despise the Saints of God because of their humility."

I soon awoke, clapping my hands together for joy.

Connections

There are many obvious connections between this dream and Lehi's vision of the tree of life recorded in 1 Nephi 8 :

- A desolate field representing the world (8:4).
- A narrow path (8:20).
- A river of water (8:13).
- A rope running along the bank of the river (similar in function to the rod of iron in 8:19, 24).
- A tree with dazzling white fruit (8:10–11).
- Joseph, Sr. desires that his family should partake of the fruit also (8:12).
- A spacious building filled with people who are mocking those who eat the fruit (8:26–27).
- Joseph, Sr. and his family ignore the mocking (8:33).
- The fruit represents the love of God (11:22).
- The building represents the world (11:36; 12:18).

Source

The source of the dream is Lucy's manuscript for Joseph Smith, The Prophet And His Progenitors For Many Generations, which she dictated to Martha Jane Coray in the winter of 1844–45. Note the date of Lucy's dictation: more than 15 years after Joseph Smith, Junior, dictated the Book of Mormon.

BOOK OF JOHN WHITMER

In volume one of the Joseph Smith Papers the historians tell us that John Whitmer refused to deliver up his papers upon his excommunication from the church. In volume two of the Joseph Smith Papers we are told "Historical evidence also suggests that Whitmer made the extant copy of the entire history in1838, Following Whitmer's excommunication in March 1838, church leaders made a concentrated effort to obtain the records in his possession. This effort was partially successful: Whitmer apparently turned over a copied list of names of members who had resided in Missouri and possibly made available some minutes he had kept." Footnote 23 page 8 Vol 2 Joseph Smith Papers Histories.

Were the historians in error when they stated in volume 1 that he refused to deliver up his papers? Why would they tell us Whitmer refused to deliver up his papers and then in volume 2 tell us the church was "partially successful" in obtaining some of his records?

In Vol. 1 of Histories, page xxii Joseph Smith "sought unsuccessfully to obtain from John Whitmer the historical materials in his custody." So was he unsuccessful or *partially* successful in obtaining John Whitmer's records?

Yet again the historians tell us on page 9 of Vol 2 Histories "After his estrangement from the church, Whitmer refused to relinquish the manuscript (History) for printing." Where is the "partial" success in gaining access to Whitmer's history?

John Whitmer was given his assignment to keep a record for the church on April 9, 1831 "when he was assigned to 'keep the Church record & history by the voice of ten Elders'." Vol. 2 Histories page 5 and as noted below on page 8 says that John Whitmer felt June 12, 1831 "corresponds to his own starting date". Why do we have two different dates for John Whitmer starting his history, April 9 and June 12, 1831?

On June 9, 1830 "Oliver Cowdery was 'appointed to keep the Church record and Conference minutes,' thus becoming the church's first official record keeper." Joseph Smith Papers Histories Volume 1 pp. xvii

On page 8 Volume 2 Histories we read: "John Whitmer's reference to 12 June 1831 as Oliver Cowdery's stopping point corresponds to his own starting date...The March 1831 revelation officially released Cowdery from his duties". We have two different dates so far for John Whitmer starting his history, let's try for three different dates. D&C 47:1 March 8, 1831 "Behold it is expedient in me that my servant John should write and keep a regular history and assist you, my servant Joseph, in transcribing all things which shall be given you, until he is called to further duties."

Joseph Smith and Sidney Rigdon wrote to John Whitmer and in the letter stated "knowing your incompetency as a historian" and then "we never supposed you capable of writing a history". Page 9 Volume 2 Histories So it would appear the appointment by the 10 elders naming him as historian shows a disagreement between them and Joseph Smith and Sidney Rigdon in their letter to Whitmer? "Knowing" his incompetency? The Lord gave a revelation to Joseph Smith about John Whitmer keeping a history of "all the important things which he shall observe and know concerning my church". D&C 47:1, D&C 69:3 Would it be wrong for us to assume the Lord felt John Whitmer was "competent"? And we may ask why Joseph Smith and Sidney Rigdon "never supposed" Whitmer "capable of writing a history". As shown from the two revelations quoted herein does it not seem that the Lord felt John Whitmer was certainly competent as an historian?

SUMMARY

So many questions and so few answers! Let us review what we have learned from this effort of inquiry.

First, Joseph Smith founded the Church of Jesus Christ of Latter-day saints. He claimed to have received a vision of Jesus Christ. At no time was he hesitant to talk about Jesus Christ, nor were any of his associates. It seems clear that Jesus Christ is the most important individual we need to relate to while in this life. Joseph Smith taught that Jesus Christ was the only begotten Son of God and thus a very sacred and holy individual. Indeed Jesus Christ is our intermediary with the Heavenly Father. He is indeed very sacred and holy.

Second, Joseph Smith established the idea of building temples. In these temples he established ordinances and ceremonies and claimed people had to follow these ordinances and ceremonies to get into the kingdom of God. Further, the current teachings of the Church of Jesus Christ of Latter-day Saints tells us these ordinances and ceremonies are so sacred and important that we cannot talk about them outside of the temples of the church. Doesn't this seem strange that these ordinances and ceremonies are more important even than Jesus Christ himself? Why can we talk about the most holy and sacred person ever in the history of the world whether we are in a temple or outside a temple, but cannot talk about secret ordinances and ceremonies that appear to certainly be subordinate to Jesus Christ himself?

Nowhere in our studies have we ever found God or Jesus Christ telling us that we cannot talk about certain things because they are too sacred. What is going on here?

While in the temple people tell us not to talk about anything that goes on in here. Where did this teaching of secrecy originate? Did Joseph Smith ever preach such an idea? Who came up with this idea?

Why do we not find any revelation of Joseph Smith regarding the temple ceremonies? He claimed to receive revelations from Jesus Christ in matters as trivial as vacations and milk skimmings that his wife was taking advantage of their neighbor yet nowhere can we find a single revelation about temple ceremonies. Why?

Who came up with the idea we had to wear special underwear after going through the temple ceremonies? Who came up with the idea this underwear is some kind of protection against accidents or whatever and we should wear them all the time outside of the temple? Can we find any support for these ideas anywhere in any of the scriptures available to us today? Do we really believe someone received a revelation from God telling us we didn't have to keep wearing this underwear down to the ankles and wrists?

Are we to believe that whenever the ordinances of the Gospel are changed it is because God has revealed this was to have to occur? While Joseph Smith lived he received revelations for virtually everything going on with the church. If any changes were made in the church you could trace the change to a particular revelation Joseph Smith claimed God gave him. If this was the way God wanted to deal with his prophet, why didn't he continue in this manner after Joseph Smith was removed from the church? Why are we now to simply assume that whenever a change is made in the church beliefs and teachings, we must accept these changes because the current leader of the church seemed to give his approval? Why did Joseph

Smith have to have a revelation about individual things but we no longer require that now Joseph Smith is gone?

Third, in keeping with this inquiry, why didn't Joseph Smith tell us the exact revelation of Peter, James and John appearing to him and conferring the Melchizedek Priesthood on him? He did this with the Aaronic Priesthood when John the Baptist appeared to him and Oliver Cowdery.

Can we have some kind of consistency in this study? Why did Joseph Smith claim the old testament prophets practiced polygamy? Did he really believe this to be the case after studying the Bible? What about Adam, and all his descendants down to Abraham? Did any of them practice polygamy? Did Noah or Job have more than one wife? Does his inference in the Book of Mormon that God might require polygamy of his people to build up a righteous following relate to the church after it was established? If so, why didn't God create a second wife or more for Adam when he was supposedly the first man on earth? Indeed did Jesus Christ have more than one wife? Did any of his followers mentioned in the Bible? Doesn't the Bible state that a deacon or bishop must be the husband of one wife? Why don't deacons in the Church of Jesus Christ of Latter-day Saints have one wife? Why are they 12 year old boys who are all single?

Even more astounding – where in any scriptures does it condone or encourage a man to have sexual relationships with another mans wife? Expand this to the entire history of the world and include any religious belief of any kind and where is this teaching approved or practiced? Has it ever been practiced by any society in the entire history of the world? Is it even condoned in those Arabic societies that practice polygamy today?

Orson Pratt and William Law both left the church due to Joseph Smith trying to claim he was to have their wives married to him at the same time so he could engage in intimate relationships with them.

There is no evidence whatsoever that Joseph Smith fathered any male children through all of his sexual activities with other women than Emma, his first wife. Yet aren't we led to believe this is the excuse he gave for having sexual relations with all these women and particularly women who were already married to other men? To raise up a righteous generation? Is immorality righteous?

SPLINTER GROUPS OFF THE CHURCH OF JESUS CHRIST OF LATTER-DAY SAINTS

Additional information that may assist the reader in understanding the nature of those individuals that were instrumental in assisting Joseph Smith Jr. to organize and develop his different ideas is presented here. What type of people are they? By studying the various splinter groups that trace their origins back to Joseph Smith Jr. Ideas and beliefs might show how stable they really were themselves. Were they seeking followers as they had done when associating with Joseph Smith Jr.? Was it recognition they were after? Did they seriously believe what they were doing was correct? Does this also show some concerns to us about whether to believe them when they were associated with Joseph Smith Jr.? Were they mentally stable people?

Is their any evidence John Whitmer ever heard of Joseph Smith Jr. claiming to have received revelations? He actually was the official church historian in 1831, a year after Joseph Smith Jr. Established his church. Is it reasonable to believe an individual of such import as the official church historian would not be aware of Joseph Smith Jr.s claim that he had seen and talked with God and angels?

What about David Whitmer? He later admitted he never actually saw or touched the gold plates but thought he witnessed them in his mind.

What kind of a testimony is this? He is one of the three witnesses to the gold plates.

By examining some of the splinter groups that trace their origin back to the Joseph Smith Jr. Group, can we learn more about what type of people these men were? What motivated them? How sincere is a person who goes from one belief to another?

Are we seriously expected to believe God began to give revelations to various men in addition to Joseph Smith Jr.? Why are many of these revelations contrary to those that Joseph Smith Jr. claimed to have?

While active in the original Mormon Church aren't we to believe these same individuals bore their testimony of the Book of Mormon and other revelations that Joseph Smith Jr. Received?

Perhaps by studying their actions throughout their lives we can understand better the type of people they really are?

Alston Church

Isaac Russell (April 13, 1807 – September 25, 1844) was a leader in the early Latter-day Saints movement. Russell held a number of positions of responsibility, including being one of the first missionaries to England, with Heber C. Kimball, Willard Richards, Orson Hyde and Joseph Fielding. He also organized the Alston branch in 1837.

As the Latter-day Saints were fleeing Missouri in the winter of 1838-1839 Russell claimed to have received revelations directing him to remain in Missouri by leading the church into Indian Territory where the three Nephites would join them to convert the Lamanites. His organization was called the Alston Church.

On April 26, 1839 Russell, along with most, if not all, of his followers were excommunicated. After his death, Russell's widow and children moved to Utah Territory and rejoined the Church of Jesus Christ of Latter-day Saints.

Apostolic Divine Church of Ghana

Joseph William Billy Johnson (Born Dec. 17, 1934) was one of the first converts to the Church of Jesus Christ of Latter-day Saints in Ghana, Africa. Prior to his baptism, he had worked for many years to spread the doctrines of the LDS Church of many of his fellow countrymen.

Johnson was born in Lagos, Nigeria. He grew up in the Roman Catholic faith. In 1964 Johnson learned about the Book of Mormon from Frank A. Mensah. Upon receiving a copy of the Book of Mormon, Johnson started "Latter-day Saint" congregations in Ghana independent from any other Latter-day sect.

Although he was not able to be baptized at this time, Johnson did receive support and encouragement in sharing the faith with others such as Marrill J. Bateman.

Johnson moved to Capt Coast, Ghana, in 1976 where he set up at least ten congregations there and in the surrounding areas. Some of Cape Coast group of these independent Latter-day Saint congregations in Ghana schismed when ongoing contact was not established with the LDS or RLDS churches. Some of the individuals in this group formed the Apostolic Divine Church of Ghana, however, this sect only lasted a few months

Johnson was finally baptized into the LDS Church on Dec. 9, 1978, a few months after Spencer w. Kimball amended the Mormon Church's postion and made a statement that allowed black people of African descent to hold the Priesthood.

Apostolic United Brethren

The Apostolic United BBrethren's claims to authority come from the accounts of John W. Woolley, Lorin Calvin Woolley and others, relating to a meeting in September 1886 between LDS Church President John Taylor, the Woolleys, and others. Prior to the meeting Taylor is said to have met with Jesus Christ and Joseph Smith, Jr. and to have received a revelation commanding that plural marriage should not cease, but be kept alive by a group separate from the LDS Church. The following day, the Woolleys, as well as Taylors' counselor, George Q. Cannon, and others, were said to have been set apart to keep "the principle" alive, the "principle" being polygamy. They claim that Jesus Christ and Joseph Smith appeared to the Wooley's and others in a special place in Bountiful, Utah and were given special ordinations to allow them to continue practicing plural marriage and keep this doctrine alive until the second coming of christ.

Members of the Apostolic United Brethren believe their history goes back to Joseph Smith and to the beliefs he preached and practices he established. They believe that the Churchof Jesus Christ of Latter-day Saints has made unacceptable changes to doctrines and ordinances. The members of the Apostolic United Brethren believe it is their responsibility to keep them alive in the same form they were originally given and to live all the laws God has commanded. Each doctrine or practice they felt had been changed or abandoned by the church of Jesus Christ of Latter-day Saints is in turn continued on by the Apostolic United Brethren.

Until the 1950s, Mormon fundamentalists were largely one group, but with the ordination in 1951 of Rulon C. Allred by Joseph W. Musser, who than presided over the fundamentalists this group broke in two with one group led by Rulon Jeffs moving to Shortcreek, Arizona, a name later changed to Colorado City for the portion of members living on the Arizona side of the border and Hilldale, Utah for the others members living on the Utah side of the border. Rulon Jeffs still resided in Salt Lake City, actually in a large mansion house located at the mouth of Little Cottonwood Canyon and directed the affairs of the group of members who moved to southern Utah. Those members in Colorado City, Arizona became more distant. Within a few years they formed their own group which is now called the Fundamentalist Church of Jesus Christ of Latter-day Saints.

The shooting and killing of Rulon C. Allred by Rena Chynoweth, a daughter of Ervil LeBaron on May 10, 1977 and acting under the direction of Ervil LeBaron, brought the Apostolic United Brethren into the spotlight. Rulon C. Allred was succeeded by his brother, Owen A. Allred, who died in February 2005 and was replaced by his successor, J. LaMoine Jenson.

The two groups now exist independently of each other.

Church of Christ – Brewsterites

This was a branch of the Latter-day Saint movement that was founded in 1848 by James C. Brewster and Hazen Aldrich. Because of the church's belief that Brewster was a prophet, the group is often called the Brewsterites.

After the death of Joseph Smith, Jr., William McLellin and other early church leaders returned to Kirtland, Ohio to pick up the remnants of the church there. The group adopted the original name of the Latter-day Saint Church, The Church of Christ. Two principles of the movement were to (1) accept David Whitmer as leader, and (2) declare Kirtland as the proper center of the church.

At the organization of the church in Springfield, Illinois, Aldrich was selected as the organization's first president. He selected Brewster and James Goodale as his counselors in the First Presidency. John

E. Page, one of the original members of the Quorum of the Twelve followed this movement.

In October 1849 a newspaper article indicated that Kirtland was a temporary headquarters, and they planned to move to California. On June 23, 1849 the group held a General Assembly in the Kirtland Temple. Six members accepted Brewster's revelation. In 1850 Brewster declared that there was a land called "Bashan" in the Rio Grande Valley that God had selected as the new gthathering place for the church. In 1851 Brewster and Goodale led a wagon train of followers to find Bashan, while Aldrich, who had began to doubt Brewster's prophetic abilities, remained behind in Kirtland. There were disagreements between Brewster and Goodale and among the other members of the church on the journey to Bashan, and most of Brewster's followers, including Olive Oatman and her family, deserted Brewster and headed for California. Brester also settled in California and the church was never reorganized.

Church of Christ – Booth

Ezra Booth (born in 1792 in Coonnecticut) was an early member in the Latter-day Saint movement. Booth had been a popular Methodiest minsiter before going to Kirtland, Ohio with John and Alice (Elsa) Johnson in 1831. After witnessing Joseph Smith, Jr. healing Elsa's arm Booth became a convert and was baptized and ordained an elder in May 1831 and later was ordained to be a high priest by Lyman Wight on June 3, 1831.

On June 6, 1831, Booth was called to go to Missouri with Isaac Morely and "preach the word by the way". Booth began his mission by preaching the Book of Mormon to a large audience in Bates Corner, Norton Township, Ohio in June 1831. On August 4, 1831, Booth was one of fourteen elders attending a "Special Conference" in Kaw township, Jackson County, Missouri, held by special commandment of the Lord" called by Joseph Smith, Jr.

On September 6, 1831, Booth was "silenced from preaching as an Elder" by Smith. Sidney Rigdon, Oliver Cowdery and others. The Prophet Joseph Smith expressed that this was because of Booth's dissension towards the leaders of the church, and his apparent lack of humility. A prophecy by Smith came a few days later and stated that:

"I the Lord, was angry with him who was my servant Ezra Booth, and also my servant Isaac Morely, for they kept not the law, neither the commandment; they sought evil in their hearts. They condemned for evil that thing in which there was no evil; nevertheless I have forgiven my servant Isaac Morely."

Less than three days after being "silenced from preaching as an Elder", and after only being a member for five months, Booth renounced Mormonism in the first of nine letters to be published in the Ohio Sar, beginning in November 1831.

Information about Booth after 1831 is scarce. However, he did marry a couple in Mentor, Ohio on January 16, 1832 and later created the "Church of Christ". His

"Church of Christ" claimed that Joseph Smith, Jr. was a false prophet and that the Book of Mormon was not true. The church had several meetings and soon disbanded.

Church of Christ (Hancock) also known as the Basement Church.

The Church of Christ (Lukeite) and the Church of Christ (Bible and Book of Mormon Teaching) was a sect of the Latter-day Saint movement founded in Indepnedence in 1946 by Pauline Hancock. This church, which became defunct in 1984 bears the distinction of being the first Latter-day Saint sect to be founded by a woman. Among its members were Jerald and Sandra Tanner, who later became well-known opponents of the Latter-day Saint movement in Utah with their "Utah Lighthouse Ministry".

Church of Christ – Hiram Page

Hiram Page (1800-August 12, 1852) was born in Vermont. Earlier in his life, he studied medicine which he practiced during his travels throughout New York and Canada. On Novembeer 10, 1825, Page married Catherine Whitmer, daughter of Peter Whitmer, Sr. and Mary Musselman. The two had nine children togetehr: John, Elizabeth, Philander, Mary, Peter, Nancy, Hiram, Oliver, and Kate.

Page became one of the eight witnesses to the gold plates during June 1829. He and Catherine were baptized on April 11, 1830 by Oliver Cowdery. On June 9, he was ordained a teacher in the church, one of the first twelve officers. Sometime after the Book of Mormon was finished, Hiram Page and Oliver Cowdery were sent to Ontario, Canada by Joseph Smith for the purpose of selling the Bok of Mormon and were promised success in their efforts. They failed completely in their mission and returned to Joseph Smith with the Book of Mormon not sold.

While Page was living with the Whitermes in Fayette, New York, Joseph Smith, Jr. arrived in August 1830 to discover Hiram using a "seerstone" to receive revelations for the church. The only available detail about the stone was that it was black. The revelations were regarding the organization and location of Zion. Oliver Cowdery and the Whitmer family (and possibly others) believed the revelations Page had received were true. In response Joseph Smith received a revelation during the conference in September of that year to have Oliver Cowdery go to Hiram and convince him that his revelations were of the devil (D&C Section 28:11). Hiram agreed to discard the stone and the revelations he received and join in following Joseph Smith as the sole revelator for the church. The members present confirmed this unanimously with a vote.

Page and other members of the Whitmer family were excommunicated from the church of Jesus Christ of Latter-day Saints in 1838. William

E. M'Lellin baptized Hiram Page, David Whitmer, John Whitmer, and Jacob Whitmer on September 6, 1847 into his newly formed Church of Christ. Williams ordained Hiram a high priest in the church. Hiram participated in the subsequent ordinations of the others. He died on his farm in Excelsior Springs, Missouri on August 12, 1852, still affirming his testimony of the Book of Mormon.

Church of Christ – Parrishites

Warren Parrish (Jan. 10, 1803 – Jan. 3, 1877) was a leader in the early Latter-day Saint movement Parrish held a number of positions of responsibility, including that of scribe to church president Joseph Smith Jr. Parrish and other leaders became disillusioned with Smith after the failure of the Kirtland Safety Society and left the church. Parrish remained in Kirtland, Ohio with other disaffected former church leaders and formed a short-lived church which they called the church of Christ, after the original name of the church organized by Joseph Smith, Jr. This church disintegrated as a result of disagreement between church leaders, and Parrish later left Kirtland and became a Baptist minister.

Church of Christ (Whitmerite)

This was a denomination of the Latter-day Saint movement based on the claims of David whitmer, one of the Three Witnesses to the Book of Mormon's Golden Plates.

There were actually two separate organization of this church. In 1847 William E. McLellin who led a congregation of Latter-day Saints in Kirtland, Ohio remembered that Joseph Smith, Jr., the movement's deceased founder, had designated David Whitmer as his successor. McLellin encouraged Whitmer to come forward and lead his church. Whitmer agreed and gathered others to his cause, including fellow Book of Mormon witnesses Olivery Cowdery, Martin Harris, Hiram Page and John Whitmer.

Taking the original name of the church, the "Church of Christ" published a periodical from Kirtland called, *The Ensign of Liberty*. Whitmer, however, never joined the main body of his followers in Kirtland and the church dissolved.

However, by 1870s David Whitmer was active again and had reorganized his Church of Christ. In 1887 he published his An Address to all Belivers in Christ which promoted his church and affirmed his testimony of the Book of Mormon.

Whitmer died in 1888, but the Whitmerite church continued on. The church published a periodical called *The Return* beginning in 1889, which became known as *The Messenger of Truth* in 1900. The church published its own edition of the Book of Mormon under the name, *The Nephite Record* and published a new edition of the *Book* united with the Church of Christ (Temple Lot). The last of the Whitmers who believed as he had was John C. Whitmer's daughter Mayme Janetta Whitmer Koontz who died in 1961.

Community of Christ

Many felt that before his death, Joseph Smith had designated his son to be the faith's rightful leader, rather than Brigham Young, the senior member of The Quorum of the Twelve Apostles.

The church traditionally known as the Reorganized Church of Jesus Christ of Latter-day Saints or RLDS, but now known as the Community of Christ, was formed. Joseph Smith III, Joseph Smith's son became its official leader.

The Community of Christ is currently a world-wide faith with approximately 250,000 members. The second-largest denomination is the Community of Christ (first named the Reorganized Church of Jesus Christ of Latter Day Saints from 1872–2001), a Missouri-based, 250,000-member denomination. Though members of this church have traditionally been called Latter Day Saints (without the hyphen), the Community of Christ has more recently stated that it rejects the use of the term Saints as a designation for its members in any official reference or publication.

The Church of Christ (Temple Lot)

This is a denomination of the Latter-day Saint movement headquartered in Independence, Missouri on what is known as the Temple Lot. Members of the chruch have been known colloquially as "Hedrickites", after Granville Hedrick, who was ordained as the church's first leader in July 1863. Unlike the Church of Jesus Christ of Latter-day Saints, and Community of Christ, the Temple Lot rejects the office of prophet or president, being led by its Quorum of Twelve Apostles. It rejects the doctrines of Baptism for the dead and Eternal Marriage as well as the Doctrine and Covenants and the Pearl of Great Price.

Its most notable claim to fame today rests in its sole ownership of the Temple Lot, which it has held for nearly 150 years. Current membership is about 2400, with members in 11 or 12 countries.

Fundamentalism" Typically Implies Polygamy

The biggest such fragment gathering is known as the Fundamentalist Church of Jesus Christ of Last day Holy people or FLDS. For the vast majority of its presence, this congregation has been situated in the twin fringe urban areas of Colorado City, Arizona and Hildale, Utah; albeit different areas do exist. As of late, critical numbers migrated to Texas; where individuals were subjected to a prominent 2008 assault, and additionally other lawful difficulties.

Nobody truly knows what number of individuals this congregation has. Traditionalist assessments recommend around 6,000. More liberal assessments put the number at 10,000 or more. Different people and gathers who hone polygamy, and guarantee some association with the standard Church, most likely number in the several thousands; albeit nobody knows for certain.

Every single such individual and gatherings are for the most part alluded to as "fundamentalists"; recommending that the standard Church has strayed from these early convictions and rehearses.

Rigdonite

Rigdonite is a name given to members of the Latter Day Saint movement who accept Sidney Rigdon as the successor in the church presidency to movement founder, Joseph Smith, Jr. The early history of the Rigdonite movement is shared with the history of the Latter Day Saint movement, but as of the 1844 succession crisis becomes distinct.

Sidney Rigdon and other church leaders, including Brigham Young and James J. Strang, presented themselves as leaders of the movement and established rival church organizations.

Rigdon's group was initially headquartered in Pittsburgh, Pennsylvania. It was known at one time as the **Church of Jesus Christ of the Children of Zion**, and its followers are referred to as Rigdonites, or sometimes "Pennsylvania Latter Day Saints" or "Pennsylvania Mormons." The only surviving organization that traces its succession back to Rigdon's organization is The Church of Jesus Christ, founded by a group of Rigdon's followers led by William Bickerton.

THE STRANGITE MOVEMENT

THE COUNCIL OF FIFTY

Joseph Smith said he got a disclosure on April 7, 1842 requiring the foundation of an association called the Living Constitution, or later the Council of Fifty. This would serve as the establishment for the foundation of Christ's Millennial government. The association was formally settled by Joseph Smith in Nauvoo, Illinois on March 11, 1844. The "assistant of the Kingdom", William Clayton, recorded that precisely one month later, Joseph Smith was "picked as our Prophet, Priest, and King by Hosannas".

The Council of Fifty was not an entirely religious gathering.. When it was shaped there were three non-Mormon individuals: Marenus G. Eaton, who had uncovered a scheme against Smith by Nauvoo dissidents; Edward Bonney who later went about as prosecutor against Joseph Smith for his part in the devastation of the Nauvoo Expositor; and Uriah Brown. Their induction demonstrated Mormon teachings about the Millennial religious government that it would be multi-denominational. While Brigham Young did not concede non-Mormons to the Council amid his organization, he welcomed both Mormons and non-Mormons to be a piece of the religious government, and even a portion of the religious government.

Smith served as the president of the Council amid his lifetime, after which Brigham Young directed, and afterward John Taylor. The greater part of the Quorum of the Twelve Apostles were individuals from the Council and had an uncommon initiative part. Amid Smith's lifetime, gatherings of the Council were held in mystery.

Part of the Council in Joseph Smith's organization

The Council was intended to be the association which could venture into any political vacuum and get the bits of a demolished world. It was not intended to overwhelm, but rather it was trusted that the framework would be uninhibitedly picked by all (Mormons and non-Mormons alike) who survived catastrophes loaded upon the world. On the other hand, the Council did perform some genuine obligations.

One obligation of the Council was to help with Joseph Smith's 1844 crusade for President of the United States. Smith kept running on a stage among chapel individuals from bringing compensation for area and property lost in Missouri, disposing of subjection, repaying slave-proprietors with the offer of private grounds, diminishing the pay rates of individuals from Congress, dispensing with obligation detainment, and so on. Individuals from the Council battled all through the United States. Other than conveying several political ministers to battle for Smith all through the U.S., they likewise designated kindred individuals from the Fifty as political envoys to Russia, the Republic of Texas, Washington D.C., England, and France. Smith was killed by a substantial horde amidst his presidential crusade. One objective of the battle was to attract more prominent consideration regarding the issues of the Mormons, who had gotten no state or government compensation for a huge number of dollars worth of property lost to horde savagery in connection to the 1838 Mormon War. Things being what they are, Smith's Presidential battle, the Nauvoo Expositor episode, and even bits of gossip about the Council of Fifty, may have made the nearby distress that prompted his death.

After Smith's passing, the Council anointed Brigham Young its pioneer, and as the "ruler and president" of the Kingdom of God. Under Young, on the other hand, the Council kept on having moderately little power.

The Council helped with the Mormon Exodus from Nauvoo, Illinois and the inevitable movement to the Great Basin zone of what is currently Utah. Brigham Young depended upon the aftereffects of scouting missions by individuals from the Council in picking the Great Basin as a destination for their departure from Nauvoo, more than a few different potential outcomes including Texas, California, Oregon, and Vancouver Island.

The board was to go about as an administrative body in the Kingdom of God, and in Utah, the Council turned into a temporary authoritative body in the legislature. This proceeded until September 1850 when Congress composed the Utah Territory upon request by the congregation. After Utah turned into a region, the American desire for a detachment in the middle of chapel and state strongly decreased the Council's official part in government. The Council then suspended gatherings in October 1851. The committee met again on October 9, 1868 and voted in favor of the foundation of Zion's Co-agent Mercantile Institution (ZCMI) which turned into the real retail chain for the Mormons in Utah.

ABOUT THE AUTHOR

All my life, I have asked the question why about life and spent many years studying philosophies and religions, particularly the Mormon Church and its history. I even went on a two-year mission to proselyte the Mormon Church's teachings in Florida, Georgia, and Alabama, where I met with ministers of other faiths and discussed many religious topics. Why do people believe in ideas about life without any positive evidence to support their beliefs? Is there really a god? Does God really speak to certain human beings? It was very startling to me to discover there wasn't a Santa Claus, and yet the same people who had been telling me there was a Santa Claus also told me there was a being like God, so if they were wrong about Santa Claus, what about their teaching about God? This study is a result of many questions about the Mormon Church and asks many questions that do not have particularly definite answers. The intent of this work is to endeavor to get people to think on their own and perhaps realize things they have been taught are not always are correct.

Printed in the United States
By Bookmasters